GOD
with
US

The Story of Jesus

The epic and complete chronicle of the life, ministry,
crucifixion, resurrection, and ascension of
our Lord Jesus Christ, told in free verse,
paraphrased from the Holy Bible.

Rev. Robert W. Gardner

GOD WITH US

The Story of Jesus

Robert W. Gardner

ISBN (Print Edition): 978-1-09835-770-2

ISBN (eBook Edition): 978-1-09835-771-9

TABLE OF CONTENTS

FOREWORD

This work was composed to harmonize and combine the New Testament Scriptures that told of the life and ministry of Jesus. I sought to learn from examining previous harmonizations and to build, if I could, upon them. This work attempts to harmonize these Scriptures from a point of faith in the inspiration that guided the original works. While the Word of God is infallible, I am not. Any errors are my own. My especial thanks to my wife, Melissa, for her encouragement, to Glen Davis who painstakingly reviewed the work, and of course, to Jesus who is indeed God with us.

Much of the original structure for this work was based upon a 19th Century work by Alfred Nevin that I encountered at https://blueletterbible.org which was derived from that public domain material.[1]

My method was to begin with Alfred Nevin's harmony, examining any difficulties that his work may have introduced. I have broken up Nevin's groupings of Scripture in some cases as seemed expedient, and conflated others. In each case, I have tried to compile discreet vignettes that each stand alone in telling some part of the story of Jesus. In a handful of cases, I rejected Nevin's chronological conclusions in favor of other solutions. My sequence of the vignettes differs where simple and logical changes of order in Scriptures were made that (to me) better relate the relationship of various journeys and events.

My desire was not to produce a new translation of Scripture. This work should be considered as no more than a (hopefully) faithful paraphrase, an attempt to present the Good News in modern English as a series of brief stories told in the approximate order of their occurrence. I hope merely to relate the full story, in one narrative, that the Gospel writers were inspired to record.

Many worthy translations, commentaries, and concordances have been consulted through the years to first develop the harmony, and then to meld the Scripture verses without losing any details. The King James Version formed the initial basis for the paraphrase.

Finally, the work was set, not into new chapters and verses, but rather into one titled vignette after another in a pattern of free verse suggested by epic poems of old. Quoted speech was indented. Divine pronouns were capitalized. As a preacher, I felt the Biblical reports of living conversations required a few more exclamation points than is usual! The quotes of angels were italicized. So was Old Testament Scripture, which was not changed from the King James Version in order to preserve the flavor of its antiquity, an antiquity that was felt even by First Century Christians. The quotes of evil spirits were rendered in a different font. US currency and measures were approximated. Though some of the vignettes are perhaps better rendered as prose, there is a grandeur of inspired thought that I felt was better related by the poetic form throughout this epic story. As one who often reads aloud, I also find that this line-by-line phrasing enhances both the reading and the listening experience, making the task of reading aloud both more joyful and meaningful for the reader, and thus more enjoyable and edifying for the listener.

Above all, a prayerful attitude was maintained in my desire to find the closest harmony and paraphrase that would provide a faithful retelling of the story of Jesus in modern language. The task took many years and was returned to again and again with fresher eyes and deeper understandings. It has been a great study of the Gospels for me and I am thankful for it. I pray that others may find it useful and that it may be used of God for a blessing and for the furtherance of His Kingdom.

Rev. Robert W. Gardner
Gulf Shores, Alabama
December 25, 2020

GOD

with

US

The Story of Jesus

1   Preamble[2]

(Mark 1:1; Luke 1:1-4)

The beginning of the Gospel of Jesus Christ, the Son of God.

Because so many have taken in hand
to set forth an orderly declaration of those things
which are most surely believed among us,
just as they delivered them to us,
who, from the beginning,
were eyewitnesses and ministers of the Word;
it seemed good to us also,
having had perfect understanding of all things from the very first,
to write to you,
so that you might know the certainty
of those things in which you have been instructed.

2   In the Beginning[3]

(John 1:1-5,10-18)

In the Beginning was the Word,
and the Word was with God,
and the Word was God.
He was with God in the Beginning.
All things were made through Him;
and without Him
nothing was made that was made.
In Him was Life;
and the Life was the Light of Man.
And the Light shines in the Darkness;
but the Darkness did not overcome it.

He was in the world,
and the world was made by Him,

but the world did not know Him.
He came to His own people,
and His own did not receive Him.
But to all who received Him,
those who believe on His Name:
He gave power to become the Children of God,
who were born,
not of blood,
nor of the will of the flesh,
nor of the will of man,
but of God.

And the Word was made flesh,
and lived among us,
and we beheld His glory,
the glory of the Only Begotten of the Father,
full of grace and truth.

3   The Genealogy of Jesus[4]
(Matthew 1:1-17; Luke 3:23-38)

This is the chronicle of the generations of Jesus Christ,
the son of David, the son of Abraham.

All the generations from Abraham to David are fourteen generations;
and from David until the captivity in Babylon are fourteen generations;
and from the captivity in Babylon until Christ are fourteen generations.

Jesus, who is called Christ, was born of Mary,
the *ward* of Joseph, the son of Jacob,
the son of Matthan, the son of Eleazar,
the son of Eliud, the son of Achim,
the son of Zadoc, the son of Azor,
the son of Eliakim, the son of Abihud,

the son of Zerubbabel, the son of Shealtiel,
the son of Jeconiah, who with his brethren was the son of Josiah
about the time they were carried away to Babylon.
Josiah was the son of Amon, the son of Manasseh,
the son of Hezkiah, the son of Ahaz,
the son of Joatham, the son of Uzziah,
the son of Joram, the son of Johoshaphat,
the son of Asa, the son of Abijah,
the son of Rheoboam, the son of Solomon,
fathered of her who had been the wife of Uriah,
by David the King.

Jesus, being (as was supposed) the son of Joseph,
the son of Eli, the son of Matthat,
the son of Levi, the son of Melchi,
the son of Jannai, the son of Joseph,
the son of Mattathiah, the son of Amos,
the son of Nahum, the son of Esli,
the son of Naggai, the son of Maath,
the son of Mattathiah, the son of Semein,
the son of Josech, the son of Joda,
the son of Joannan, the son of Rhesa,
the son of Zerubabel, the son of Shealtiel,
the son of Neri, the son of Melchi,
the son of Addi, the son of Cosam,
the son of Elmadam, the son of Er,
the son of Joshua, the son of Eliezer,
the son of Jorim, the son of Matthat,
the son of Levi, the son of Simeon,
the son of Judah, the son of Joseph,
the son of Jonam, the son of Eliakim,
the son of Melea, the son of Menna,
the son of Mattatha, the son of Nathan,
the son of David, the son of Jesse,

the son of Obed, the son of Boaz,
the son of Salmon, the son of Nahshon,
the son of Aminadab, the son of Admin
the son of Aram, the son of Hezron,
the son of Perez, the son of Judah,
the son of Jacob, the son of Isaac,
the son of Abraham, the son of Terah,
the son of Nahor, the son of Serug,
the son of Reu, the son of Peleg,
the son of Heber, the son of Shela,
the son of Cainan, the son of Arphaxad,
the son of Shem, the son of Noah,
the son of Lamech, the son of Methusalah,
the son of Enoch, the son of Jared,
the son of Mahalaleel, the son of Cainan,
the son of Enosh, the son of Seth,
the son of Adam,
the son of God.

4   John the Baptist Was Sent[5]

(John 1:6-9)

There was a man sent from God,
whose name was John.
He came as a witness,
to tell of the Light,
so that all through Him might believe.
John was not the Light,
but was sent to tell of the Light,
the true Light,
who shines upon all who came into the world.

5   The Testimony of John the Baptist

(John 1:15-18)

John told of Him, crying out,
  "This was He of whom I said,
    'He who comes after me is before me:
    because He was before me.'"

From His fullness,
we have all received grace upon grace.
For the Law was given through Moses,
but grace and truth came through Jesus Christ.
None have ever seen God,
except the Only Begotten of God,
who is in the heart of the Father.
He has revealed Him.

6   Gabriel Announces John's Birth

(Luke 1:5-25)

There was in the days of Herod, the king of Judea,
a certain priest named Zachariah,
of the lineage of Abijah:
and his wife was of the daughters of Aaron,
and her name was Elizabeth.
They were both righteous before God,
walking blamelessly
in all the commandments and ordinances of the Lord.
Now they had no child,
because Elizabeth was barren,
and they were both well advanced in years.

It came to pass,
that while he served as priest before God in the order of his lineage,

according to the custom of the priests,
it was his lot to enter and burn incense in the Temple of the Lord.
And the whole multitude of the people were praying outside,
at the time of incense.
And there appeared to him an angel of the Lord
standing on the right side of the Altar of Incense.
When Zachariah saw him,
he was troubled
and fear fell upon him.
But the angel said,

> *"Fear not, Zachariah:*
> *for your prayer is heard;*
> *and your wife Elizabeth shall bear you a son,*
> *and you shall call his name John.*
> *And you shall have joy and gladness;*
> *and many shall rejoice at his birth.*
> *For he shall be great in the sight of the Lord,*
> *and shall drink neither wine nor strong drink;*
> *and he shall be filled with the Holy Spirit,*
> *even from his mother's womb.*
> *He shall turn many of the children of Israel*
> *to the Lord their God,*
> *and he shall go before Him*
> *in the spirit and power of Elijah,*
> *to turn the hearts of the fathers*
> *to the children,*
> *and the disobedient*
> *to the wisdom of the just;*
> *to make ready a people prepared for the Lord."*

And Zachariah said to the angel,

> "How shall I know this?
> for I am an old man,
> and my wife is well advanced in years."

The angel answered,

"I am Gabriel,
who stands in the presence of God;
and was sent to speak to you,
and to show you these glad tidings.
Behold,
you shall be mute,
and unable to speak,
until the day that these things shall take place,
because you did not believe my words,
which shall be fulfilled in their season."

And the people waited for Zachariah,
amazed that he lingered so long in the Temple.

And when he came out,
he could not speak to them,
and they perceived that he had seen a vision in the temple:
for he made signs to them and remained speechless.

And it came to pass that
as soon as the days of his ministry were finished,
he returned to his own home.
After those days, his wife Elizabeth conceived,
and hid herself five months, saying,

"Thus, has the Lord dealt with me
in the days he looked upon me,
to take away my reproach among men."

7   Gabriel Visits Mary

(Luke 1:26-38)

In the sixth month
the angel Gabriel was sent from God
to Nazareth, a city of Galilee,

to a virgin engaged to a man whose name was Joseph,
of the House of David;
and the virgin's name was Mary.
And the angel came to her and said,

> *"Hail! Highly favored one!*
> *The Lord is with you!*
> *Blessed are you among women!"*

And when she saw him,
she was troubled at what he said,
and wondered what kind of greeting this was.
And the angel said to her,

> *"Fear not, Mary:*
> *for you have found favor with God.*
> *And, behold,*
> *you shall conceive in your womb,*
> *and bear a son,*
> *and shall call His name JESUS.*
> *He shall be great,*
> *and shall be called the Son of the Highest.*
> *And the Lord God shall give Him the throne of His father David,*
> *and He shall reign over the House of Jacob forever;*
> *and of His Kingdom there shall be no end.*

Then Mary said to the angel,
"How can this be, since I have never intimately known a man?"
And the angel answered her,

> *"The Holy Spirit shall come upon you,*
> *and the power of the Highest shall overshadow you:*
> *thus, the Holy Infant who will be born of you*
> *shall be called the Son of God.*
> *And, behold,*
> *your cousin Elizabeth,*
> *has also conceived a son in her old age:*
> *and this is the sixth month with her,*

who was called barren.
For with God nothing shall be impossible."
And Mary said,
"Behold,
    I am the handmaid of the Lord;
    May it be with me as you have said."
    And the angel departed from her.

8   Mary Visits Elizabeth

(Luke 1:39-56)

In those days, Mary arose
and went speedily into the hill country,
into a city of Judah,
and entered the house of Zachariah,
and greeted Elizabeth.
And it came to pass that,
when Elizabeth heard Mary's greeting,
the baby leaped in her womb;
and Elizabeth was filled with the Holy Spirit,
and she cried out with a loud voice,
    "Blessed are you among women,
    and blessed is the fruit of your womb!
    And how wonderful is this to me
    that the mother of my Lord should come to me!
    For, see?
    As soon as the sound of your greeting rang in my ears,
    the baby leaped in my womb for joy!
    And blessed is she who believed
    those things shall be done
    that she was told from the Lord!"

And Mary said,
    "My soul magnifies the Lord,

And my spirit rejoices in God my Savior.
For He has looked upon His lowly handmaiden.
And see!
From now on, all generations shall call me blessed
because He who is mighty has done great things to me,
and Holy is His name.
And His mercy is on those who revere Him
from generation to generation.
He has shown strength with His arm.
He has scattered the proud in the imagination of their hearts.
He has put down the mighty from their thrones,
and raised up those of low degree.
He has filled the hungry with good things;
and the rich, He has sent away empty.
He has helped His servant Israel,
in remembrance of His mercy;
that He spoke to our fathers,
to Abraham,
and to his children
forever."

And Mary stayed with her about three months,
and then returned to her own home.

9 The Birth of John the Baptist

(Luke 1:57-80)

Now Elizabeth's full term came to give birth,
and she delivered a son.
Her neighbors and her cousins heard
how the Lord had showed great mercy to her;
and they rejoiced with her.
And it came to pass that on the eighth day
they came to circumcise the child

and they thought to call him Zachariah,
after his father.
But his mother answered and said,
    "No. He shall be called John."
And they said to her,
    "None of your kindred is called by that name."
And they made signs to his father,
asking what he wanted him to be called.

He asked for a writing table and wrote,
    "His name is John."
And they were all surprised.
And his mouth was opened immediately,
and his tongue freed,
and he spoke, praising God.
Awe struck all who dwelt around them:
and all this news was the talk of all the hill country of Judea.
All who heard
kept it in their hearts, saying,
    "What kind of child will this be!"
For the hand of the Lord was with him.
And his father Zachariah was filled with the Holy Spirit,
and prophesied,
    "Blessed be the Lord God of Israel;
    for He has visited and redeemed His people.
    And has raised up the horn of salvation for us
    in the House of His servant David,
    as He spoke by the mouth of His holy prophets,
    from the Beginning,
    that we should be saved from our enemies,
    and from the hand of all who hate us;
    to provide the mercy promised to our fathers,
    and to remember His Holy Covenant;
    the oath which He swore to our father Abraham,

to grant us,
that being delivered out of the hand of our enemies
we might serve Him without fear,
in holiness and righteousness before Him,
all of our days."

"And you, child,
shall be called the prophet of the Highest:
for you shall go before the face of the Lord
to prepare His ways,
to give knowledge of salvation to His people
by the remission of their sins,
through the tender mercy of our God.
So, shall the Dayspring from on high visit us,
to give light
to those who sit in darkness
and in the shadow of death,
to guide our feet
into the way of peace."
And the child grew, and became strong in spirit,
and was in the deserts until the day of his appearing to Israel.

10   The Angel Appears to Joseph in a Dream
(Matthew 1:18-25)

Now the birth of Jesus Christ was as follows:
When His mother Mary was engaged to Joseph,
before they came together,
she was found with child of the Holy Spirit.
Then Joseph her husband,
being a reasonable man, and not willing to disgrace her,
had considered discreetly divorcing her.
But while he thought on these things,
the angel of the Lord appeared to him in a dream, saying,

"Joseph, son of David,
do not fear to take Mary to be your wife,
because that which is conceived in her
is of the Holy Spirit.
She shall bear a son,
and you shall call His name JESUS:
for He shall save his people from their sins."

All this was done to fulfill
that which was spoken of the Lord by the prophet,
'Behold, a virgin shall be with child,
and shall bring forth a son,
and they shall call his name Emmanuel,'
(which means, 'God with us').

Then Joseph was awakened from sleep
and did as the angel of the Lord commanded him,
and received his betrothed,
but did not intimately know her
until after she had given birth to her firstborn son:
and he called His name JESUS.

11   The Birth of Jesus in Bethlehem

(Luke 2:1-7)

It came to pass in those days,
that there went out a decree from Augustus Caesar,
that all the world should be taxed.
(This was the first tax census made
when Quirinus was Governor of Syria.)
And all went to be taxed,
everyone into his own city.

Joseph also went up from Galilee,

out of the city of Nazareth,
into Judea,
to the city of David called Bethlehem;
(because he was of the House and lineage of David:)
to be taxed with Mary his betrothed,
who was late in her pregnancy.

So it was,
that while they were there,
the time came when she gave birth.
And she delivered her firstborn son,
and wrapped Him in swaddling clothes,
and laid Him in a manger;
because there was no room for them in the inn.

12   Shepherds Visit Jesus at the Manger
(Luke 2:8-20)

In the same area
there were shepherds living in the fields,
keeping watch over their flock by night.

The angel of the Lord came to them,
and the glory of the Lord shone around them,
and they were struck with great dread.
And the angel said to them,
   "Fear not!
   For, behold!
   I bring you good tidings of great joy,
   which shall be to all people!
   For to you is born this day in the city of David
   a Savior, who is Christ the Lord!
   And this shall be a sign for you:
   you shall find the Baby

wrapped in swaddling clothes,
and lying in a manger."
And suddenly there was with the angel
a multitude of the Heavenly host
praising God, and saying,
"Glory to God in the highest,
and on Earth peace,
good will toward men!"

And it came to pass,
as the angels were gone away from them into Heaven,
the shepherds said to one another,
"Let us go into Bethlehem now,
and see this thing that has come to pass,
which the Lord has made known to us!"
With haste they came
and found Mary and Joseph,
and the Baby lying in a manger.
And when they saw these things,
they made known what they were told about this Child,
and all who heard it were astonished
about what the shepherds told them,
but Mary kept and pondered all these things in her heart.

And the shepherds returned,
glorifying and praising God
for all that they had heard and seen,
as it was told to them.

13 Jesus Is Presented in the Temple

(Luke 2:21-38)

When eight days had passed and He was circumcised,
He was called JESUS,

as named by the angel
before He was conceived in the womb.
And when the days were finished for purification
according to the Law of Moses,
they brought Him to Jerusalem,
to present Him to the Lord,
since it is written in the Law of the Lord,
> *"Every male who opens the womb*
> *shall be called holy to the Lord,"*

and to offer a sacrifice
according to what is commanded in the Law of the Lord,
> *"A pair of turtledoves, or two young pigeons."*

Also, there was a man in Jerusalem,
whose name was Simeon,
a just and devout man,
waiting for the Consolation of Israel,
and the Holy Spirit was upon him.
And it was revealed to him by the Holy Spirit,
that he would not see death,
before he had seen the Lord's Christ.

He was led by the Spirit into the Temple,
and when the parents brought in the child Jesus,
to do for Him according to the custom of the Law,
then took he Him up in his arms,
and blessed God and said,
> "Lord, now Your servant departs in peace,
> according to Your Word;
> for my eyes have seen Your Salvation,
> which You have prepared before the face of all peoples:
> a Light for enlightening the Gentiles,
> and the glory of Your people, Israel."

And his father and his mother were astonished

at what was said of Him.
And Simeon blessed them
and said to Mary, His mother,

"This child is set for the fall and rising of many in Israel;
and for a sign which shall be spoken against;
that the thoughts of many hearts may be revealed.
(Yes, and a sword shall also pierce through your own soul.)"

There was also a prophetess, Anna,
the daughter of Phanuel, of the tribe of Asher.
She was of a great age,
and had lived with a husband seven years from her virginity;
and was a widow of about eighty-four years.
She never left the Temple,
serving God with fasting and prayer night and day.
And she was there in that moment
and gave thanks to the Lord,
and spoke of Him to all who waited for redemption in Jerusalem.

14   The Magi

(Matthew 2:1-12)

Now when Jesus was born in Bethlehem of Judea
in the days of Herod the king,
there came Magi from the east to Jerusalem, saying,

"Where is He who is born King of the Jews?
For we saw His star when it rose in the east,
and have come to worship Him."

When Herod the king heard this,
he was troubled,
and all Jerusalem with him.
Gathering all the Chief Priests and Scribes of the people,
he demanded they tell where the Christ should be born.

They told him,
 "In Bethlehem of Judea:
 for so it is written by the prophet,
  'And you O Bethlehem, in the land of Judah,
  are in no way the least among the princes of Judah
  for out of you shall come a Prince
  who shall shepherd my people Israel.'"
Then Herod secretly called the wise men,
diligently inquiring of them what time the star appeared.
He sent them to Bethlehem and said,
 "Go and search diligently for the child,
 and when you have found him,
 bring me word,
 so that I may also come and worship him."
When they had heard the king, they departed;
and the star which they saw rising in the east,
went before them until it came to stand still
over where the Child was.
When they saw the star,
they rejoiced with exceedingly great joy.
Entering the house
they saw the Child with Mary, His mother,
and fell down and worshiped Him.
Then they had opened their treasures,
and presented Him with gifts
of gold and frankincense and myrrh.
And being warned of God in a dream
that they should not return to Herod,
they left another way into their own country.

15 The Escape into Egypt

(Matthew 2:13-15)

When they had gone,

the angel of the Lord appeared to Joseph in a dream, saying,
> *"Arise!*
> *and take the Child and His mother,*
> *and flee into Egypt,*
> *and stay there until I tell you,*
> *because Herod will seek the Child to destroy Him!"*

Then he got up and took the Child and his mother by night,
and departed into Egypt
and stayed there until the death of Herod.
This fulfilled that which the Lord spoke by the prophet,
> *"Out of Egypt have I called my son."*

16   The Slaughter of the Children of Bethlehem

(Matthew 2:16-18)

Then Herod,
when he saw that the wise men had deceived him,
was overcome with rage,
and sent out and murdered all the children in Bethlehem
and in all the region,
from two years old and under,
according to the time which he had diligently inquired of the Magi.
This fulfilled that which was spoken by the prophet Jeremiah:
> *"In Rama*
> *there was heard a voice,*
> *weeping,*
> *lamentation,*
> *and great mourning.*
> *Rachel weeping for her children,*
> *beyond consolation,*
> *because they are no more."*

17 The Return to Israel

(Matthew 2:19-23; Luke 2:39-40)

When Herod was dead,
the angel of the Lord appeared in a dream to Joseph in Egypt, saying,
  "Arise and take the Child and His mother,
  and go into the land of Israel,
  because those who sought the Child's life, are dead."
And he got up and took the Child and his mother,
and came into the land of Israel.
But when he heard that Archelaus ruled in Judea
in the room of his father Herod,
he was afraid to go there,
moreover, being warned in a dream,
he returned to the region of Galilee.

Having performed all things
according to the Law of the Lord,
he came and dwelt in the city called Nazareth,
so that which was spoken by the prophets was fulfilled,
  "He shall be called a Nazarene."
And the child grew,
and became ever stronger,
filled with wisdom:
and the grace of God was upon Him.

18 The Childhood of Jesus

(Luke 2:41-52)

Now his parents went to Jerusalem every year
at the Feast of the Passover.
When He was twelve years old,
they went up as was the custom.
And when the Feast was finished,

as they returned,
the Child Jesus remained behind in Jerusalem,
and His parents did not know it.
Moreover, thinking Him to have been in the caravan,
they went a day's journey;
and then sought for Him among their kinsfolk and acquaintances.
When they did not find Him,
they turned back to Jerusalem, seeking Him.

And it came to pass,
that after three days
they found Him in the Temple,
sitting among the rabbis,
hearing them and asking them questions.
All who heard Him
were astonished at His understanding and answers.

When they saw Him,
they were amazed,
and His mother said to Him,
  "Son! Why have you done us this way?
  Look how your father and I have sought you in such sorrow!"
And He said to them,
  "Why were you looking for Me?
  Didn't you know that I had to be with My Father?"
And they did not understand what He told them.

But He went down with them,
and came to Nazareth,
and was submissive to them,
and His mother kept all these words in her heart.
And Jesus increased in wisdom and stature,
and in favor with God and man.

19 The Ministry of John the Baptist

(Matthew 3:1-12; Mark 1:2-8; Luke 3:1-18; John 1:19)

This is the story of John.

In those days,
in the fifteenth year of the reign of Tiberius Caesar,
when Pontius Pilate was Governor of Judea,
and Herod was Tetrarch of Galilee,
and his brother Philip was Tetrarch of Ituraea
(and of the region of Trachonitis),
and Lysanias was the Tetrarch of Abilene.
Annas and Caiaphas were the High Priests.

As it is written in the prophets,
the Word of God came to John the Baptist, son of Zachariah,
in the wilderness;
and he came into all the country about Jordan,
baptizing in the wilderness of Judea,
and preaching the baptism of repentance
for the remission of sins, saying,
    "Repent! For the Kingdom of Heaven is at hand!"
For it was he who was spoken of by the prophet Isaiah,
    "Behold, I send My messenger before Thy face,
    who shall prepare thy way before thee;
    the voice of one crying in the wilderness,
        'Prepare ye the way of the Lord,
        make His paths straight!'
    Every valley shall be filled,
    and every mountain and hill shall be brought low;
    and the crooked shall be made straight,
    and the rough ways shall be made smooth;
    And all flesh shall see the Salvation of God."
And John had clothing of camel's hair,
and a leather belt around his hips;

and his diet was locusts and wild honey.

Then the people of Jerusalem,
and all Judea,
and all the region around the River Jordan,
went out to him and confessed their sins,
and were baptized by him in the Jordan.
But when he saw many of the Pharisees and Sadducees
had come to his baptism,
among the multitude that came out to be baptized by him,
he said to them,

> "Oh, generation of vipers!
> Who has warned you to flee from the wrath to come?
> So, bear the fruits that show repentance!
> Do not think to say among yourselves,
>> 'But we have Abraham for our father:'
> for I tell you that from these stones
> God can raise up children for Abraham!
> And now, too, the ax is laid to the root of the trees!
> So, every tree that does not bear good fruit is chopped down,
> and cast into the fire."

And the people asked him,
> "Then what will we do?"
He answered,
> "Let him who has two coats
> give to him who has none;
> and let him who has food
> do likewise."
Then tax collectors also came to be baptized,
and said to him,
> "Master, what will we do?"
And he told them,
> "Take no more than what you are appointed."

And the soldiers likewise demanded of him,
    "And what will we do?"
And he told them,
    "Do no one harm,
    nor falsely accuse any.
    Be content with your wages."

Since the people were in expectation,
and all men considered in their hearts
whether or not John was the Christ;
John answered, telling them all,
    "I indeed baptize you with water for repentance:
    but He who comes after me is mightier than I,
    He whose shoes I am not worthy to carry:
    the strap of whose shoes I am not worthy to loosen!
    I have indeed baptized you with water.
    He shall baptize you with the Holy Spirit and with fire!
    His fan is in His hand,
    and He will thoroughly purge his floor,
    and gather His wheat into the garner.
    But He will burn up the chaff with unquenchable fire!"
And he preached many other things as he exhorted the people.

20   John Foretells Christ

(John 1:19-28)

When the Jews sent Priests and Levites from Jerusalem to ask him,
    "Who are you?"
he confessed, not denying, but confessing, said,
    "I am not the Christ."
They asked him,
    "What then? Are you Elijah?"
And he said,
    "I am not."

"Are you that prophet?"
And he answered,
"No."
Then they said to him,
"Who are you?
We need an answer for those who sent us.
What do you say for yourself?"
He said,
"*I am the voice of one crying in the wilderness,*
"Make straight the way of the Lord!"
as the prophet Isaiah said."
Also, those who were sent by the Pharisees asked him,
"Then why do you baptize,
if you are neither the Christ,
nor the prophet Elijah?"
John answered them,
"I baptize with water:
but there stands among you
one whom you do not know;
It is He who comes after me but is before me,
whose sandals I am unworthy to unstrap."
These things happened in Bethabara beyond Jordan,
where John was baptizing.

21   The Baptism of Jesus

(Matthew 3:13-17; Mark 1:9-11; Luke 3:21-23)

It came to pass in those days,
when all the people were being baptized,
that Jesus, who was about thirty years old,
came from Nazareth of Galilee to John
to be baptized by him in the Jordan River.
But John stopped Him, saying,
"I need to be baptized by you,

yet You come to me?"
And Jesus answered him,
    "Let it be so now:
    because it is suitable for us
    to do every righteous thing."
Then John agreed to baptize Him
and when Jesus was baptized,
He went straight up out of the water,
and the Heavens were opened to Him,
and He saw the Spirit of God
descending in a bodily shape like a dove,
and alighting upon Him,
and a voice from Heaven said,
    "This is my beloved Son,
    in whom I am well pleased."

22   Temptation in the Wilderness

(Matthew 4:1-11; Mark 1:12-13; Luke 4:1-13)

Then, being full of the Holy Spirit,
Jesus was led and immediately driven into the wilderness
with the wild beasts,
where there was temptation of the Devil.
When He had fasted forty days and forty nights,
He was afterwards famished.

When the Tempter came to Him, he said,
    "If You are the Son of God,
    command these stones be made bread."
But He answered and said,
    "It is written,
        'Man shall not live by bread alone,
        but by every word that proceeds out of the mouth of God.'"

Then the Devil took Him up into the Holy City,
and set Him on a pinnacle of the Temple,
and said to Him,
> *"If You are the Son of God,*
> *cast Yourself down:*
> *for it is written,*
>> *'He shall give His angels charge concerning You:*
>> *and in their hands they shall bear You up,*
>> *lest at any time You dash Your foot against a stone.'"*

Jesus said to him,
> "It is written again,
>> *'You shall not tempt the Lord your God.'"*

Again, the Devil took Him up into an exceedingly high mountain,
and, in a moment of time,
showed Him all the kingdoms of the world,
and the glory of them;
and said to Him,
> *"All this power will I give You,*
> *and their glory:*
> *for that is delivered to me;*
> *and to whomsoever I will,*
> *I give it.*
> *If You will fall down and worship me,*
> *All shall be Yours."*

Then Jesus told Him,
> "Be gone, Satan!
> For it is written,
>> *'You shall worship the Lord your God,*
>> *and only Him shall you serve.'"*

Then, when the Devil had ended all the temptations,
he left Him for a season,
and angels came and cared for Him.

23 Behold the Lamb of God

(John 1:29-34)

The next day John saw Jesus coming to him and said,
    "Behold the Lamb of God,
    who takes away the sin of the world!
    This is He of whom I said,
        'After me comes a man who is before me,'
    because He was before me.
    I did not know Him,
    but so that He would be revealed to Israel,
    I came baptizing with water."

And John testified,
    "I saw the Spirit descend from Heaven like a dove,
    and it remained on Him!
    I did not know Him,
    but He who sent me to baptize with water said to me,
        'Upon whom you shall see the Spirit descend and remain,
        it is He who baptizes with the Holy Spirit.'
    I saw this, so I testify,
    He is the Son of God!"

24 The First to Follow[6]

(John 1:35-51)

The next day, John and two of his disciples stood;
looking at Jesus as He walked,
and he again said,
    "Behold the Lamb of God!"
And the two disciples heard this and followed Jesus.

Then Jesus turned,
saw them following,

and said to them,
　　"What do you seek?"
They said,
　　"Master, where are You staying?"
He said,
　　"Come and see."
They came and saw where he stayed,
and stayed with Him that day:
because it was about four in the afternoon.

One of the two who heard John and followed Jesus,
was Andrew, Simon Peter's brother.
He quickly found his brother Simon and said,
　　"We have found the Christ."
Andrew brought him to Jesus.
When Jesus saw Simon, he said,
　　"You are Simon the son of Jonah;
　　　you shall be called Cephas (or Peter, meaning Rock)."

The next day Jesus wanted to go into Galilee,
and there He found Philip and said to him,
　　"Follow Me!"
Now Philip was from Bethsaida, the city of Andrew and Peter.
Philip found Nathanael and said,
　　"We have found Him,
　　　of whom Moses in the law, and the prophets, wrote!
　　　Jesus of Nazareth, the son of Joseph!"
And Nathanael replied,
　　"Can anything good come out of Nazareth?"
Philip said,
　　"Come and see!"
Jesus saw Nathanael coming to Him and said,
　　"Behold an Israelite indeed, in whom is no deceit!"
Nathanael said,

"How do you know me?"
Jesus answered him saying,
   "Before Philip called you,
   when you were under the fig tree,
   I saw you."
Nathanael answered Him,
   "Master, you are the Son of God!
   You are the King of Israel!"
Jesus said to him,
   "You believe because I said
   I saw you under the fig tree?
   You shall see greater things than this."
And He said to him,
   "Truly, truly, I tell you,
   after this you shall see Heaven open,
   and the angels of God
   ascending and descending upon the Son of Man."

25   Water Made into Wine[7]

(John 2:1-12)

Three days later there was a marriage in Cana of Galilee;
and the mother of Jesus was there,
and both Jesus and His disciples were invited to the wedding.
When wine was lacking,
the mother of Jesus said to Him,
   "They have no wine!"
Jesus said to her,
   "Dear woman, what am I to do with you?
   My hour has not yet come."
His mother said to the servants,
   "Whatever He says to you, do it!"

There were six stone water-pots sitting there

for the purifying customs of the Jews,
holding between *twenty and thirty gallons* each.
Jesus said to them,
    "Fill the water-pots with water."
And they filled them up to the brim.
And He said to them,
    "Draw some out now,
      and take it to the master of the feast."
They took it and when the master of ceremonies had tasted
the water that was made into wine,
not knowing where it was from
(though the servants who drew the water knew),
he called the bridegroom,
and said to him,
    "Every man puts out the good wine first;
      and when men have drunk plenty,
      then the cheaper wine.
    But you held back the good wine until now!"
Jesus did this first of miracles in Cana of Galilee,
openly displaying His glory,
and His disciples believed in Him.

26 The First Cleansing of the Temple[8]

(John 2:13-25)

After this He went down to Capernaum
with His mother, His brothers, and His disciples,
and stayed there a few days.
It was almost the Jewish Passover,
and Jesus went up to Jerusalem,
and in the Temple
found sellers of oxen and sheep and doves,
and the moneychangers sitting there.
When He had made a whip of small cords,

He drove them all out of the Temple,
with the sheep and the oxen;
and poured out the changers' money,
and overthrew the tables;
and said to those who sold doves,
    "Take these things away!
    Do not make My Father's house a marketplace!"
His disciples remembered that it was written,
    "The zeal of Thine house hath eaten Me up."
Then the Jews said to Him,
    "What sign can you show us,
    that you rightfully do these things?"
Jesus answered them,
    "Destroy this Temple,
    and in three days I will raise it up."
Then the Jews said,
    "It took forty-six years to build this temple,
    and you will raise it up in three days?"
But He spoke of the Temple of His body.
So, when He had risen from the dead,
His disciples remembered that He had said this to them;
and they believed the Scriptures,
and the words which Jesus had said.

Now while He was in Jerusalem
on the Feast Day of the Passover,
many believed in His Name
when they saw the miracles that He did.
But Jesus did not fully reveal Himself to them,
because He knew all men
and did not need any testimony of man:
for He knew what was in Humanity.

27   You Must Be Born Again

(John 3:1-21)

There was a man of the Pharisees, named Nicodemus,
a ruler of the Jews.
He came to Jesus by night,
and said to Him,
>"Master, we know that you are a teacher from God:
>for no man can do these miracles that you do,
>unless God is with him."

Jesus answered him,
>"Truly, truly, I tell you,
>unless a man is born again,
>he cannot see the Kingdom of God.

Nicodemus said,
>"How can a man be born when he is old?
>Can he enter a second time into his mother's womb
>and be born?"

Jesus answered,
>"Truly, truly, I tell you,
>unless a man is born of water and of the Spirit,
>he cannot enter the Kingdom of God.
>That which is born of the flesh is flesh;
>and that which is born of the Spirit is spirit.
>Do not wonder that I told you,
>>'You must be born again.'
>
>The wind blows where it goes,
>and you hear the sound of it,
>but cannot tell its beginning,
>or its end.
>So it is with everyone who is born of the Spirit."

Nicodemus asked,
>"How can these things be?"

Jesus answered him,

"Are you the teacher of Israel,
and yet do not know these things?"

"Truly, truly, I tell you,
we speak what we know,
and testify to what we have seen;
and you do not receive our witness.
If I have told you earthly things,
and you do not believe,
how can you believe,
if I tell you of Heavenly things?

No man has ascended up to Heaven,
except He who descended from Heaven:
the Son of Man who is in Heaven.
And as Moses lifted up the serpent in the wilderness,
just so must the Son of Man be lifted up.
This is so that whoever believes in Him should not perish,
but will have Eternal Life."

"For God so loved the world,
that He gave His only begotten Son,
so that whoever believes in Him should not perish,
but will have Everlasting Life.
For God did not send His Son into the world
to condemn the world;
but so that the world through Him might be saved.
He who believes in Him is not condemned:
but He who does not believe is already damned,
because he has not believed
in the Name of the only begotten Son of God."

"And this is the judgment,
that Light has come into the world,
and men loved darkness rather than Light,

because their deeds were evil.
For everyone who does evil hates the Light,
and will not come to the Light,
lest his deeds be exposed.
But he who acts truly comes to the Light,
so that his deeds may be seen to be works of God."

28   Lingering by the Jordan
(John 3:22-36)

After this, Jesus and His disciples went into the land of Judea;
and there He lingered with them and baptized.
And John was also baptizing in Aenon near Salim,
because there was an abundance of water there:
and people came and were baptized,
for John was not yet imprisoned.
Then there arose a question about purifying
between some of John's disciples and the Jews.
And they came to John and said to him,
　　"Master, look!
　　He who was beyond Jordan with you,
　　of whom you testified:
　　he baptizes and everyone goes to him."

John answered,
　　"A man can receive nothing,
　　unless it is given to him from Heaven.
　　You yourselves can testify that I said,
　　　　'I am not the Christ,'
　　but that I was sent before Him.
　　He who has the Bride is the Bridegroom:
　　but the friend of the Bridegroom,
　　who stands and hears Him,
　　takes great joy at the Bridegroom's voice.

My joy is now complete!"

"He must increase,
but I must decrease.
He who comes from above is above all.
He who is of the Earth is of the Earth,
and speaks of the Earth.
He who comes from Heaven is above all.
And what He has seen and heard is what He testifies;
but none receive His testimony.
He who has received His testimony
has verified that God is true.
For He whom God has sent speaks the words of God:
for He does not measure out the Spirit.
The Father loves the Son,
and has given all things into His hand.
He who believes in the Son has Everlasting Life:
and he who does not believe in the Son will not see Life;
instead, the wrath of God remains on him."

29   John the Baptist Imprisoned

(Matthew 4:12; Mark 1:14; Luke 3:19-20)

But Herod the Tetrarch,
being convicted by him
and for all the evils which he had done,
because of Herodias, his brother Philip's wife,
yet added this above all,
that he shut up John in prison.

Now after He had heard that John was cast into prison,
Jesus came into Galilee,
preaching the Gospel of the Kingdom of God.

30   The Woman at the Well

(John 4:1-26)

So, when the Lord knew that the Pharisees had heard
that Jesus made and baptized more disciples than John,
(though Jesus Himself did not baptize,
instead, His disciples did,)
He left Judea, going again into Galilee,
and He had to pass through Samaria.

Then He came to Sychar,
a city of Samaria near the parcel of ground
that Jacob gave to his son Joseph.
Now Jacob's Well was there,
so, Jesus, being weary from His journey,
sat at the well at about noon.
A woman of Samaria came to draw water:
Jesus said to her,
　　"Give Me a drink."
(Because His disciples had gone to the city to buy food.)
Then the woman of Samaria said to Him,
　　"How is it that you, a Jew,
　　ask a drink from me, a woman of Samaria?"
(For Jews have nothing to do with Samaritans.)
Jesus answered her,
　　"If you knew the gift of God,
　　and Who it is who says to you,
　　　　'Give me a drink;'
　　you would have asked Him,
　　and He would have given you Living Water."
The woman said,
　　"Sir, you have nothing to draw with,
　　and the well is deep:
　　where do you keep that living water?

Are you greater than our Father Jacob,
who gave us the well,
and drank from it himself,
as well as his children and his cattle?"
Jesus answered her, saying,
"Whoever drinks of this water shall thirst again.
But whoever drinks of the water that I shall give him
shall never thirst.
The water that I shall give him
will become a spring of water in him
welling up into Everlasting Life."

The woman said to Him,
"Sir, give me this water,
so that I will never thirst,
nor come here to draw!"
Jesus said,
"Go, call your husband and come back here."
The woman said,
"I have no husband."
Jesus said to her,
"You are right to say,
'I have no husband:'
because you have had five husbands;
and he whom you now have is not your husband.
In that, you spoke truly."
The woman said to Him,
"Sir, I see that you are a Prophet!
Tell me how it is
that our Forefathers worshiped on this mountain;
but you Jews say that Jerusalem
is where men ought to worship."
Jesus said,
"Woman, believe Me,

the hour comes when you shall worship the Father
neither on this mountain,
nor even at Jerusalem.
You Samaritans do not know what you worship.
We know what we worship:
for salvation is of the Jews.
But the hour comes and is now here,
when the true worshipers shall worship the Father
in spirit and in truth:
for the Father seeks such as these to worship Him.
God is a Spirit:
and those who worship Him must worship Him
in spirit and in truth."
The woman said,
    "I know that Christ comes.
    When He comes,
    He will tell us all things."
Jesus said to her,
    "I who speak to you am He."

31   The Fields Are Ripe for Harvest

(John 4:27-38)

At this moment His disciples returned,
and were astonished that He talked with the woman.
But no one said,
    "What do you want?"
    or, "Why do You talk with her?"
Then the woman left her water-pot,
and went into the city and said to the men,
    "Come! See a man who told me all I ever did!
    Is he the Christ?"
Then they left the city and came to Him.

Meanwhile, His disciples urged Him,
    "Master, eat."
But He said to them,
    "I have food to eat that you know nothing about."
So, the disciples said to each other,
    "Has anyone brought Him anything to eat?"
Jesus said,
    "My sustenance is to do the will of Him who sent Me,
    and to finish His work.
    Don't you say,
        'There are four months until the harvest?'
    Look, I tell you!
    Lift up your eyes and look on the fields;
    for they are already ripe for harvest.
    And he who reaps receives wages,
    and gathers fruit for Eternal Life:
    so that both he who sows and he who reaps
    may rejoice together.
    And in this the saying is true,
        One sows and another reaps.
    I sent you to reap where you did not work:
    other men have worked
    and you have entered into their labors.

32   The Samaritans Believe

    (John 4:39-42)

Many of the Samaritans of that city believed in Him
because of what the woman said, who swore,
    "He told me all I ever did!"
So, when the Samaritans came to Him,
they pleaded with Him to linger with them:
and He stayed there two days.
And many more believed because of His own words;

and they said to the woman,
    "Now, we too, believe,
    not because of what you said:
    but because we have heard Him ourselves,
    and know that He is indeed the Christ,
    the Savior of the world!"

33   Rejected in Nazareth; Accepted in Galilee
(Mark 1:14-15; Luke 4:14-30; John 4:43-45)

Now after two days He left there
and came to Nazareth,
where He had been brought up:
and, as was His custom,
He went into the synagogue on the Sabbath Day,
and stood up to read.

There, the book of the prophet Isaiah was given to Him.
And when He opened the book,
He found the place where it was written,
    "The Spirit of the Lord is upon Me,
    because He hath anointed Me to preach the gospel to the poor;
    He hath sent Me to heal the brokenhearted,
    to preach deliverance to the captives,
    and recovering of sight to the blind,
    to set at liberty them that are bruised,
    to preach the acceptable year of the Lord."
And He closed the book,
and gave it again to the minister,
and sat down.
The eyes of all those who were in the synagogue were fastened on Him
and he began to say to them,
    "This day is this Scripture fulfilled in your ears."

And all approved of Him,
and were astonished at the gracious words
which proceeded out of His mouth.
And they said,
    "Is this not Joseph's son?"
And He said to them,
    "You will surely tell Me this proverb,
        'Physician, heal yourself!'
        'What we have heard was done in Capernaum,
        do here in your country, as well!'"
And He said,
    "Truly, I tell you,
    no prophet is accepted in his own country.
    But I will tell you a true story.
    Many widows were in Israel
    in the days of Elijah,
    when the Heavens were shut up three years and six months,
    and when great famine was throughout all the land.
    But Elijah was sent to none of them,
    except to Sarepta, a city of Sidon,
    to a woman who was a widow.
    Many lepers were in Israel
    in the time of Elijah the prophet;
    and none of them was cleansed,
    except Naaman the Syrian."

All those in the synagogue,
when they heard these things,
were filled with wrath,
and got up and thrust Him out of the city,
and led Him to the edge of the cliff on which their city was built,
so that they might hurl Him down headfirst.
But He passed through the middle of them
and went on His way.

He left there and went into Galilee,
preaching the Gospel of the Kingdom of God,
and saying,

> "The time is fulfilled,
> and the Kingdom of God is at hand:
> repent and believe the good news!"

For Jesus Himself testified,
that a prophet has no honor in his own country.

He returned in the power of the Spirit into Galilee:
the Galileans received Him,
having seen all that He did at the Feast in Jerusalem:
because they also went to the Feast,
and there went out a fame of Him
through all the surrounding region.
And He taught in their synagogues,
and was glorified by all.

34   The Healing in Capernaum

(John 4:46-54)

So, Jesus came back to Cana of Galilee,
where He made the water into wine.
And there was a certain nobleman,
whose son was sick in Capernaum.
When he heard that Jesus had come from Judea into Galilee,
he went to Him,
and begged Him that He would come down and heal his son:
for he was at the point of death.
Then Jesus said to him,

> "Unless you see signs and wonders, you will not believe."

The nobleman said to him,

> "Sir, come down before my child dies."

Jesus said to him,

"Go your way.
Your son lives."

And the man believed what Jesus told him,
and he went on his way.
Just as he was going down,
his servants met him and said,
    "Your son lives!"
Then he asked them the time when he began to mend.
And they said to him,
    "Yesterday afternoon at one o'clock the fever left him."
The father knew that it was at that same time
that Jesus said to him,
    "*Your son lives.*"
So, he himself, and his whole household, believed.
This is the second miracle that Jesus did,
when He came out of Judea into Galilee.

35   Jesus Settles in Capernaum

(Matthew 4:13-17; Luke 4:31-32)

After leaving Nazareth,
he came and dwelt in Capernaum,
a city of Galilee which is on the seacoast,
in the borders of Zebulon and Nephthalim:
to fulfill that which was spoken by Isaiah the prophet,
    "The land of Zebulon,
    and the land of Nephthalim,
    by the way of the sea,
    beyond Jordan,
    Galilee of the Gentiles;
    The people which sat in darkness saw great light;
    and to them which sat in the region and shadow of death
    light is sprung up."

From that time Jesus began to preach,
and taught them on the Sabbath days, saying,
"Repent! For the Kingdom of Heaven is at hand."
And they were astonished by his teaching:
for His word was with power.

36   Fishermen Called to Be Disciples

(Matthew 4:18-22; Mark 1:16-20; Luke 5:1-3)

And it came to pass that,
Jesus was walking by the sea of Gennesaret (or Galilee),
and the people pressed in on Him
to hear the Word of God.

As He stood by the water,
He saw two brethren,
Simon called Peter,
and Andrew his brother,
casting a net into the water:
for they were fishermen.
He saw two boats standing by on the sea:
but the fishermen had left them,
and were washing their nets.
He said to them,
"Follow Me,
and I will make you fishers of men."
And they immediately abandoned their nets,
and followed Him.

Going on a little farther from there,
He saw two other brothers,
James and John,
in a ship with Zebedee their father,
mending their nets.

He called them
and they immediately left the boat and their father
and the hired servants
and followed Him.
He got into Simon's boat,
and asked Him if he would push out a little from the land.
Then He sat down and taught the people out of the boat.

37　A Miraculous Catch of Fish

(Luke 5:4-11)

Now, when He had finished speaking,
He said to Simon,
　　"Launch out into the deep,
　　and let down your nets for a catch."
Simon answered Him,
　　"Master, we have worked all night and caught nothing!
　　Nevertheless, at Your word, I will let down the net."
When they had done this,
they enclosed a great multitude of fishes
and their net broke,
and they motioned to their partners,
who were in the other boat,
to come and help them,
and they came and filled both of the boats,
so much that they began to sink.

When Simon Peter saw it,
he was astonished,
at the volume of fish they had caught,
as also were James and John, the sons of Zebedee,
who were partners with Simon,
and all who were with him.
He fell down at the knees of Jesus, saying,

"Leave me!
For I am a sinful man, O Lord."
Jesus said to Simon,
"Fear not! From now on you shall catch men."
When they had brought their boats to the shore,
they abandoned it all and followed Him.

38 A Demon in the Synagogue of Capernaum

(Mark 1:21-28; Luke 4:33-37)

They went into Capernaum;
and on the Sabbath day
He entered the synagogue and immediately taught.
They were astonished at His teaching:
for He taught them as one who had authority,
and not as the Scribes.
There was in their synagogue
a man with an unclean spirit of a demon;
and he cried out with a loud voice,

"Leave us alone!
What have we to do with Thee,
thou Jesus of Nazareth?
Art Thou come to destroy us?
I know thee who Thou art,
the Holy One of God!"

Jesus rebuked him, saying,

"Hold your peace,
and come out of him!"

And when the unclean spirit had torn him,
and cried with a loud voice,
and thrown him down in their midst,
he came out of him
and he was unhurt.

And they were all amazed,
so much that they questioned one another, saying,
    "What is this thing?
    What is this new teaching?
    He commands even the unclean spirits,
    with authority and power!
    And they obey him and come out!"
And immediately His fame spread abroad
throughout all the region around Galilee.

39   More Healings in Capernaum
(Matthew 8:14-17; Mark 1:29-38; Luke 4:38-43)

Afterwards, they left the synagogue,
and Jesus came to the house of Simon Peter,
with James and John.
But Simon's mother-in-law lay sick with a severe fever,
and right away they told Him about her.

He saw her and stood over her and rebuked the fever,
and took her by the hand and lifted her up.
Immediately, the fever left her:
and she got up and started serving them.

When evening came, as the sun set,
all the city gathered together at the door.
And they brought to Him all who were diseased,
and many who were possessed with devils:
and He cast the spirits out with His word.
Demons also came out of many, crying out,
    "Thou art Christ the Son of God!"
And He rebuked them,
not permitting them to speak:
for they knew that He was Christ.

He laid His hands on every one of them,
and healed all the crowd who were sick.
So, what was spoken by Isaiah the prophet was fulfilled, who said,
"Himself took our infirmities,
and bare our sicknesses."

And in the morning, rising up a great while before day,
He departed and went out into a solitary place,
and there prayed.
And the people sought Him,
and came to Him,
and detained Him,
so that He would not leave them.
And Simon and those who were with him followed after Him.

When they had found Him,
they said to Him,
"All men look for you."
And He said to them,
"Let us go into the next towns,
so that I may preach the Kingdom of God there also:
for that is why I came forth."

40   The Multitudes Gather

(Matthew 4:23-25, 8:2-4; Mark 1:39-45; Luke 4:44, 5:12-16)

Jesus went about all Galilee,
teaching in their synagogues,
and preaching the Gospel of the Kingdom,
healing all kinds of sickness and disease among the people.

His fame spread throughout all Syria:
and they brought to Him

all the sick people who were stricken with various diseases
and torments,
and those who were possessed with demons,
and those who were lunatics,
and those who were paralyzed,
and He healed them.
Great multitudes of people followed Him from Galilee,
and from Decapolis,
and from Jerusalem,
and from Judea,
and from beyond Jordan.

It came to pass,
when He was in a certain city,
a man full of leprosy came there to Him,
who begged Him,
kneeling down and worshiping, saying,
    "Lord, if it is your will,
      you can make me clean."
And Jesus, moved with compassion,
put out His hand,
and touched him, saying,
    "I would have it so. Be clean!"
Immediately the leprosy left him,
and he was cleansed.
And Jesus strictly charged him,
and promptly sent him away;
saying to him,
    "See that you tell no one;
    but go on your way,
    show yourself to the priest,
    and offer for your cleansing the gift that Moses commanded,
    as a testimony to them."
But he went out and began to proclaim it everywhere,

and spread the matter abroad like a fire.

Great multitudes gathered to hear Him
and to be healed by Him of their infirmities.
So much more did fame go ahead of Him,
that Jesus could no longer enter the city openly,
but was out in the wilderness
and still they came to Him from every quarter.
So, He withdrew into the wilderness and prayed.

41   Jesus Heals and Forgives a Paralyzed Man
(Matthew 9:2-8; Mark 2:1-12; Luke 5:17-26)

After a while He returned to Capernaum;
and it came to pass on a certain day as He was teaching,
that there were Pharisees and doctors of the Law sitting by,
and the word spread that He was in the house.
Right away many gathered together,
from out of every town of Galilee, and Judea, and Jerusalem:
so many that there was no room for them,
not even around the door.
And the power of the Lord was there to heal them.
and He preached the Word to them.

They brought Him a paralyzed man,
lying on a bed carried by four.
And they looked for a way to bring him in,
and to lay him before Jesus.
When they could not bring him near to Jesus
because of the press of the multitude,
they went up on the housetop where He was.
They uncovered the roof:
and when they had broken it up,

through the tiling,
they let down the bed
on which the paralyzed man lay.

Seeing their faith,
Jesus said to the paralyzed man;
 "Son be of good cheer!
 Your sins are forgiven!"
Certain Scribes sitting there,
debating in their hearts, said within themselves,
 "Why does this man speak blasphemies?
 Who can forgive sins but God alone?"

Immediately, when Jesus perceived in His spirit
that they debated like this within themselves,
knowing their thoughts, He said,
 "Why do you think these evil things in your hearts?
 For what is easier,
 to say to the paralyzed man,
  'Your sins are forgiven;'
 or to say,
  'Arise. Pick up your bed and walk?'
 But so that you may know
 that the Son of Man has power on earth to forgive sins
(He then said to the paralyzed man):
 I say to you,
 Get up!
 Pick up your bed,
 and go to your own house."
And he immediately got up,
took up the bed,
and went out before them all,
and left for his house,
glorifying God.

But when the multitudes saw it,
they marveled and were all amazed and glorified God,
who had given such power to men, saying,
    "We never saw anything like this!"
And they were filled with fear, saying,
    "We have seen strange things today."

42   Jesus Calls Levi (Matthew)

(Matthew 9:9; Mark 2:13-14; Luke 5:27-28)

After these things,
as Jesus again went from there to the seaside,
all the multitude followed Him,
and He taught them.
He saw a man sitting at the tax office:
a tax collector called Matthew,
Levi the son of Alphaeus,
and He said to him,
    "Follow Me!"
And he got up, left it all,
and followed Him.

43   Parables at Levi's Feast

(Matthew 9:10-17; Mark 2:15-22; Luke 5:29-39)

Levi made Him a great feast in his own house.
It came to pass,
as Jesus sat to dinner in the house,
many tax collectors and sinners came
and sat down with Him and His disciples:
for there were many and they followed Him.
When the Scribes and Pharisees
saw Him eat with tax collectors and sinners,

they said to His disciples,
    "Why do you and your Master eat and drink,
    with tax collectors and sinners?"

But when Jesus heard that,
He answered them,
    "Those who are whole do not need a physician,
    like those who are sick.
    But as for you,
    go and learn what this means,
        'I will have mercy,
        and not sacrifice:'
    for I have not come to call the righteous to repentance,
    but sinners instead,"

Then the disciples of John and of the Pharisees came to him, saying,
    "Why do we and the Pharisees often fast,
    but your disciples eat and drink?"
And Jesus said to them,
    "Can you make
    the children of the Bride-chamber
    fast and mourn,
    while the Bridegroom is with them?
    But the days will come when the Bridegroom
    will be taken from them,
    and then, in those days,
    they will fast."

He also told them a parable;
    "Also, no man having drunk old wine
    immediately wants the new:
    for he says,
        'The old is better.'
    Nor do men put new wine into old wine-skins:

or else the new wine bursts the skins,
and the wine will be spilled and run out,
and the skins will be ruined.
Instead, they put new wine into new skins,
and both are preserved.
Also, no one sews a piece of new cloth on old clothing,
for the new piece that is put in to patch it
pulls apart the old clothing,
and the tear is made worse."

44   The Second Passover

(John 5:1-15)

Afterwards there was a Feast of the Jews;
and Jesus went up to Jerusalem.

Now in Jerusalem by the Sheep Market there was a pool,
which is called in Hebrew, "Bethesda," since it had five porches.
In these lay a great multitude of handicapped folk,
the blind,
the lame,
the withered,
all waiting for the movement of the water.
At certain times an angel went down into the pool
and stirred the waters.
Whoever stepped in first was healed of whatever disease he had.

A certain man was there,
who had been handicapped thirty-eight years.
When Jesus saw him lying there
He knew that he been that way a long time,
and He said to him,

"Do you want to be healed?"
The handicapped man answered Him,

"Sir, when the water stirs,
I have no one to put me into the pool.
But while I am still coming,
another steps in before me."

Jesus said,
"Rise, pick up your bed, and walk."
And immediately the man was healed,
picked up his bed and walked:
on that very Sabbath day.

So, the Jews said to him who was healed,
"It is the Sabbath day:
it is not lawful for you to carry your bed."
He answered,
"He who healed me said to me,
'Pick up your bed and walk.'"
Then they asked,
"What man told you,
'Pick up your bed and walk'?"
But he who was healed did not know who it was:
for Jesus had walked away through the multitude in that place.
Afterwards Jesus found him in the Temple and said,
"Look! You are made whole.
Sin no more
or a worse thing may happen to you."
The man left and told the Jews
that it was Jesus who had made him whole.

45   The Testimony of God the Father

(John 5:16-47)

For this reason,
the Jews persecuted Jesus,

and sought to slay Him,
because He had done these things on the Sabbath day.
But Jesus answered them,
    "My Father works today and so I also work."
So, the Jews sought even more to kill Him,
not only because He had broken the Sabbath,
but also said that God was His Father,
making Himself equal with God.

Then Jesus answered them,
    "Truly, truly, I tell you,
    the Son can do nothing through Himself,
    except what He sees the Father do:
    because whatever He does,
    the Son does likewise.
    For the Father loved the Son,
    and showed Him all things that He, Himself, does.
    He will show Him greater works than these,
    such that you will be astonished!
    Just as the Father raises up the dead
    and gives them life;
    even so the Son gives life to whoever He desires.
    For the Father judges no one,
    but has committed all judgment to the Son:
    so that all should honor the Son,
    just as they honor the Father.
    He who does not honor the Son
    does not honor the Father who has sent Him."

    "Truly, truly, I tell you,
    He who hears My Word,
    and believes in Him who sent Me,
    has Everlasting Life,
    and shall not come into damnation;

but passes from death to Life."

"Truly, truly, I tell you,
The hour comes, and is now,
when the dead shall hear the voice of the Son of God:
and those who hear shall live.
Just as the Father has Life in Himself;
so has he granted it to the Son to have Life in Himself;
and has also granted Him authority to execute judgment,
because He is the Son of Man.
Do not be astonished at this:
for the hour is coming,
in which all who are in the graves shall hear His voice,
and shall come forth;
those who have done good,
to the Resurrection of Life;
and those who have done evil,
to the Resurrection of Damnation."

"By Myself
I can do nothing:
as I hear, I judge:
and My judgment is just;
because I do not seek My own will,
but instead the will of the Father who sent Me.
If I testify alone for Myself,
my witness is not true.
There is another who testifies for Me;
and I know that the testimony that he witnessed about Me is true."

"You sent to John,
and he testified to the Truth.
I do not require testimony from man for Myself:
but I say these things so that you might be saved.

He was a burning and a shining light:
and you were willing for a season to rejoice in his light.
But I have greater testimony than that of John:
for the works that the Father has given Me to finish,
the very works that I do,
testify for Me that the Father has sent Me.
And the Father Himself, who has sent Me,
has testified for Me.
You have never heard His voice,
nor seen His shape.
And you do not have His Word living in you:
for you do not believe
He whom He has sent.
Search the Scriptures,
because you think you have Eternal Life in them,
but they testify for Me.
Yet you will not come to Me,
so that you might have Life."

"I do not receive honor from Mankind.
But I know you,
and how you do not have the love of God in you.
I have come in My Father's Name,
and you do not believe Me.
If another comes in his own name,
him you believe.
How can you believe,
who receive honor from one another,
but do not seek the honor that comes only from God?

Do not think that I will accuse you to the Father.
There is another who accuses you:
indeed, it is Moses, in whom you trust.
If you had believed Moses,

you would have believed Me:
because he wrote about Me.
But if you do not believe his writings,
how can you believe My words?"

46   Lord of the Sabbath

(Matthew 12:1-8; Mark 2:23-28; Luke 6:1-5)

At that time, it came to pass,
on the second Sabbath after the first,
that Jesus went on the Sabbath day through the grain fields;
and His disciples were hungry.
As they went,
they began to pluck the heads of grain to eat,
rubbing them in their hands.
When the Pharisees saw it,
they said to Him,

 "Look! Why are your disciples doing
 what is not lawful on the Sabbath Day?"
But He said to them,
 "Have you not read so much as this,
 what David did,
 when he and those who were with him,
 had need and were hungry?
 How he entered the House of God
 in the days of Abiathar the High Priest,
 and took and ate the showbread,
 which was not lawful for him or those with him to eat,
 but only for the priests?
 Or have you not read in the Law,
 how, on the Sabbath days,
 the Priests in the Temple profane the Sabbath,
 and are blameless?
 But I tell you,

that in this place
there is One greater than the Temple!"

And He said to them,
"The Sabbath was made for man!
Not man for the Sabbath!
But if you had known what this means,
'*I will have mercy,*
and not sacrifice',
you would not have condemned the guiltless.
For the Son of Man is Lord even of the Sabbath day!"

47   A Healing on the Sabbath

(Matthew 12:9-14; Mark 3:1-6; Luke 6:6-11)

After He left there,
it also came to pass on another Sabbath,
that He again entered their Synagogue and taught,
and a man was there whose right hand was withered.
The Scribes and Pharisees watched Him
so that they might accuse Him,
and asked Him,
"Is it lawful to heal on the Sabbath Days?"
But He knew their thoughts,
and He said to the man who had the withered hand,
"Get up and stand in front of the rest."
And he got up and stepped forward.
Then Jesus said to them,
"I will ask you one thing;
Is it lawful to do good on the Sabbath days
or to do evil?
to save life
or to kill?"
But they held their peace.

And He said to them,
  "What man is there among you,
  who has a sheep,
  and if it falls into a pit on the Sabbath day,
  will not take hold of it and lift it out?
  How much better then,
  is a man than a sheep?
  So! It is lawful to do good deeds on the Sabbath days!"

He looked around on them in anger and grief
for the hardness of their hearts,
and then He said to the man,
"Stretch out your hand!"

He stretched it out;
and it was wholly restored,
and was just like the other.

The Pharisees were filled with wrath
and immediately went out
to scheme together with the Herodians against Him,
on how they could destroy Him..

48 Jesus Withdraws from the Multitudes

(Matthew 12:14-21)

But when Jesus knew of it,
He withdrew from there.
Great multitudes followed Him,
and He healed them all
and charged them not to make Him known:
so that what Isaiah the prophet said could be fulfilled,
who said,
  "Behold My Servant,

whom I have chosen;
my Beloved, in whom My soul is well pleased:
I will put My spirit upon Him,
and He shall shew judgment to the Gentiles.
He shall not strive, nor cry;
neither shall any man hear His voice in the streets.
A bruised reed shall He not break,
and smoking flax shall He not quench,
till He send forth judgment unto victory.
And in His Name shall the Gentiles trust."

49   Multitudes Follow for Healing

(Mark 3:7-12)

Jesus withdrew with His disciples to the sea.
When they had heard of the great things He did,
a great multitude followed Him from Galilee,
and came to Him
from Judea, Jerusalem, Idumea,
from around Tyre and Sidon,
and from beyond Jordan.
He spoke to His disciples,
saying that because of the multitude,
a small boat should carry Him
or else they would crush Him.

He had healed so many;
that they now pressed in upon Him to touch Him.
All who had plagues and unclean spirits,
fell down before Him when they saw Him,
and cried out,
   "Thou art the Son of God!"
And He strictly charged them not to make Him known.

50 The Twelve Apostles

(Mark 3:13-19; Luke 6:12-16)

It came to pass in those days,
that He went up into a mountain to pray,
and continued all night in prayer to God.
When it was day,
He called to Him those
whom He chose from His disciples:
and they came to Him and went into a house.

He chose and ordained twelve to be with Him,
whom He named Apostles,
so that He might send them out to preach,
and to have power to heal sicknesses,
and to cast out demons:
Simon (whom He called Peter)
and Andrew, his brother;
James, the son of Zebedee,
and John the brother of James
(whom He called Boanerges,
which means 'The Sons of Thunder');
Philip and Bartholomew;
Matthew and Thomas;
James, the son of Alphaeus,
and Judas Thaddaeus the brother of James;
Simon the Canaanite, who was called the Zealot,
and Judas Iscariot, who also betrayed Him.

51 Healing the Multitude

(Luke 6:17-19)

He came down with them,
and stood in the plain,

with the company of His disciples,
and a great multitude of people out of all Judea and Jerusalem,
and from the seacoast of Tyre and Sidon,
who came to hear Him and to be healed of their diseases.
Those who were vexed with unclean spirits were healed.
And the whole multitude sought to touch Him:
for power went out of Him that healed them all.

52　Sermon on the Mount[9]

(Matthew 5:1)

Seeing the multitudes,
He went up into a mountain:
and when He was ready,
His disciples came to Him.

53　Sermon on the Mount: The Blessed

(Matthew 5:2-12, Luke 6:20-23)

He lifted up His eyes on His disciples,
and He opened His mouth and taught them, saying,
　　"Blessed are you, the poor in spirit:
　　for yours is the Kingdom of Heaven.
　　Blessed are you who mourn:
　　for you shall be comforted.
　　Blessed are you who now weep:
　　for you shall laugh.
　　Blessed are the meek:
　　for they shall inherit the Earth.
　　Blessed are you who now hunger and thirst for righteousness:
　　for you shall be filled.
　　Blessed are the merciful:
　　for they shall receive mercy.

Blessed are the pure in heart:
for they shall see God.
Blessed are the peacemakers:
for they shall be called the Children of God.
Blessed are those who are persecuted for righteousness' sake:
for theirs is the Kingdom of Heaven.

Blessed are you,
when men hate you,
and revile you,
and persecute you,
and when they drive you from their company,
and reproach you,
and falsely say all manner of evil against your name,
for the Son of Man's sake.

Rejoice on that day,
and leap for joy,
and be exceedingly glad!
Because, see! your reward in Heaven is great!
For so too did their fathers persecute the prophets
who were before you."

54   Sermon on the Mount: The Cursed

(Luke 6:24-26)

"But woe to you who are rich!
because you have received your consolation.
Woe to you who are full!
for you shall hunger.
Woe to you who laugh now!
for you shall mourn and weep.
Woe to you, when all men speak well of you!
for so too did their fathers speak of the false prophets."

55   Sermon on the Mount: The Salt and the Light

(Matthew 5:13-16, Luke 14:34-35)

"You are the salt of the earth:
Salt is good:
but if the salt has lost its flavor,
what can flavor it?
It is neither fit for the land,
nor yet for the dunghill;
it has become good for nothing,
but to be thrown out and trampled under the feet of men.
He who has ears to hear, let him hear."

"You are the light of the world.
A city that is set on a hill cannot be hid.
Nor do men light a candle,
and put it under a basket,
but instead, on a candlestick;
and it gives light to all who are in the house.
Let your light so shine before men,
that they can see your good works,
and glorify your Father who is in Heaven."

56   Sermon on the Mount: The Law and the Prophets

(Matthew 5:17-20)

"Do not think that I have come
to destroy the Law or the Prophets:
I have not come to destroy them,
but to fulfill them.
For truly, I tell you,
until Heaven and Earth pass,
not one dot nor one stroke shall in any way pass from the Law,
until all is fulfilled.

So, whoever breaks one of these least commandments,
and teaches men likewise,
will be called the least in the Kingdom of Heaven:
but whoever shall do and teach them,
will be called great in the Kingdom of Heaven.
For I tell you,
unless your righteousness
exceeds the righteousness of the Scribes and Pharisees,
you can in no way enter into the Kingdom of Heaven."

57   Sermon on the Mount: Be Reconciled[10]

(Matthew 5:21-26)

"You have heard that it was said of old,
   'Thou shalt not kill;
   and whosoever shall kill shall be in danger of the judgment.'
But I tell you,
whoever is angry with his brother without cause
shall be in danger of the judgment."

"And whoever will say to his brother,
   'You are worthless!'
shall be in danger of the council:
but whoever will say,
   'You fool!'
shall be in danger of hellfire."

"So, if you bring your gift to the altar,
and remember there that your brother has something against you;
leave your gift there before the altar,
and go on your way.
First be reconciled to your brother,
and then come and offer your gift."

"Agree with your adversary quickly,
while you are on the way with him;
or else your adversary might at any time deliver you to the judge,
and the judge to the officer,
and you are thrown into prison.
Truly, I tell you,
by no means will you come out of there,
until you have paid the last *dime*."

58 Sermon on the Mount: Lust and Divorce

(Matthew 5:27-32)

You have heard that it was said of old,
 'Thou shalt not commit adultery.'
But I tell you,
whoever looks on a woman to lust after her
has committed adultery with her already in his heart.
If your right eye makes you sin,
pluck it out and throw it away from you:
for it is more profitable for you that one of your parts should perish,
than that your whole body should be cast into Hell.
If your right hand makes you sin,
cut it off and throw it away from you:
for it is more profitable for you that one of your parts should perish,
than that your whole body should be cast into Hell.

"It has been said,
 'Whosoever shall put away his wife,
 let him give her a writing of divorcement.'
But I tell you,
whoever divorces his wife,
except for the cause of fornication,
causes her to commit adultery:
and whoever marries her who is divorced

commits adultery."

59   Sermon on the Mount: Swearing and Oaths
(Matthew 5:33-37)

"Again, you have heard that it has been said old,
  'Thou shalt not forswear thyself,
  but shalt perform unto the Lord thine oaths.'"
"But I tell you,
swear not at all:
neither by Heaven, for it is God's Throne,
nor by the Earth, for it is His Footstool;
neither by Jerusalem, for it is the City of the great King.
Nor shall you swear by your head,
because you cannot make one hair white or black.
But let your communication be,
'Yes,' for yes;
'No,' for no;
because whatever is more than these proceeds from evil."

60   Sermon on the Mount: Love Your Enemies
(Matthew 5:38-48, Luke 6:27-36)

"You have heard that it has been said,
  'An eye for an eye,
  and a tooth for a tooth.'
But I tell you,
do not oppose evil.
Whoever shall strike you on your right cheek,
turn to him and offer the other also.
If any man will sue you in court,
and take away your coat,
let him also have your overcoat.

Whoever shall compel you to go a mile,
go with him two.

Give to him who asks you,
and do not turn away
from him who wants to borrow from you.
As for him who borrows your goods
do not ask for them again."

"You have heard that it has been said,
    'Thou shalt love thy neighbor,
    and hate thine enemy.'
But I tell you who will listen,
love your enemies,
bless those who curse you,
do good to those who hate you,
and pray for those who treat you spitefully and persecute you;
so that you may be the Children of your Father who is in Heaven:
for He makes His sun rise on the evil and on the good,
and sends rain on the just and on the unjust."

"As you would have men do to you,
You likewise do to them."

"If you love those who love you,
what reward do you have?
Even the tax collectors do the same, don't they?
If you do good to those who do good to you,
what thanks have you earned?
Sinners also do exactly the same.
If you only greet your brethren,
what are you doing more than others?
Even the tax collectors do so, don't they?"

"But love your enemies,

and do good,
and lend hoping for nothing in return;
and your reward will be great,
and you shall be the Children of the Highest:
for He is kind to the thankless and to the evil.
So be merciful,
as your Father also is merciful.
So be perfect,
even as your Father who is in Heaven is perfect."

61   Sermon on the Mount: Charity and Prayer
(Matthew 6:1-8, 16-21)

"Be careful that you do not give charity
in sight of men,
to be seen by them:
or you have no reward from your Father who is in Heaven.
So, when you give your charities,
do not sound a trumpet ahead of yourself,
as the hypocrites do in the synagogues and in the streets,
so that they may have the praise of men.
Truly, I tell you,
they have their reward.
But when you give charity,
do not let your left hand know what your right hand is doing:
so that your charities may be in secret:
and your Father,
who sees in secret
Himself shall reward you openly.

"When you pray,
do not be as the hypocrites are:
for they love to pray
standing in the synagogues and in the street corners,

so that they may be seen by men.
Truly, I tell you,
they have their reward.
But when you pray,
enter your closet,
and when you have shut your door,
pray to your Father who is in secret;
and your Father,
who sees in secret
shall reward you openly."

"When you pray,
do not use vain repetitions, as the heathen do:
for they think that they will be heard
because of their many words.
So, do not be like them.
Your Father knows what things you have need of,
before you ask Him."

"Also, when you fast,
do not put on a sad face like the hypocrites,
for they disfigure their faces,
so that they can be seen by men to fast.
Truly, I tell you,
they have their reward.
But when you fast,
anoint your head,
and wash your face;
so that you are not seen fasting by men,
but only by your Father who is in secret:
and your Father,
who sees in secret,
will reward you openly."

62   Sermon on the Mount: Treasures in Heaven
(Matthew 6:24, Luke 6:34)

"Do not lay for yourselves treasures on Earth,
where moth and rust corrupt,
and where thieves break through and steal."

"Instead, lay up for yourselves treasures in Heaven,
where neither moth nor rust corrupts,
and where thieves do not break through or steal.
Where your treasure is,
there your heart will be also.
No man can serve two masters:
for either he will hate the one,
and love the other;
or else he will hold to the one,
and despise the other.
You cannot serve God and greed."

63   Sermon on the Mount: Do Not Be Anxious[11]
(Matthew 6:25-34, Luke 6:22-40)

"So, I tell you,
do not be worried about your life,
what you will eat,
or what you will drink;
nor yet for your body,
what you will wear.
Is not life more than food,
and the body more than clothing?"

"See the birds of the air?
Consider the ravens:
for they do not plant,

nor do they harvest,
or gather into storehouses or barns;
yet your Heavenly Father feeds them.
Are you not much better than them?

Who among you can add *a foot* to his height by worrying?
So, if you are not able to do that little thing,
why do you anxiously worry about the rest?"

"And why do you worry about clothing?
Consider the lilies of the field, how they grow;
they do not work,
nor do they weave:
And yet I tell you that even Solomon in all his glory
was not clothed like one of these."

"So, if God clothes the grass of the field in such a way,
which is in the field today
and is thrown into the oven tomorrow,
shall he not care much more to clothe you?
Oh, you of little faith!"

"So, take no thought, saying,
    'What will we eat?' or,
    'What will we drink?' or,
    'What will we wear?'
Nor be of a doubtful mind.
Your Heavenly Father knows that you have need of all these things.
The Gentiles, the nations of the world, seek after all these things.
But you seek the Kingdom of God and His righteousness first;
and all these things will be added to you.
So, do not worry about tomorrow;
tomorrow can worry about itself.
Each day's evil is enough for itself."

"Do not fear, little flock!
It is your Father's good pleasure to give you the Kingdom!
Sell what you have and give charitably!
Provide yourselves bags that do not grow old,
a treasure in the Heavens that does not fail,
where no thief approaches,
where no moth corrupts.
Where your treasure is,
there your heart will be also."

64   Sermon on the Mount: Do Not Be Judgmental
(Matthew 7:1-5, Luke 6:37,41-42)

"Do not judge,
and you shall not be judged.
Do not condemn,
and you shall not be condemned.
Forgive,
and you shall be forgiven"

"With the judgment you judge,
you will be judged:
and the measurement you measure out,
will be measured back to you."

"Why do you look for the speck in your brother's eye,
but do not see the beam in your own eye?
How can you say to your brother,
     'Let me take the speck out of your eye'
but cannot see the beam in your own eye?
You hypocrite!
First, take the beam out of your own eye;
and then you can see clearly
to take the speck out of your brother's eye."

65   Sermon on the Mount: Giving and Receiving

(Matthew 7:6-12, Luke 6:38)

"Do not give that which is holy to the dogs,
nor throw your pearls before swine,
or they may trample them under their feet,
and turn around and rip into you."

"But give and it will be given to you.
In good measure,
pressed down,
shaken and settled,
and running over,
men shall give into your pocket.
The same measurement you measure out
will be measured back to you."

"Ask, and it will be given to you.
Seek, and you will find.
Knock, and it will be opened to you.
For everyone who asks, receives;
and he who seeks, finds;
and to him who knocks, it will be opened."

"What man is there among you, who,
if his son asks for bread,
will give him a stone?
Or, if he asks for a fish,
will give him a serpent?
If you then, being evil,
know how to give good gifts to your children,
how much more shall your Father who is in Heaven
give good things to those who ask Him?

"So, in whatever and in all things

you would have men do to you,
do just so to them in the same way:
for this is the Law and the Prophets."

66   Sermon on the Mount: The Narrow Gate

(Matthew 7:13-14, Luke 6:39-40)

He told them a parable:
    "Can the blind lead the blind?
    Shall they not both fall into the ditch?
    The disciple is not above his master:
    but everyone who is perfect shall be as his master."

    "Enter in at the narrow gate:
    for the gate is wide and the way is broad
    that leads to Damnation,
    and there are many who go that way.
    Because the gate is narrow and the way is hard,
    which leads to Life,
    and there are few who find it."

67   Sermon on the Mount: False Prophets

(Matthew 7:15-23, Luke 6:43-46)

"Beware of false prophets,
who come to you in sheep's clothing,
but inwardly they are ravening wolves!
You will know them by their fruits!
Do men gather grapes from thorns, or figs from thistles?
Just so, every good tree produces good fruit;
but a corrupt tree produces evil fruit.
A good man out of the good treasure of his heart
produces that which is good;

and an evil man out of the evil treasure of his heart
produces that which is evil:
because the mouth speaks
from the abundance of the heart.
A good tree cannot produce evil fruit;
nor can a corrupt tree produce good fruit.
Every tree that does not produce good fruit is chopped down,
and cast into the fire.
So, you will know them by their fruits."

"Not everyone who says to Me,
    'Lord! Lord!'
shall enter the Kingdom of Heaven;
but only he who does the will of My Father who is in Heaven.
Many will say to Me in that day,
    'Lord! Lord!
    Have we not prophesied in Your name?
    In Your name we have cast out demons
    and in Your name done many wonderful works!'
And then I will say to them,
    'Why do you call Me,
        "Lord! Lord!"
    and do not do the things I say?
    I never knew you.
    Depart from Me,
    you workers in unrighteousness!'"

68   Sermon on the Mount: Building on Sand

(Matthew 7:24-8:1, Luke 6:47-49, 7:1)

"So, whoever comes to Me,
and hears these sayings of Mine,
and does them,
I compare to a wise man,

who built his house upon a rock.
The rain fell,
the floodwaters rose,
the winds blew and beat upon that house,
the stream broke upon that house and could not shake it;
and it did not fall,
because it was founded upon a rock."

"Everyone who hears these sayings of Mine,
and does not do them,
is like a foolish man,
who built his house upon the sand.
The rain fell,
the floodwaters came,
the winds blew and beat upon that house,
the stream broke upon that house;
and it fell.
Great was the fall and ruin of it."

And it came to pass,
when Jesus had ended these sermons,
in the hearing of the people,
they were astonished at His teaching:
because He taught them as one with authority,
and not as the Scribes taught.
Now when he came down from the mountain,
great multitudes followed Him.

69   The Faith of the Centurion

(Matthew 8:5-13; Luke 7:1-10)

And when Jesus entered Capernaum,
a certain Centurion,
who had a dear servant who was sick and ready to die,

heard of Jesus,
and sent the elders of the Jews to Him,
to entreat that He would come and heal the servant.

When they came to Jesus,
they immediately entreated Him,
saying that the one for whom He should do this was worthy:
 "For he loves our nation,
 and he has built us a synagogue."
And saying,
 "Lord, his servant is grievously tormented
 and lies at home sick and paralyzed."
And Jesus said to them,
 "I will come and heal him."

Then Jesus went with them
and when He was not far from the house,
the Centurion sent friends to Him, saying,
 "Lord, do not trouble yourself:
 for I am not worthy
 that you should enter under my roof:
 Nor did I think myself worthy to come to You.
 Only say the word,
 and my servant will be healed.
 I am a man under authority,
 having soldiers under me:
 I say to this man, 'Go,' and he goes;
 to another, 'Come,' and he comes;
 to my servant, 'Do this,' and he does it."

When Jesus heard it, He was astonished,
and turned around and said to the people who followed,
 "Truly, I tell you,
 I have not found such great faith,

no, not in Israel.
I tell you that many will come from the east and west,
and shall sit down with Abraham, and Isaac, and Jacob,
in the Kingdom of Heaven.
But the children of the Kingdom
will be cast into the outer darkness:
there will be weeping and gnashing of teeth."
And Jesus said to those who were sent by the Centurion,
    "Go on your way;
    and say to him that as he has believed,
    so, too, will it done to him."
And returning to the house,
they found his servant was healed in the same hour.

70   A Resurrection in Nain

(Luke 7:11-17)

It came to pass the day after,
that He went into a city called Nain;
and many of His disciples and people went with Him.
Now when He came near the gate of the city,
they saw there was a dead man being carried out.
He was the only son of his mother,
and she was a widow:
and many people of the city were with her.
When the Lord saw her,
He had compassion for her,
and said to her,
    "Do not weep."
He came and touched the bier:
and those who carried him stood still.
He said,
    "Young man, I say to you, "Arise!"
He who was dead sat up and began to speak

and He delivered him to his mother.
There came a fear on them all:
and they praised God, saying,

"A great prophet has risen up among us!
God has visited His people!"

And this story about Him spread throughout all Judea,
and throughout all the surrounding region.

71   John's Disciples Question Jesus

(Matthew 11:2-6; Luke 7:18-23)

Now, at that same time,
He cured many of their infirmities and plagues and evil spirits;
and He gave sight to many who were blind.
When the disciples of John told him in the prison
of all these works of Christ,
he called two of his disciples to him
and sent them to Jesus,
to say to Him,

"Are you He who should come,
or do we look for another?"

At that same time,
He cured many of their infirmities and plagues and evil spirits;
and He gave sight to many who were blind.

Then Jesus answered them,

"Go on your way and show John again
those things which you hear and see.
The blind received their sight
and the lame walk;
the lepers are cleansed
and the deaf hear;
the dead are raised up
and the poor have the gospel preached to them!

Whoever is not offended by Me is blessed."

72   Jesus Commends John the Baptist

(Matthew 11:7-19; Luke 7:24-35)

When the messengers of John had gone,
Jesus began to speak to the multitudes about John,
    "What did you go out into the wilderness to see?
    A reed shaken with the wind?
    What did you go out to see?
    A man dressed in effeminate apparel?
    Look, those who wear soft, lavish clothing
    and who live luxuriously
    are in houses and courts of kings.
    What did you go out to see?
    A prophet?
    Yes, I tell you,
    and much more than a prophet."

"This is he of whom it was written,
    'Behold, I send My messenger before Thy face,
    which shall prepare Thy way before Thee.'
Truly, I tell you,
Among those born of women,
there has not risen a greater prophet than John the Baptist."

"Even so,
he who is least in the Kingdom of Heaven
is greater than him.
From the days of John the Baptist until now
the Kingdom of Heaven suffers violence,
and the violent take it by force.
All the Prophets and the Law prophesied until John;
and, if you will accept it,

this is Elijah, who was to come.
He who has ears to hear, let him hear."

And all the people and the tax collectors who heard Him,
declared the righteousness of God,
having been baptized by John.
But the Pharisees and Scribes
rejected the will of God for themselves,
not being baptized by him.

And the Lord said,
    "But to what shall I compare this generation?
    It is like children sitting in the markets,
    and calling to their friends, and saying,
        'We have played the flute for you,
        and you have not danced.
        We have mourned for you,
        and you have not wept.'
    John the Baptist came neither eating nor drinking, and they said,
        'He has a demon!'
    The Son of Man came eating and drinking, and they say,
        'Look a man who is gluttonous and a drunkard,
        a friend of tax collectors and sinners!'
    But wisdom is declared by her children."

73   Jesus Rebukes Three Cities

(Matthew 11:20-30; Luke 10:13-15)

Then He began to reproach the cities
where most of His great works were done,
because they did not repent.
    "Woe to you, Chorazin!
    Woe to you, Bethsaida!
    If the great works done in you,

had been done in Tyre and Sidon,
they would have repented long ago in sackcloth and ashes.
But I tell you,
it shall be more bearable for Tyre and Sidon
in the Day of Judgment,
than for you.
And you, Capernaum,
who are exalted to Heaven,
shalt be brought down to Hell:
for if the great works, which were done in you,
had been done in Sodom,
it would have remained until this day.
But I tell you,
that it shall be more bearable for the land of Sodom
in the Day of Judgment,
than for you."

Then Jesus continued,
  "I thank you, Father,
  Lord of Heaven and Earth,
  because you hid these things from the wise and learned,
  and revealed them to infants.
  Justly so, Father:
  for that seemed good in Your sight."

"All things are delivered to Me from My Father:
and no man knows the Son,
except the Father;
nor does any man know the Father,
except the Son,
and to whomever the Son reveals Him."

"Come to Me,
all you who labor and are heavily burdened,

and I will give you rest.
Take up My harness and learn from Me;
for I am gentle and humble of heart:
and you will find rest for your souls.
For My harness is easy,
and My burden is light."

74   The Sinful Woman of The City[12]

(Luke 7:36-50)

One of the Pharisees wanted Jesus to eat with him.
So, He went into the Pharisee's house,
Then a sinful woman of the city came to Him
when she knew that Jesus sat at the feast
in the Pharisee's house.
She brought an alabaster box of ointment
and stood behind Jesus at His feet,
weeping,
and began to wash His feet with tears,
and wiped them with the hair of her head,
and kissed His feet,
and anointed them with the ointment,

Now when the Pharisee who had invited Him saw this,
he spoke within himself, saying,
        "This man,
        if he were a prophet,
        would have known who
        and what manner of woman this is
        that touches him:
        since she is a sinner."
And Jesus said to him,
        "Simon, I have something to say to you."
And he said,

"Master, speak."

"There was a certain creditor who had two debtors:
the one owed a sum worth five hundred day's labor,
and the other fifty.
And when they had nothing to pay,
he frankly forgave them both.
Tell me therefore,
which of them will love him most?"
Simon answered and said,
"I suppose that he to whom he forgave most."
And He said to him,
"You have judged rightly."

He turned to the woman,
and said to Simon,
"Do you see this woman?
I entered your house,
and you gave me no water for my feet:
but she has washed my feet with her tears,
and wiped them with the hair of her head.
You gave me no kiss [of greeting]:
but this woman, since the time I came in,
has not ceased to kiss my feet.
You did not anoint my head with oil:
but this woman has anointed my feet with ointment.
So, I tell you,
her sins, which are many, are forgiven;
for she loved much:
but he who is forgiven little,
loves little."
And He said to her,
"Your sins are forgiven."

And those who sat at supper with Him
began to say within themselves,
    "Who is this who also forgives sins?"
And He said to the woman,
    "Your faith has saved you!
    Go in peace."

75   The Generous Women

(Matthew 11:1; Luke 8:1-3)

Afterwards, it came to pass,
when Jesus had finished instructing His twelve disciples,
that He went throughout every city and village,
teaching and preaching and showing
the joyful news of the Kingdom of God:
and the Twelve were with Him,
as well as certain women,
who had been healed of evil spirits and infirmities:
Mary "Magdalene", out of whom went seven devils,
and Joanna the wife of Chuza, Herod's steward,
and Susanna, and many others,
who provided for Him from what they had.

76   Jesus Heals a Possessed Man

(Matthew 12:22-23; Mark 3:20-21; Luke 11:14)

And the multitude gathered together again,
so many they could not even eat bread.
Then one was brought to Him
who was blind and mute
and possessed by a demon.
It came to pass,
when the demon was gone,

that He healed him,
and he who had been blind and mute
could both speak and see.
All the people were astonished and amazed, and said,
    "Is this not the Son of David?"
When His family heard of it,
they went out to restrain Him, saying,
    'He is beside himself!"

77   Blasphemy of the Pharisees
    (Matthew 12:24-37,43-45; Mark 3:22-30; Luke 11:15-26)

When the Scribes and Pharisees heard it,
who came down from Jerusalem,
some of them said,
    "This fellow does not cast out demons,
    unless through Beelzebub the prince of the demons!"
Others, testing Him, wanted a sign from Heaven through Him.

And Jesus knew their thoughts,
and said to them,
    "Every kingdom divided against itself
    is brought to desolation.
    Every city or house divided against itself
    shall not stand.
    And if Satan casts out Satan,
    he is divided against himself,
    and he cannot stand,
    but has an end.
    How then shall his kingdom stand?
    And if through Beelzebub I cast out demons,
    by whom do your children cast them out?
    So, they will be your judges.
    But if I, with the finger of God,

cast out demons by the Spirit of God,
then the Kingdom of God has come to you."

"Or else how can one enter a strong man's house,
and steal his goods,
unless he first binds the strong man?
Then he can plunder his house.
When a man, strong and well-armed,
keeps his palace,
his goods are in peace.
But when a stronger one overcomes him,
he takes from him all his armor in which he trusted,
and plunders his property."

"He who is not with Me is against Me;
and he who does not gather with Me scatters abroad."

"When the unclean spirit is gone out of a man,
he walks through dry places seeking rest;
and finding none, he says,
    'I will return to my house which I left.'
And when he comes,
he finds it swept and put in order.
Then he goes,
and gathers seven more spirits
more wicked than himself;
and they enter in, and dwell there:
and the last state of that man is worse than the first.
Just so shall it be to this wicked generation."

"Truly, I tell you,
all manner of sin and blasphemy
will be forgiven of men:
except blasphemy against the Holy Spirit.
That shall not be forgiven of men.

Whoever speaks a word against the Son of Man,
it will be forgiven him:
however they blaspheme.
Because they said,
    'He has an unclean spirit',
whoever speaks against the Holy Spirit
is in danger of eternal damnation.
It shall not be forgiven him,
neither in this world,
nor in the world to come."

"Either make the tree good,
and his fruit good;
or else make the tree corrupt,
and his fruit corrupt:
for the tree is known by his fruit."

"Oh, generation of vipers!
How can you, being evil, speak good things?
Out of the abundance of the heart, the mouth speaks.
But I tell you,
men shall be held accountable in the Day of Judgment
for every idle word that they will speak.
For by your words you will be declared righteous,
and by your words you will be condemned."

78   The Sign of Jonah

(Matthew 12:38-42; Luke 11:29-32)

Then certain Scribes and Pharisees answered,
    "Master, we want to see a sign from you."
When the people were gathered thickly together,
He began to say,
    "An evil and adulterous generation seeks after a sign;

and there will no sign be given to it,
but the sign of the prophet Jonah.
Just as Jonah was a sign to the Ninevites,
so, too, shall the Son of Man be to this generation.
Just as Jonah was three days and three nights
in the belly of the whale;
so, the Son of Man will be three days and three nights
in the heart of the Earth.
The men of Nineveh
shall rise in the Judgment with this generation,
and will condemn it:
because they repented at the preaching of Jonah;
Behold! One greater than Jonah is here!
The Queen of the South
shall rise up in the Judgment with this generation,
and will condemn it:
because she came from the uttermost parts of the earth
to hear the wisdom of Solomon;
Behold! One greater than Solomon is here!"

79   The Family of Jesus

(Matthew 12:46-50; Mark 3:31-35; Luke 8:19-21)

While He still talked to the people,
His mother and his brothers came to Him and stood outside,
and could not come to Him for the crowd,
and sent to Him,
wanting to speak with Him.
The multitude sat about Him,
and then a certain one said to Him,
   "Look, your mother and your brothers stand outside,
   wanting to speak with you!"
But He answered and said to him,
   "Who is My mother?

and who are My brothers?"

He looked about on those who sat around Him,
and He stretched out His hand toward His disciples and said,
"See My mother and My brothers!
Whoever shall hear the Word of God,
and do the will of My Father who is in Heaven,
they are My brother, and sister, and mother."

80   Parables by the Sea

(Matthew 13:1-2; Mark 4:1; Luke 8:4)

The same day Jesus went out of the house,
and He sat by the seaside
and began to teach again.
Great multitudes gathered
and came to Him out of every city,
so that He went into a boat and sat in the sea;
and the whole multitude stood on the shore by the sea.

81   Parables by the Sea: The Parable of the Seeds

(Matthew 13:3-9; Mark 4:2-9; Luke 8:5-8)

He taught them many things in parables,
saying in His teachings,
"Listen. A planter went out to sow his seed.
It came to pass when he sowed,
that some seeds fell by the path,
and were trampled down,
and the birds of the air came and ate them up.
Some fell on stony places,
where there was not much soil:
and immediately they sprung up,

because they had no depth of soil.
When the sun was up,
they were scorched;
and, because they had no root and lacked moisture,
they withered away.

"Some fell among thorns;
and the thorns sprung up with them,
and choked them:
and they yielded no fruit.

"But some fell into good ground,
sprang up and produced fruit and increased;
some a hundred-fold,
some sixty-fold,
some thirty-fold."

And He told them,
"He who has ears to hear,
let him hear."

82   Parables by the Sea: The Parable of the Seeds Explained
(Matthew 13:18-23; Mark 4:13-20; Luke 8:11-15)

When He was alone the twelve disciples came, and asked Him,
"What does this parable mean?"
And He said to them,
"Do you not know this parable?
How then will you know all parables?
Hear then the parable of the sower."

"The sower plants seed that is the Word of God.
When anyone hears the Word of the Kingdom,
and does not understand it,

then immediately the wicked one, the devil, Satan,
comes and snatches away the Word
which was sown in his heart,
or else they might believe and be saved.
This is he who received seed by the path."

"Likewise is He who received the seed in stony places.
This is he who hears the Word,
and immediately receives it with joy and gladness.
Yet he has no root in himself,
and endures for only a little while.
Afterwards, when tribulation or persecution arises
because of the Word,
he immediately stumbles,
and in times of temptation,
falls away."

"He who received seed among the thorns
is he who hears the Word;
and the care of this world,
and the deceitfulness of riches,
and the lusts for pleasures and other things
enters in choking the Word,
and he becomes unfruitful,
and bring no fruit to perfection.

"But he who received seed into the good ground
is he who hears the Word,
and receives it in an honest and good heart,
and understands it and keeps it;
and who also produces fruit with patience,
and increased,
some a hundred-fold, some sixty-fold, some thirty-fold."

83 Parables by the Sea: Parables Fulfill Prophecy

(Matthew 13:10-17; Mark 4:10-12; Luke 8:9-10,18)

His disciples asked Him,
> "Why do you speak to them in parables?"

He answered,
> "Because it is given to you
> to know the mysteries of the Kingdom of Heaven,
> but it is not given to those who are outside.
> So, all of these things are done in parables.

> "Whoever has,
> to him more will be given,
> and he shall have greater abundance:
> but whoever does not have,
> from him shall be taken away even what he has."

> "So, I speak to them in parables:
> because seeing, they do not see;
> and hearing, they do not hear,
> nor do they understand."

> "In them the prophecy of Isaiah is fulfilled, which says,
>> *'By hearing ye shall hear,*
>> *and shall not understand;*
>> *and seeing ye shall see,*
>> *and shall not perceive:*
>> *For this people's heart is waxed gross,*
>> *and their ears are dull of hearing,*
>> *and their eyes they have closed;*
>> *lest at any time*
>> *they should see with their eyes*
>> *and hear with their ears,*
>> *and should understand with their heart,*
>> *and should be converted,*

and I should heal them.

and their sins should be forgiven them.'

But your eyes are blessed, because they see:

and your ears, because they hear."

"Truly, I tell you,

many prophets and righteous men have wanted to see

those things which you see,

and have not seen them;

and to hear those things which you hear,

and have not heard them."

84   Parables by the Sea: All Will Be Revealed

(Mark 4:21-25; Luke 8:16-17)

He told them,

"No man, when he has lit a candle,

covers it with a pot,

or puts it under a basket,

or under a bed.

Instead he sets it on a candlestick,

so that those who enter in may see the light.

There is nothing hidden,

which will not be revealed;

nor was anything kept secret,

that will not be known near and far.

If any man has ears to hear,

let him hear."

And He told them,

"So be mindful how you hear:

with the measurement you measure out,

it will be measured out to you:

and to you who hear,

more will be given.
Because more will be given
to him who has,
and all he seems to have will be taken
from him who has not."

85   Parables by the Sea: The Kingdom

(Matthew 13:24-35; Mark 4:26-34)

He said,
    "The Kingdom of God is like this:
    as if a man should plant seed into the ground;
    and should sleep and rise night and day,
    and the seed should spring and grow up.
    He does not know how.
    For the Earth produces fruit by herself;
    first the blade, then the head,
    after that the full grain in the head.
    But when the grain is ripe,
    immediately he puts in the sickle,
    because the harvest has come."

He told them another parable, saying,
    "The Kingdom of Heaven is like a man
    who sowed good seed in his field.
    But while men slept,
    his enemy came
    and planted weeds among the wheat,
    and went his way.
    When the blade sprang up,
    and brought forth fruit,
    then the weeds also appeared.
    So, the servants of the man of the house

came and said to him,
> 'Sir, didn't you sow good seed in your field?
> Where did the weeds come from?'

He said to them,
> 'An enemy has done this.'

The servants said to him,
> 'Then do you want us to go and gather them up?'

But he said,
> 'No. Or else while you gather up the weeds,
> you may also root up the wheat with them.
> Let both grow together until the harvest:
> and in the time of harvest
> I will say to the reapers,
>> "Gather the weeds together first,
>> and bind them in bundles to burn them:
>> but gather the wheat into my barn."''"

He told them another parable, saying,
> "What is the Kingdom of God like?
> and to what shall I compare it?
> The Kingdom of Heaven
> is like a grain of mustard seed,
> which a man took,
> and planted into his garden field.
> It is indeed the smallest of all the seeds in the world:
> but when it is grown,
> it is the greatest among the herbs,
> shooting out great branches and becoming a great tree,
> so that the birds of the air come and lodge in the branches
> and under the shadow of it."

He told them another parable, saying,
> "To what shall I compare the Kingdom of God?

The Kingdom of Heaven is like leaven,
which a woman took and hid in three measures of meal,
until it was all leavened."

Jesus spoke all these things to the multitude in many such parables;
and He did not speak to them without a parable.
When they were alone,
He explained everything to His disciples.
This was to fulfill what was spoken by the prophet who said,
    'I will open my mouth in parables;
    I will utter things
    which have been kept secret
    from the foundation of the world.'

86   Parables by the Sea: The Kingdom Explained
(Matthew 13:36-53)

Then Jesus sent the multitude away and went into the house:
and His disciples came to Him, saying,
    "Explain the parable of the weeds of the field to us."
He answered,
    "He who plants the good seed is the Son of Man;
    The field is the World;
    the good seed are the Children of the Kingdom;
    but the weeds are the children of the Wicked One;
    The enemy who sowed them is the Devil;
    the harvest is the End of the World;
    and the reapers are the angels.
    Therefore, as the weeds are gathered and burned in the fire;
    so shall it be in the End of the World.
    The Son of Man will send out His angels,
    and they shall gather out of His Kingdom
    everything that causes sin,
    and those who do wickedness;

and will hurl them into a furnace of fire.
There will be wailing and gnashing of teeth.
Then the righteous shall shine forth like the sun
in the Kingdom of their Father.
Whoever has ears to hear,
    let him hear."

"Again, the Kingdom of Heaven is like treasure hid in a field;
which, when a man finds it,
he hides it,
and for joy goes and sells all that he has,
and buys that field."

Again, the Kingdom of Heaven is like a merchant,
seeking precious pearls:
who, when he had found one pearl of great price,
went and sold all that he had,
and bought it."

Again, the Kingdom of Heaven is like a net cast into the sea,
gathering fish of every kind:
which, when it was full, they drew to shore,
and sat down, and gathered the good fish into vessels,
but cast the bad fish away."

So shall it be at the End of the World:
the angels will come forth,
and cut away the wicked from among the just,
and will hurl them into the furnace of fire.
there will be wailing and gnashing of teeth."

Jesus said to them,
    "Have you understood all these things?"
They said to Him,
    "Yes, Lord."

Then He told them,
   "Therefore, every Scribe
   who is instructed about the Kingdom of Heaven
   is like a man who is a man of the house,
   who brings forth out of his treasure things new and old."

When Jesus had finished these parables,
he left that place.

87   Jesus Calms a Storm

(Matthew 8:18,23-27; Mark 4:35-41; Luke 8:22-25)

Now it came to pass on a certain day,
when Jesus saw great multitudes around Him, He said,
   'Let us pass over to the other side of the sea.'
When they had sent the multitude away,
they took Him just as He was
and when He entered a boat,
His disciples followed Him,
and they launched out,
with some other small boats.

But as they sailed, He fell asleep:
and there arose a great tempest of wind in the sea,
such that the ship was covered with waves:
and the waves beat into the ship,
so that it was soon full
and they were in jeopardy.

He was in the stern of the boat, asleep on a pillow.
And His disciples came to Him, and woke Him, saying,
   "Master! Master!
   Don't you care that we are dying?

Lord, save us!"

And He told them,
 "Why are you fearful?
 Oh, you of little faith!"

He got up and rebuked the wind and the raging of the water;
and said to the sea,
 "Peace! Be still!"
The wind ceased and there was a great calm.
He said to them,
 "Where is your faith?
 Why are you so fearful?
 How is it that you have no faith?"

But the men were astonished,
And they were exceedingly fearful,
and said to one another,
 "What manner of man is this,
 that even the wind and the water obey Him?"

88   Jesus Casts Out the Demon, Legion[13]
(Matthew 8:28-34; Mark 5:1-20; Luke 8:26-39)

He came to the other side of the sea
near the city of the Gergesenes
in the country of the Gadarenes,
which is across from Galilee.
When He got out of the ship,
and went out onto land,
immediately two who were possessed with demons
met Him there, coming out of the tombs,
so exceedingly fierce that no man could pass by that way.

One had demons a long time, and wore no clothes,
nor lived in any house, but in the tombs instead.
No man could bind him, not even with chains:
because he had often been bound with fetters and chains,
and had pulled apart the chains,
and broke the fetters in pieces.
Nor could any man tame him.
And always, night and day,
he was in the mountains and in the tombs,
crying out and cutting himself with stones.

But when he saw Jesus from afar,
they ran and worshiped Him,
and he cried out with a loud voice and said,
"Jesus, thou Son of the Most High God?
I adjure Thee by God,
I beseech Thee that thou Torment me not."
And they cried out, saying,
"What have we to do with Thee,
Jesus, Thou Son of the Most High God?
Art Thou come hither to torment us before the Time?"
And Jesus said to the one,
"Come out of the man,
you unclean spirit!"
And he cried with a loud voice, and said,
"What have I to do with Thee,
Jesus, Thou Son of the Most High God?
I adjure Thee by God, that Thou torment me not."
And He asked him,
"What is your name?"
And he answered, saying,
"My name is Legion:
for we are many."
And he begged Him many times

that He would not send them away out of the country,
into the Abyss.

A good way off from them, near the mountains,
there was a great herd of many pigs feeding.
So, all the demons begged Him, saying,
   "If thou cast us out,
   suffer us to go away into the herd of swine,
   that we may enter into them."
Immediately, Jesus gave them permission
and He told them,
   "Go!"
And the unclean spirits went out
into the herd of swine:
and the whole herd of about two thousand pigs
ran violently down a steep slope into the sea,
and were drowned in the sea and perished in the waters.
Those who kept and fed the pigs fled,
and went on their way into the city,
and told everything in the city and in the country,
about what happened to the ones possessed by demons.

The whole city came out to meet Jesus,
to see what had happened.
When they saw Him,
and saw him who was possessed with the demon,
and him who had the Legion,
sitting at the feet of Jesus, clothed, and in his right mind:
they were afraid.
And those who saw it
told how he who was possessed by the demons was healed,
and also told about the pigs.
Then the whole multitude of the surrounding country of the Gadarenes
begged Him to leave their shores.

When He got into the boat,
he who had been possessed with the demon
begged Him that he might be with Him.
However, Jesus did not let him,
but instead told him,

"Return to your own house.
Go home to your friends,
and show the great things the Lord has done for you,
and tell them He has had compassion on you!"

And he left and began to tell the news in the Decapolis
of the great things Jesus had done for him
and everyone was astonished.

89   The Daughter of Jairus

(Matthew 9:1,18-19; Mark 5:21; Luke 8:40-41)

When Jesus passed over again by boat to the other side,
and returned to His own city,
many people gathered and received Him gladly:
for they were all waiting for Him.
and He was nearby the sea.

There came a certain ruler of the synagogue,
by name the name of Jairus;
and when he saw Him,
he fell at His feet and worshiped Him.
He had one only daughter, about twelve years of age,
and she lay dying.

He insistently begged Him to come to his house, saying,

"My little daughter lies at the point of death!
I beg You!
Come and lay Your hands on her,
so that she may be healed and will live!"

Jesus got up and followed him,
as did His disciples.
But as He went the people pressed in on Him.

90   A Woman Is Healed by Touching Jesus
(Matthew 9:20-22; Mark 5:24-34; Luke 8:42-48)

And a certain woman,
who was diseased with an issue of blood for twelve years,
had suffered many things of many physicians,
and had spent all that she had,
and was not improved.
Nor could any heal her,
but instead she grew worse.

When she heard of Jesus,
she came in the crowd from behind,
and touched the hem of His cloak.
She said,
   "If I can only touch His clothes,
   I will be made whole!"
Immediately, the fountain of her blood stopped and dried up;
and she felt in her body that she was healed of that illness.
Immediately, Jesus, knowing in Himself
that power had gone out of Him,
turned around in the crowd, and said,
   "Who touched Me?
   Who touched My clothes?"
His disciples,
Peter and those who were with Him, said to Him,
   "Master, You see the multitude
   crushing You and pressing in on You,
   and You say, 'Who touched Me?'"

And Jesus said,
> "Somebody has touched Me:
> for I know that power went out of Me."

He looked around to see her who had done this thing.
When the woman saw that she was not hidden,
fearing and trembling,
knowing what was done in her:
she came and fell down before Him,
and she declared to Him, in front of all the people,
why she had touched Him,
and how she was healed immediately,
and told Him all the truth.
He said to her,
> "Daughter take courage!
> Your faith has made you whole!
> Go in peace and be healed of your illness."

And the woman was whole from that very hour.

91   Jesus Resurrects the Daughter of Jairus

(Matthew 9:23-26; Mark 5:35-43; Luke 8:49-56)

While He still spoke,
one came up from the ruler of the synagogue's house telling him,
> "Your daughter is dead.
> Do not trouble the Master any longer."

As soon as Jesus heard what was said,
He told the ruler of the synagogue,
> "Do not fear!
> Just believe, and she shall be made whole!"

When Jesus came into the house,
He permitted no one to go in,
except Peter, and James, and John,
and the father and the mother of the maiden.

When He saw the tumult,
and the minstrels and the people making a noise,
and those who wept and wailed greatly.
He told them,
    "Make way!
    Why do you make this weeping commotion?
    The maiden is not dead, just sleeping."

And they laughed at Him scornfully,
knowing that she was dead.
But when He had put them all out,
He took the father and the mother of the maiden,
and those who were with Him,
and entered in where the maiden was lying.

He took the maiden by the hand, and said to her,
    "Talitha cumi!"
which is interpreted,
    "Maiden, I tell you to rise!"
Immediately, the maiden got up and walked
and they were astonished with a great wonder.
He strictly charged them that no man should know of it;
and commanded that food should be given to her to eat.
And the news of it went out into all that land.

92   Jesus Heals the Blind and the Mute

    (Matthew 9:27-34)

When Jesus left there,
two blind men followed Him, crying out,
    "You! The Son of David!
    Have mercy on us!"
When He had come into the house,
the blind men came to Him:

and Jesus said to them,
    "Do you believe that I am able to do this?"
They told Him,
    "Yes, Lord!"
Then He touched their eyes, saying,
    "According to your faith,
    let be it done to you."
And their eyes were opened;
and Jesus strictly charged them,
    "See that no man knows of it."
But when they left,
they spread his fame abroad in all that country.

As they went out,
there was brought to Him
a mute man possessed by a demon.
When the demon was cast out,
the mute man spoke:
and the multitudes marveled at it, saying,
    "This has never been seen in Israel!"
But the Pharisees said,
    "He casts out demons
    through the prince of demons."

93 The Second Rejection in Nazareth

(Matthew 13:54-58; Mark 6:1-6)

He left there and His disciples followed Him.
When He had come into His own country
it was the Sabbath day
and He began to teach them in their synagogue.
Many were astonished who heard Him, and said,
    "Where did this man get these things?
    What wisdom is given to him,

that these mighty works are done by his hands?
Is this not the carpenter's son?
Is this not the carpenter, the son of Mary,
the brother of James, Joseph, Judas, and Simon?
and are not his sisters here with us?"
And they were offended by Him.

But Jesus told them,
"A prophet is not without honor,
except in his own country,
and among his own family,
and in his own house."
And he did not do many mighty works there
because of their unbelief,
except that He laid His hands upon a few sick folk
and healed them.
And He was astonished because of their unbelief.

94 Jesus Sends the Twelve
(Matthew 9:35-11:1; Mark 6:7-13; Luke 9:1-6)

And Jesus went to all the cities and villages,
teaching in their synagogues,
and preaching the Gospel of the Kingdom,
and healing every sickness and every disease among the people.
But when He saw the multitudes,
He was moved with compassion for them,
because they were despairing and cast aside,
like sheep without a shepherd.
Then He told His disciples,
"The harvest is truly great,
but the laborers are few;
Therefore, pray to the Lord of the harvest,
that He will send out laborers into His harvest."

When He had called His twelve disciples to Himself,
He gave them power against unclean spirits,
to cast them out,
and to heal all manner of sickness and disease.
Now the names of the Twelve Apostles are these;
The first, Simon, who is called Peter, and Andrew his brother;
James the son of Zebedee, and John his brother;
Philip, and Bartholomew;
Thomas, and Matthew the tax collector;
James the son of Alphaeus,
and Lebbaeus, who was called Thaddaeus;
Simon the Canaanite,
and Judas Iscariot, who also betrayed Him.

These twelve Jesus sent out, two by two
and commanded them,
    "Do not go among the Gentiles,
    and do not enter any city of the Samaritans.
    Instead, go to the lost sheep of the House of Israel.
    Preach as you go, saying,
        'The Kingdom of Heaven is at hand!'"

    "Heal the sick,
    cleanse the lepers,
    raise the dead,
    cast out unclean spirits and demons!
    You have freely received,
    so freely give!
    Procure no gold, silver, or brass in your purses,
    Do not bring a pack for your journey,
    or two coats, or shoes,
    Take only a staff and
    wear sandals on your feet.
    The worker deserves his wages."

"In whatever city or town you enter,
ask who is worthy;
and stay there until you leave.
When you come into a home, greet them.
and if the household is worthy,
let your peace rest upon them."

"But if they are not worthy,
let your peace return to you.
And if they do not receive you,
or listen to your message,
when you leave that house or city,
shake off even the dust on your feet
as a testimony against them.
Truly I tell you,
it will be more bearable
for the land of Sodom and Gomorrah
in the Day of Judgment,
than for that city."

"Look! I send you out as sheep among wolves:
so, you must be as wise as serpents,
and as harmless as doves.
Beware of men:
for they will arrest you for the tribunals,
and they will beat you in their synagogues;
And you will be brought before governors and kings for My sake,
for a testimony against them and the Gentiles.
But when they arrest you,
take no thought how or what you will say:
for in that same hour what you will say
shall be given to you.
For it is not you who speaks,
but instead the Spirit of your Father who speaks in you.

And the brother will betray the brother to death,
and the father the child:
and the children will rebel against their parents,
and cause them to be put to death.
And you will be hated by all men for the sake of My name:
but he who endures to the end shall be saved."

"When they persecute you in one city,
flee into another:
for truly, I tell you,
you will not have gone over all the cities of Israel,
until the Son of Man has come.
The disciple is not above his master,
nor the servant above his lord.
It is enough for the disciple that he be as his master,
and the servant as his lord.
If they have called the master of the house Beelzebub,
how much more likewise shall they call those of his household?"

"Do not think that I have come to send peace on Earth:
I did not come to send peace, but a sword.
I am come to cut a man apart from his father,
And the daughter from her mother,
and the daughter-in-law from her mother-in-law.
A man's foes will be those of his own household."

"He who loves father or mother more than Me
is not worthy of Me:
and he who loves son or daughter more than Me
is not worthy of Me.
And he who does not take his cross and follow Me,
is not worthy of Me.
He who finds his life will lose it:
and he who loses his life for My sake shall find it."

"He who receives you receives Me,
and he who receives Me receives Him who sent Me.
He who receives a prophet in the name of a prophet
will receive a prophet's reward;
and he who receives a righteous man
in the name of a righteous man
will receive a righteous man's reward.
And whoever will give a drink to one of these little ones,
even a cup of cold water in the name of a disciple,
truly, I tell you,
he will in no way lose his reward."

And it came to pass,
when Jesus had finished instructing His twelve disciples,
He left to teach and to preach in their cities.
And they left and went out,
preaching the gospel, so that men should repent.
And they cast out many demons,
and anointed many with oil who were sick,
and healed them everywhere.

95   The Beheading of John the Baptist

(Matthew 14:1-12; Mark 6:14-29; Luke 9:7-9)

At that time, King Herod, the Tetrarch, heard of the fame of Jesus
and of all that was done by Him
(for His name was spread abroad);
and he was perplexed,
because some said that
John the Baptist had risen from the dead,
and that was why mighty works showed themselves in Him.

Others said,
  "It is Elijah!"

Others said that it is a prophet,
or like one of the prophets.
And Herod said to his servants,
    "John I have beheaded:
    but who is this,
    of whom I hear such things?"
And he wanted to see Him.

For Herod himself had sent forth and laid hold upon John,
and bound him in prison for the sake of Herodias,
his brother Philip's wife:
because he had married her.
John had told Herod,
    "It is not lawful for you
    to have your brother's wife!"
Thus, Herodias had a quarrel against him,
and would have killed him;
but she could not:
and when he would have put him to death,
he feared the multitude,
because they considered him to be a prophet.
So, Herod feared John.
Knowing that he was a holy and just man,
he often observed him and gladly heard him.

When a convenient day had come,
Herod on his birthday held a feast
for his lords, high captains, and the chief estate-holders of Galilee.
But on Herod's birthday,
the daughter of Herodias danced for them,
and so pleased Herod and those who sat with him,
that at that very moment
the king promised with an oath to the maiden and swore to her,
    "Whatever you shall ask from me,

I will give it to you,
   even half of my kingdom!"
And she went out and said to her mother,
   "For what shall I ask?"
And she said,
   "The head of John the Baptist."

She immediately went to the king in haste,
and being previously instructed by her mother, said,
   "I want you to give me,
   here and now,
   on a platter,
   the head of John the Baptist!"

And the king was exceedingly sorry;
yet for the sake of his oath,
and for the sake of those who sat with him at the supper,
he would not deny her.
Immediately, the king sent an executioner
and commanded his head to be brought and given to her.
He went and beheaded John in the prison,
and brought his head on a platter,
and gave it to the maiden:
and the maiden gave it to her mother.

And when his disciples heard of it,
they came and took his corpse,
and laid it in a tomb,
and buried it,
and went and told Jesus.

96 The Twelve Return

(Matthew 14:13; Mark 6:30-32; Luke 9:10; John 6:1)

Jesus heard of it,
and when the Apostles returned,
they gathered together with Jesus,
and told him all the things
that they had done and had taught.

He told them,
    "Come away into the wilderness,
    and rest yourselves for a while."
because there were so many coming and going,
that they did not have leisure enough even to eat.
He left there with them privately in a boat
over the Sea of Tiberias,
which is called Galilee,
away into the wilderness,
across from the city called Bethsaida.

97 Jesus Teaches and Heals a Multitude

(Matthew 14:14; Mark 6:33-34; Luke 9:11; John 6:2-4)

Jesus went up into a mountain,
and sat there with His disciples,
near the time of the Jewish Passover.
A great multitude followed Him,
because they saw the miracles He performed on the diseased.
Many knew Him and saw them leaving.
When the people knew it,
they followed Him and went ahead of them,
and ran there on foot out of all the cities,
and came together to Him.
And when Jesus went out,

He saw many people, a great multitude,
and was moved with compassion toward them,
because they were like sheep without a shepherd.
He received them,
and told them about the Kingdom of God,
and healed their sick and those who had need of healing.
and He began to teach them many things.

98   Jesus Feeds Five Thousand Men[14]

(Matthew 14:15-21; Mark 6:35-44; Luke 9:12-17; John 6:5-14)

When the day began to wear away,
and was far spent in the late afternoon,
the Twelve, His disciples came to Him, and said,
  · "This is wilderness,
    and now the hour is late."
When Jesus lifted up his eyes,
and saw a great company had come to Him,
He said to Philip,
    "Where shall we buy bread,
    so that all these can eat?"
This He said to test him:
for He himself knew what He would do.
Philip answered Him,
    "More than seven months pay would not buy enough bread
    for all of them to have even a little!"
    Send the multitude away,
    so that they may go into the country around here,
    into the villages to lodge
    and to buy themselves food and bread:
    because they have nothing to eat."

But Jesus answered and said to them,
    "They do not need to go.

You give them food to eat."
And they said to Him,
"Shall we go and buy two hundred days wages worth of bread
to feed all these people?"
He said to them,
"Go and see how many loaves you have"
One of His disciples, Andrew, Simon Peter's brother, said to Him,
"Here is a boy who has five barley loaves and two small fishes:
but what is that among so many?"
He said,
"Bring them here to Me."
And Jesus said,
"Make the men sit down."
It was a grassy place,
so, the men sat down,
and there were about five thousand in number.

He commanded them to make the multitude all sit down
by fifties in companies upon the green grass.
They did so and made them all sit down.
And they sat down in ranks, by hundreds, and by fifties.

When He had taken the five loaves and the two fish,
He looked up to Heaven, and blessed and broke the loaves,
and gave them to His disciples to set before the multitude;
and the two fishes he divided among them all.
and they likewise divided the fishes
as much as the multitude wanted,
and they all ate and were filled.

When they were filled,
He said to His disciples,
"Gather up what is left over, so that nothing is lost."
So, they gathered the leftovers together,

and filled twelve baskets
with the fragments of the five barley loaves and the fish
that remained over and above what had been eaten.
There were about five thousand men who ate from the loaves,
not counting the women and children.

When they had seen the miracle that Jesus did,
then those men said,
>   "This truly is that prophet
>   who is supposed to come into the world!"

99 Jesus Prays Alone

(Matthew 14:22-23; Mark 6:45-46; John 6:15)

But when Jesus saw that they meant
to come and force Him to be a king,
He immediately compelled His disciples
to get into the boat and to go on ahead
across to Bethsaida,
while He sent the people away.
When He had sent them away,
He went upon a mountain alone by Himself to pray.

100 Jesus Walks on Water[15]

(Matthew 14:24-33; Mark 6:47-52; John 6:16-21)

Evening had come,
when His disciples went down to the sea,
and got into a boat,
and went over the sea toward Capernaum.
Though it had gotten dark,
Jesus had not come to them.
And when night fell,

the ship was in the middle of the sea,
and He was alone on the land.

The sea arose because of a great blowing wind.
So, when they had rowed *about three miles*,
He saw them rowing hard;
because the wind was against them.

He came to them *in the hours before sunrise*,
walking upon the sea,
and would have passed by them.
The disciples saw Jesus walking on the sea and drawing near the boat:
and they were troubled and afraid,
and cried out in fear, saying,
 "It is a spirit!"

Immediately He spoke to them, saying,
 "It is Me!
 Do not be afraid!"
Peter answered him and said,
 "Lord, if it is You,
 tell me to come to You on the water!"
And He said,
 "Come!"

When Peter came down out of the boat,
he walked on the water, going to Jesus.
But when he saw the violent wind,
he was afraid and began to sink
He cried out, saying,
 "Lord! Save me!"

Immediately, Jesus stretched out His hand,
and caught him,
and said to him,

"Oh, you of little faith!
Why did you doubt?"
Because they did not consider the miracle of the loaves:
since their hearts were hardened.
Then He went up to them
and they gladly took Him into the boat:
and the wind ceased.
Then those who were in the ship came and worshiped Him, saying,
"It is true! You are the Son of God!"
They were utterly amazed
and then astounded beyond measure within themselves,
when immediately the ship was at their destination.

101 The Healings in Gennesaret

(*Matthew 14:34-36; Mark 6:53-56*)

They crossed over,
and came to the land of Gennesaret.
When they drew near the shore
and got out of the boat,
right away the men of that place knew Him,
and when they were aware of Him,
they ran throughout and around that whole region,
and brought to Him all who were diseased;
carrying on stretchers those who were sick,
to where they heard He was.
And wherever He entered,
into villages, or cities, or countryside,
they laid the sick in the streets,
and begged Him to let them touch
just the fringe of His shawl.
And all who touched Him
were made perfectly whole.

102 The Bread of Life

(John 6:22-7:1)

The following day,
the people who stood on the other side of the sea
saw that there was no other boat,
except the one His disciples had entered,
and that Jesus did not go with His disciples into that boat,
and that His disciples had gone away alone;
(even though other boats from Tiberias
came near the place where they ate bread
after the Lord had given thanks).
So, when the people saw
that neither Jesus nor His disciples were there,
they also found boats
and came to Capernaum looking for Jesus.

When they found Him on the other side of the sea,
they said to Him,
    "Master, when did you come here?"
Jesus answered them,
    "Truly, truly, I tell you,
    you do not seek me because you saw the miracles,
    but because you ate bread and were filled.
    Do not labor for the food which perishes,
    but for the food which endures into Everlasting Life,
    which the Son of Man shall give you:
    for God the Father has sealed Him."
Then they said to Him,
    "How shall we do the works of God?
Jesus answered and said to them,
    "This is the work of God,
    that you believe in Him whom He has sent."
So, they said to Him,

"Then what sign do you show us,
for us to see and believe you?
What will you do?
Our fathers ate manna in the desert; as it is written,
'He gave them bread from Heaven to eat.'"
Then Jesus said to them,
"Truly, truly, I tell you,
Moses did not give you that bread from Heaven;
but My Father gives you the true Bread from Heaven.
For the Bread of God is He who comes down from Heaven,
and gives Life to the World."
Then they said to Him,
"Lord, give us this bread forever."
And Jesus said,
"I am the Bread of Life:
he who comes to Me will never hunger;
and he who believes in Me will never thirst.
But I told you that,
even though you have seen Me,
you do not believe.
All who the Father gives Me
shall come to Me;
and he who comes to Me
I will by no means cast out.
For I came down from Heaven,
not to do My own will,
but the will of Him who sent Me.
And this is the Father's will who has sent Me,
that of all whom He has given Me
I should lose none,
but should raise them up again at the Last Day.
And this is the will of Him who sent Me,
that everyone who sees the Son,
and believes in Him,

may have Everlasting Life:
and I will raise him up at the Last Day."

The Jews then murmured against Him, because He said,
"I am the Bread who came down from Heaven."
And they said,
"Is this not Jesus, the son of Joseph,
whose father and mother we know?
how can he say,
'I came down from Heaven?'"
So, Jesus answered and said to them,
"Do not murmur among yourselves.
No man can come to Me,
unless the Father who has sent Me draws him.
And I will raise him up at the Last Day.
It is written in the prophets,
'And they shall be all taught of God.'
So, every man who has heard,
and has learned from the Father,
comes to Me.
Not that any man has seen the Father,
except He who is of God.
He has seen the Father.

"Truly, truly, I tell you,
He who believes in Me has Everlasting Life.
I am the Bread of Life.
Your fathers ate manna in the wilderness and are dead.
This is the Bread which comes down from Heaven,
so that a man may eat from it and not die.
I am the Living Bread who came down from Heaven:
if any man eats from this Bread,
he shall live forever:
and the bread that I will give is My flesh,

which I will give for the life of the World."

So, the Jews argued among themselves, saying,
    "How can this man give us his flesh to eat?"

Then Jesus said,
    "Truly, truly, I tell you,
    Unless you eat the flesh of the Son of Man
    and drink His blood,
    you have no life in you.
    Whoever eats My flesh
    and drinks My blood,
    has Eternal Life;
    and I will raise him up at the Last Day.
    For my flesh is food indeed,
    and my blood is drink indeed.
    He who eats My flesh
    and drinks My blood,
    dwells in Me,
    and I in him.
    As the living Father has sent Me,
    and I live by the Father:
    so it is that he who eats of Me shall live by Me.
    This is the Bread which came down from Heaven:
    but not as your fathers ate manna and are dead.
    He who eats from this Bread shall live forever."

He said these things in the synagogue as he taught in Capernaum.
For this reason, many of His disciples,
when they had heard this, said,
    "This is a hard teaching:
    who can understand it?"
When Jesus knew in Himself that His disciples murmured about it,
He said to them,

"Does this offend you?
What if you shall see the Son of Man
rise to where He was before?
It is the spirit that gives life;
the flesh gives no profit:
the words that I speak to you,
they are Spirit,
and they are Life.
But there are some of you who do not believe."
For Jesus knew from the Beginning who did not believe,
and who would betray Him.
And He said,
  "That is why I told you
  that no man can come to Me,
  unless it is given to him by My Father."

From that time many of His disciples turned,
and walked with Him no more.
Then said Jesus to the Twelve,
  "Will you also go away?"
Then Simon Peter answered Him,
  "Lord, to whom will we go?
  You have the words of Eternal Life.
  We believe and are sure that you are the Christ,
  the Son of the living God."
Jesus answered them,
  "Have I not chosen you Twelve?
  But one of you is a devil."
He spoke of Judas Iscariot the son of Simon:
because, among the Twelve,
it was he who would betray Jesus.

After this Jesus walked in Galilee:
because He would not walk in Judea,

since the Jews sought to kill Him.

103 Jesus Rebukes the Traditions of Men
(Matthew 15:1-11; Mark 7:1-16)

Then the Pharisees came to Jesus,
along with certain Scribes from Jerusalem.
They found fault when they saw some of His disciples eat bread
with defiled, that is to say, with unwashed, hands.

For the Pharisees, and all the Jews,
unless they often wash their hands,
do not eat,
holding the tradition of the Elders.
When they come from the market,
unless they wash, they do not eat.
And there are many other things
which they have received and observe,
regarding the washing of cups, pots, brass vessels, and tables.
Then the Pharisees and Scribes asked Him,
 "Why do your disciples transgress
 the tradition of the Elders?
 Why do your disciples not walk
 according to the tradition of the Elders?
 For they do not wash their hands,
 but eat bread with unwashed hands!"

But He answered and said to them,
 "Why do you also transgress the commandment of God
 by your tradition?
 Isaiah prophesied well about you hypocrites, as it is written,
  'This people honoureth Me with their lips,
  but their heart is far from Me.
  Howbeit in vain do they worship Me,

teaching for doctrines the commandments of men.'
Laying aside the commandment of God,
you observe the tradition of men,
regarding the washing of pots and cups!
And you do many other things like this!"

And He said to them,
"Full well you reject the commandment of God,
so that you may keep your own tradition.
For Moses said God commanded,
'Honour thy father and thy mother;'
and, *'Whoso curseth father or mother,*
let him die the death.'

But you say,
'If a man shall say to his father or mother,
"However it is you might be helped by me;
it is Corban, *offered to God instead*,"
he will be free of obligation.'
And you let him get away with doing nothing
to help his father or his mother!
You make the Word of God impotent
by teaching your traditions!
And you do many things just like this!"

And when He had called all the people to Him, He told them,
"Listen to Me every one of you and understand!
It is not what goes into the mouth that defiles a man;
but what comes out of the mouth.
This is what defiles a man.
If any man has ears to hear,
let him hear!"

104 A Parable Privately Explained
(Matthew 15:12-20; Mark 7:17-23)

When He had entered the house away from the people,
then His disciples came and asked Him about the parable,
and said to Him,
> "You do know that the Pharisees were offended
> after they heard this speech?"

But He answered and said,
> "Every plant,
> which My Heavenly Father has not planted,
> will be rooted up.
> Let them be!
> They are blind leaders of the blind!
> And if the blind lead the blind,
> they will both fall into the ditch."

Then Peter answered and said to him,
> "Explain this parable to us."

And He said to them,
> "Are you also still so much without understanding?
> Do you not yet understand,
> that whatever a thing is that enters a man from outside,
> it cannot defile him,
> because it does not enter his heart,
> but instead enters the belly,
> and goes out into the privy,
> as all foods are purged?"

And He said,
> "It is what comes out of the mouth
> that defiles a man.
> Because it is from within,
> out of the heart of men,
> that evil thoughts proceed:

adultery, sexual sin,
murder, theft,
envy, wickedness,
deceit, lust,
an evil mind, blasphemy,
pride, foolishness...
All these evil things come from within,
defiling a man:
but eating with unwashed hands
does not defile a man."

105 The Faith of The Gentile Woman

(Matthew 15:21-28; Mark 7:24-30)

From there Jesus got up,
and went to the coasts of Tyre and Sidon,
and entered a house,
and wanted no man to know of it:
but He could not be hidden.
A certain woman of Canaan from the same coasts,
whose young daughter had an unclean spirit,
heard of Him,
and came and fell at his feet.

The woman was a Greek,
a Syrophoenician by nation;
and she begged Him to cast the demon out of her daughter,
and cried out to Him,
    "Have mercy on me!
    O Lord! You, the Son of David!
    My daughter is grievously tormented with a demon!"
But He gave her no answer, not even word.
His disciples came and entreated Him, saying,
    "Send her away,

for she cries behind us, loudly!"
He answered and said,
    "I was only sent
    to the lost sheep of the House of Israel.
    Let the children be fed first:
    For it is not right to take the children's food,
    and toss it to the dogs."
And she answered and said to him,
    "Yes, Lord."
    But the little dogs under the table
    do eat what the children drop!"
Then Jesus answered and said to her,
    "Oh, woman! Your faith is great!
    It shall be for you just as you desire!
    For what you have said:
    be on your way;
    the demon is cast out of your daughter."
And her daughter was made whole from that very hour.
And when she had come to her house,
she found the demon gone,
and her daughter laid upon the bed.

106 Jesus Heals A Deaf Man

    (Mark 7:31-37)

Again, leaving the coasts of Tyre and Sidon,
He came to the sea of Galilee,
through the middle of the region of Decapolis.
And they brought to Him one who was deaf,
and had a speech impediment;
and they begged Him to lay His hand upon him.

And He took him aside from the multitude,
and put His fingers into his ears,

and He spit,
and touched his tongue;
And looking up to Heaven,
He sighed, and said to him,
    "Ephphatha" that is, "Be opened."
Right away his ears were opened,
and his speech impediment was removed,
and he spoke plainly.
And He charged them not to tell any man:
but the more He charged them,
that much more greatly they spread the story;
and were astonished beyond measure, saying,
    "He has done all good things!
    He both makes the deaf hear,
    and the mute speak!"

107 Jesus Heals Multitudes on A Mountain

(Matthew 15:29-31)

Jesus left there and came near the sea of Galilee;
and went up into a mountain,
and sat down there.
Great multitudes came to Him,
bringing with them
those who were lame, blind, dumb, maimed,
and many others,
and laid them down at the feet of Jesus.
He healed them:
and the multitude was astonished,
because they saw the mute speak,
the maimed made whole,
the lame walk and the blind see:
and so, they glorified the God of Israel.

108 Jesus Feeds Four Thousand Men

(Matthew 15:32-39; Mark 8:1-10)

In those days the multitude was very great,
and had nothing to eat.
Jesus called His disciples to Him,
and said to them,

> "I pity the multitude,
> because they have been with Me now for three days,
> and have nothing to eat.
> If I send them away still fasting
> to their own houses,
> they will faint along the way:
> because some of them came a long way."

And His disciples answered Him,

> "From where in the wilderness,
> can a man find enough bread
> to satisfy such a great multitude?"

And He asked them,

> "How many loaves do you have?"

And they said,

> "Seven, and a few little fishes."

He commanded the multitude to sit down on the ground:
and He took the seven loaves,
and gave thanks and broke them,
and gave it to His disciples to set before them;
and they set it before the people.
They had a few small fishes:
and He blessed them and commanded
that these also be set before them.
So, they all ate and were satisfied:
and they took up seven baskets full
of the broken food that was left over.

There were about four thousand men,
who had eaten, beside women and children.
He sent the multitude away
and immediately got into a boat with His disciples,
and came to the area of Dalmanutha
on the coasts of Magdala.

109 The Pharisees Seek a Sign

(Matthew 16:1-4; Mark 8:11-13)

The Pharisees, along with the Sadducees, came out,
and began to debate with Him,
seeking from Him a sign from Heaven, testing Him.
He sighed deeply in His spirit, and answered,
    "When it is evening, you say,
        'It will be fair weather:
        because the sky is red.'
    And in the morning,
        'It will be foul weather today:
        because the sky is red and overcast.'
    Oh, you hypocrites!
    You can see the face of the sky;
    but you cannot see the signs of the times?
    Why does this generation seek for a sign?
    Truly, I tell you,
    no sign will be given to this generation!
    A wicked and adulterous generation seeks for a sign;
    and there will be no sign given to it,
    but the sign of the prophet Jonah."
He left them,
and got into the boat
and again, went to the other side.

110 The Leaven of the Pharisees

(Matthew 16:5-12; Mark 8:13-21)

Now the disciples had forgotten to take bread,
nor did they have with them more than one loaf in the boat.
Then Jesus charged them, saying,
　　"Take heed!
　　Beware of the leaven of the Pharisees,
　　and of Herod and the Sadducees.
They debated among themselves, saying,
　　"This is because we have brought no bread?"

When Jesus knew it, He said to them,
　　"Oh, you of little faith!
　　Why do you debate among yourselves,
　　that I said this because you brought no bread?
　　Do you still neither see nor understand?
　　Have you still hardened your hearts?
　　Having eyes,
　　do you not see?
　　and having ears,
　　do you not hear?
　　Do you still not understand
　　and do you not remember?
　　When I broke the five loaves among five thousand,
　　how many baskets full of fragments did you take up?"
They told Him,
　　"Twelve."
　　"And when I broke the seven among four thousand,
　　how many baskets full of fragments did you take up?"
And they said,
　　"Seven."
And He said to them,
　　"How is it that you do not understand

that I did not say this to you about bread,
but that you should instead beware
of the leaven of the Pharisees and of the Sadducees?"
Then they understood that He was not teaching them
to beware of the leaven of bread,
but instead of the teaching of the Pharisees and of the Sadducees.

111 A Blind Man Cured in Bethsaida

(Mark 8:22-26)

He came to Bethsaida;
and they brought a blind man to Him,
and begged Him to touch him.
He took the blind man by the hand,
and led him out of the town;
and when He had spit on his eyes,
and put His hands upon him,
He asked him if he saw anything.
And he looked up, and said,
    "I see men like walking trees."

After that, He put his hands upon his eyes again,
and made him look up
and he was restored
and saw every man clearly.
He sent him away to his house, saying,
    "Neither go into the town,
    nor tell this to any in the town."

112 Peter Confesses Jesus is the Son of God

(Matthew 16:13-20; Mark 8:27-30; Luke 9:18-21)

When Jesus came to the coasts of Caesarea Philippi,

it came to pass, as He was alone praying,
His disciples were with Him.
He asked His disciples,
    "Whom do men say that I, the Son of Man, am?"
And they said,
    "Some say that you are John the Baptist:
    some, Elijah; and others, Jeremiah,
    or that one of the old prophets is risen again."
He said to them,
    "But whom do you say that I am?"
And Simon Peter answered,
    "You are the Christ of God,
    the Son of the living God!"
And Jesus said to him,
    "You are blessed, Simon Bar Jonah:
    for flesh and blood did not reveal it to you,
    but it was revealed by My Father who is in Heaven.
    And I also tell you,
    that you are "Peter",
    and upon this rock I will build My church;
    and the gates of Hell will not prevail against it.
    I will give to you the keys of the Kingdom of Heaven:
    and whatever you shall bind on Earth
    will be bound in Heaven:
    and whatever you shall release on Earth
    will be released in Heaven."
Then He strictly charged and commanded His disciples
that they should not tell any man that He was Jesus the Christ.

113 Jesus Rebukes Peter

    (Matthew 16:21-28; Mark 8:31-9:1; Luke 9:22-27)

From that time onward
Jesus began to show His disciples,

how He must go to Jerusalem,
and that the Son of Man must suffer many things,
and be rejected by the Elders and Chief Priests and Scribes,
and be killed,
and be raised again the third day.
And He spoke that teaching only.

Then Peter took Him,
and began to rebuke Him, saying,
    "Far be that from you, Lord!
    This will not be done to You!"
But He turned around
and looked upon His disciples
and said to Peter,
    "You get behind Me, Satan!
    You are a snare to Me:
    because you do not consider the things that are of God,
    but those that are of men!"

And when he had called the people to Him with His disciples also,
then Jesus said to His disciples and to them all,
    "If any man at all will follow Me,
    let him deny himself,
    and take up his cross daily,
    to follow Me.
    For whoever will save his life
    shall lose it:
    and whoever will lose his life
    for My sake and that of the Gospel,
    shall find it and save it.
    For what does a man gain,
    what is a man's advantage,
    if he gains the whole world and loses himself,
    or is cast away and loses his own soul?

What shall a man give in exchange for his soul?"

"Therefore, whoever shall be ashamed of Me and of My words
in this adulterous and sinful generation;
the Son of Man shall also be ashamed of him,
when He will come in His own glory.
The Son of Man will come
in the glory of His Father with His angels;
and then He shall reward every man
according to his works.
Truly, I tell you,
there are some standing here,
who will not taste of death,
until they see the Son of Man
coming in His Kingdom with power."

114 The Transfiguration
(Matthew 17:1-8; Mark 9:2-8; Luke 9:28-36)

After six days Jesus took Peter, James, and John his brother,
and brought them apart,
up into a high mountain to pray.
About eight days after these teachings,
He was transfigured in front of them.
His face shone as white as the light of the sun,
and His raiment grew bright,
as exceedingly white as glistening snow,
such as no laundry on earth could whiten them.

There appeared to them
two men talking with Him,
Moses and Elijah,
who appeared in glory,
and spoke of His death,

which He would fulfill in Jerusalem.
But Peter and those who were with him
were weighed down with sleep:
and when they were awake,
they saw His glory,
and the two men who stood with Him.
And it came to pass, as they left Him, that Peter,
not knowing what he was saying, said to Jesus,
>"Lord, it is good that we are here!
>If you desire,
>let us make three tabernacles here;
>one Master, for you,
>and one for Moses,
>and one for Elijah!"

While he still spoke,
a bright cloud overshadowed them:
and they were afraid as they entered the cloud.
and there came a voice out of the cloud that said,
>*'This is My beloved Son,*
>*in whom I am well pleased.*
>*Listen to Him."*
When the disciples heard it,
they fell on their faces and were greatly frightened.

Suddenly, the voice was past,
and when they looked all round,
they no longer saw any man
except Jesus with them.
Jesus came and touched them and said,
>"Get up and do not be afraid."
And they kept the matter closely,
and told no man in those days
any of those things which they had seen.

115 Elijah and John the Baptist

(Matthew 17:9-13; Mark 9:9-13)

As they came down from the mountain,
Jesus charged them,
    "Tell the vision to no man,
    until the Son of Man is risen again from the dead."
And they kept that saying with themselves,
debating with one another
what the rising from the dead should mean.
His disciples asked Him,
    "Then why do the Scribes say
    that Elijah must first come?
Jesus answered and said to them,
    "Elijah truly shall first come,
    and restore all things.
    But I tell you,
    that Elijah has come already,
    and they did not know him,
    but have done to him whatever they desired.
    Likewise, shall the Son of Man suffer by them
    as it is written."
Then the disciples understood
that He spoke to them about John the Baptist.

116 Jesus Casts a Demon out of a Boy

(Matthew 17:14-18; Mark 9:14-27; Luke 9:37-43)

When He came to His disciples,
He saw a great multitude around them,
and the Scribes debating with them.
Right away, all the people,
when they saw Him,
were greatly amazed,

and running to Him hailed Him.
And He asked the Scribes,
    "Why do you debate with them?"
And a certain man, one of the multitude,
came to Him, kneeling down and saying,
    "Master, I have brought my son to You,
    my only child,
    who has a mute spirit.
    And wherever it possesses him,
    it tears at him:
    and he foams and gnashes with his teeth,
    and pines away!
    Lord, have mercy on my son:
    for he is driven insane,
    and is grievously tormented:
    for often he falls into fire,
    and often into water!
    It bruises him and hardly ever leaves him!
    I brought him to your disciples
    and begged them to cast him out,
    and they could not cure him."

Then Jesus answered and said,
    "Oh, faithless and perverse generation!
    How long will I be with you!
    How long will I tolerate you!
    Bring him here to Me."
And they brought him to Him:
and when he saw Him,
immediately the spirit tore him;
and he fell foaming
and wallowing on the ground,
and He asked his father,
    "How long ago is it since this came to him?"

And he said,
    "As a child!
    And it has often cast him into the fire,
    and into the waters,
    to destroy him!
    But if you can do anything,
    have compassion on us,
    and help us!"
Jesus said to him,
    "If you can believe.
    All things are possible
    to him who believes."
Right away the father of the child cried out,
and said with tears,
    "Lord, I believe.
    Help my unbelief!"
When Jesus saw that the people came running together,
He rebuked the foul spirit, saying to him,
    "You! Deaf and speechless spirit!
    I command you!
    Come out of him,
    and enter him no more!"
And as he was still coming,
the demon threw him down,
and cried out,
and ripped him sorely,
and he was as one dead;
so much so that many said,
    "He is dead!"
Jesus rebuked the devil;
and he went out of him;
Jesus healed the child,
and he arose.
He took him by the hand,

and lifted him up
and gave him to his father again.
The child was cured from that very hour
and they were all amazed at the mighty power of God.
But while each one of them
wondered at all the things
that Jesus had done,
He spoke to His disciples.

117 Why the Disciples Failed

(Matthew 17:19-21; Mark 9:28-29)

When He had come into the house,
then the disciples came to Jesus apart from the crowds,
and asked Him privately,
    "Why could we not cast him out?"
And Jesus told them,
    "Because of your unbelief."
    Truly, I tell you,
    If you have faith like a grain of mustard seed,
    you shall say to this mountain,
        'Move from here to that place yonder;'
    and it will move;
    and nothing shall be impossible to you.
    However, this sort can come out
    only by prayer and fasting."

118 Jesus Foretells His Death

(Matthew 17:22-23; Mark 9:30-32; Luke 9:44-45)

They left there,
and passed through Galilee;
and He did not want any man to know it.

While they stayed in Galilee,
Jesus told them,
> "Let these sayings sink down into your ears:
> because the Son of Man will be delivered,
> betrayed, into the hands of men.
> They will kill Him,
> and after He is killed,
> the third day He shall be raised again."
They were greatly distressed.
But they did understand these words,
and it was hidden from them,
so that they did not perceive it:
and they feared to ask Him about those words.

119 Jesus Miraculously Pays Taxes[16]
  (Matthew 17:24-27)

When they came to Capernaum,
those who collected the Temple tribute came to Peter and said,
> "Does your master not pay tribute?"
He said,
> "Yes,"
and when he came into the house,
Jesus anticipated him, saying,
> "What do you think, Simon?
> From whom do the kings of the earth take custom or tribute:
> from their own children or from strangers?"
Peter said to Him,
> "From strangers."
Jesus said to him,
> "Then the children are free.
> Nevertheless, so that we will not offend them,
> go to the sea, and cast a hook,
> and take up the first fish that comes up;

and when you have opened his mouth,
you shall find *a silver coin worth a shekel.*
Take that, and give it to them for you and Me."

120 The Disciples Argue about Their Greatness

(Matthew 18:1-6; Mark 9:33-37,42; Luke 9:46-48, 17:2)

Then there arose a debate among them,
about which of them should be greatest.
Jesus came to Capernaum,
seeing the thoughts of their heart:
and being in the house He asked them,
    "What was it that you disputed among yourselves along the way?"
But they held their peace:
for along the way they had argued among themselves,
who should be the greatest.
He sat down and called the Twelve, and told them,
    "If any man desires to be first,
        that one shall be last of all,
        and servant of all."

At that same time the disciples came to Jesus, asking,
    "Who is the greatest in the Kingdom of Heaven?"

And Jesus called a little child to Him,
and set him by Him, in the middle of them,
and when He had taken him in His arms, He said to them,
    "Whoever shall receive
    one of such children in My name:
    receives Me.
    And whoever shall receive Me:
    does not receive Me,
    but Him who sent Me.
    Because he who is least among you all,

is the one who will be great."

Truly, I tell you,
unless you turn yourselves,
and become like little children,
you will not enter the Kingdom of Heaven!

So, whoever shall humble himself
like this little child,
that one is greatest in the Kingdom of Heaven.
Whoever will receive
one such little child in My name:
receives Me.
But whoever will entice one of these little ones
who believes in Me
to fall away:
it would be better for him
if a millstone was hanged around his neck,
and he was drowned in the depths of the sea."

121 He Who Is Not Against Us

(Mark 9:38-42; Luke 9:49-50)

John said to Him,
    "Master, we saw someone
    casting out demons in Your name.
    He does not follow us:
    so, we forbade him!"
But Jesus said,
    "Do not forbid him:
    because there is no man
    who shall do a miracle in My name,
    who can speak evil of Me lightly!"

"He who is not against us is for us!
Whoever will give you a cup of water
to drink in My name,
because you belong to Christ,
truly, I tell you,
he shall not lose his reward."

122 Warnings about Sin

(Matthew 18:7-11; Mark 9:43-50)

"Woe to the world because of sinful snares!
Opportunities to sin must come;
but woe to that man through whom the sin comes!"

"If your hand makes you sin,
cut it off!
It is better for you to enter Life maimed,
than with two hands to be thrown into Hell,
into the fire that shall never be quenched:
where the maggots do not die,
and the fire is never quenched."

"And if your foot makes you sin,
cut it off!
It is better for you to enter Life lame,
than with two feet to be thrown into Hell,
into the fire that shall never be quenched:
where the maggots do not die,
and the fire is never quenched."

"So, if your hand or your foot makes you sin,
cut them off,
and cast them away from you!
It is better for you to enter Life maimed or lame,

than to be cast into everlasting fire
with two hands or two feet."

"And if your eye makes you sin,
pluck it out,
and cast it away from you!
It is better for you to enter Life,
to enter the kingdom of God with one eye,
than to be cast into hellfire with two eyes
where the maggots do not die,
and the fire is never quenched."

"Everyone shall be seasoned with fire,
and every sacrifice shall be seasoned with salt.
Salt is good:
but if the salt has lost its flavor,
with what will you season it?
Have salt in yourselves,
and have peace with one another.
Take care that you do not disdain one of these little ones;
for I say tell you,
that in Heaven their angels always see
the face of My Father who is in Heaven,
for the Son of Man has come to save that which was lost."

123 Church Discipline

(Matthew 18:15-20)

"Moreover, if your brother will sin against you,
go and tell him his fault between you and him alone.
If he shall hear you,
you have gained your brother.
But if he will not hear you,
then take one or two more with you,

so that in the mouth of two or three witnesses
every word can be established.
If he shall be unwilling to hear them,
tell it to the church:
but if he is unwilling to hear the church,
let him be as a heathen and a tax collector to you."

"Truly, I tell you,
whatever you shall bind on Earth
will be bound in Heaven:
and whatever you shall release on Earth
will be released in Heaven."

"Again, I tell you,
that if two of you will agree on earth
concerning anything that they shall ask,
it will be done for them by My Father who is in Heaven.
For where two or three are gathered together in My name,
there, in the middle of them, am I."

124 Forgiveness[17]

(Matthew 18:21-35)

Then Peter came to Him, and said,
    "Lord, how many times
    can my brother sin against Me,
    and I still must forgive Him?
    Up to seven times?"
Jesus told him,
    "I do not tell you,
       'Up to seven times,'
    but seventy times seven!"

"Consider that the Kingdom of Heaven is like a certain king,

who examined the accounts of His servants.
And when he began the reckoning,
one was brought to him,
who owed him *nearly sixty million dollars.*
But since he had no means to pay,
his lord commanded that he be sold to make payment,
along with his wife and children and all that he had.
So, the servant fell down prostrate before him, saying,
    'Lord, have patience with me,
    and I will pay you everything!'
Then the lord of that servant was moved with compassion,
and released him and forgave his debt."

"But the same servant went out,
and found one of his fellow-servants,
who owed him *not quite four hundred dollars*:
and he grabbed him,
and took him by the throat, saying,
    'Pay me what you owe!'"

"And his fellow-servant fell down at his feet
and begged him, saying,
    'Have patience with me,
    and I will pay you everything!'
But he would not wait:
and instead had him thrown into prison,
until he paid the debt."

"So, when his fellow-servants saw what had been done,
their grief was great,
and they came and told their lord all that had happened.
Then, after the lord had called him,
he said to him,
    'Oh you wicked servant!

I forgave you all that debt,
just because you asked me!
Should you not have also had compassion
on your fellow-servant,
just as I had pity on you?'"

"And his lord was furious,
and delivered him to the torturers,
until he paid all that was due him.
So likewise, shall my Heavenly Father do to you all,
if, from your hearts,
you do not forgive your brothers for their sins."

125 Tempting Jesus to Show Himself

(John 7:2-10; Luke 9:51)

At this time, the Jewish Feast of Tabernacles was approaching.
So, His brothers said to Him,
  "Leave here and go into Judea,
  so that your disciples may also see
  the works you do.
  No man does anything in secret,
  if he wants himself to be known.
  If you really do these things,
  show yourself to the world."
For His brothers did not believe in Him.

Then Jesus said to them,
  "My time has not yet come:
  but your time is anytime.
  The world cannot hate you;
  but it hates Me,
  because I testify that the works in it are evil.
  You go to the Feast.

I am not going to the Feast yet.
My time has not come yet."
When He had said this to them,
He still remained in Galilee.

And it came to pass,
when the time came that He should ascend,
but after His brothers had gone,
then He steadfastly set His face to go to Jerusalem,
and He also went to the Feast,
not openly, but secretly.

126 James and John Are Rebuked

(Luke 9:52-56)

He sent messengers before His face:
and they went and entered a village of the Samaritans,
to make things ready for Him.
They did not receive Him,
because His face was set go to Jerusalem.
When His disciples, James and John, saw this, they said,
    "Lord, would You have us command fire
    to come down from Heaven and consume them,
    just as Elijah did?
But He turned, and rebuked them, and said,
    "You do not know what manner of spirit you are of!
    The Son of Man has not come to destroy men's lives,
    but to save them!"
And they went to another village.

127 Unfit Followers

(Matthew 8:19-22; Luke 9:57-62)

It came to pass, as they went along the way,
that a certain Scribe came and said to Him,
> "Master, I will follow you wherever you go!"

And Jesus said to him,
> "The foxes have holes,
> and the birds of the air have nests;
> but the Son of Man has nowhere to lay His head."

He said to another of His disciples,
> "Follow Me!"

But he said,
> "Lord, first let me go and bury my father."

Jesus said to him,
> "Follow Me and let the dead bury their dead:
> but you go preach the Kingdom of God!"

Another also said,
> "Lord, I will follow You;
> but first let me go say farewell,
> to those at home in my house."

And Jesus said to him,
> "No man who has put his hand to the plow,
> but looks backwards,
> is fit for the Kingdom of God."

128 Jesus at the Feast of Tabernacles

(John 7:11-24)

Then the Jews sought Him at the Feast, and said,
> "Where is he?"

There was much murmuring among the people about Him:

for some said,

    "He is a good man,"

others said,

    "No, he just deceives the people."

However, no man spoke openly about Him

for fear of the Jews.

At about the middle of the feast

Jesus went into the Temple and taught.

And the Jews were astonished, saying,

    "How does this man have an education, having never learned?"

Jesus answered them,

    "My doctrine is not Mine,

    but His who sent Me.

    If any man will do His will,

    he shall know whether the doctrine is of God,

    or whether I speak on My own.

    He who speaks on his own seeks his own glory:

    but He who seeks the glory of He who sent Him,

    is true,

    and unrighteousness is not in Him.

    Did not Moses give you the Law?

    But none of you keeps the Law!

    Why do you seek to kill me?"

The people answered and said,

    "You have a devil.

    Who seeks to kill you?"

Jesus answered them,

    "I have done one work and you are all astonished.

    Now Moses gave you circumcision

    (not because it is from Moses, but from the Patriarchs);

    and you on the Sabbath day will circumcise a man.

    If a man receives circumcision on the Sabbath day,

    so that the Law of Moses is not broken;

how can you be angry at Me
for making a man completely whole on the Sabbath day?
Do not judge according to appearances,
judge instead with righteous judgment."

129 Jesus Cries Out in the Temple

(John 7:25-36)

Then some of those from Jerusalem said,
"Is this not he, whom they seek to kill?"
"But, look, he speaks boldly, and they say nothing unto him."
"Do the rulers know that this is indeed the Christ?"
"How is it we know where this man is from:
but when Christ comes,
no one knows where he is from?"

Then, as He taught,
Jesus cried out in the Temple,
"You know Me
and you know where I am from.
I have not come on My own,
but He who sent Me is true,
whom you do not know.
But I know Him:
for I am from Him,
and He has sent Me."

Then they tried to take Him:
but no man laid hands on Him,
because His hour had not yet come.

Many of the people believed in Him and said,
"When Christ comes,
will He do more miracles

than this man has done?"

The Pharisees heard that the people murmured such things about Him;
and so, the Pharisees and the Chief Priests sent officers to arrest Him.

Then Jesus said to them,
    "I will be with you only a little longer
    and then I will go to Him who sent Me.
    You shall seek Me,
    and will not find Me:
    and where I am,
    there you cannot come."

Then the Jews said among themselves,
    "Where will he go, that we cannot find him?"
    "Will he go to the Dispersed among the Gentiles
    and teach the Gentiles?
    "What kind of talk is this when he said,
        'You shall seek me,
        and will not find me:
        and where I am,
        there you cannot come?'"

130 Rivers of Living Water

    (John 7:37-44)

In the last day, that great day of the Feast,
Jesus stood and cried out,
    "If any man thirsts,
    let him come to Me and drink!
    For He who believes in Me,
    it will be as the Scripture has said,
        'Out of his belly shall flow rivers of living water.'"
(He spoke this about the Spirit,

which they who believe in Him should receive:
for the Holy Spirit had not yet been given;
because Jesus had not yet been glorified.)

So many of the people when they heard this saying said,
    "Truly this is the Prophet."
Others said,
    "This is the Christ."
But some said,
    "How can Christ come out of Galilee?
    The Scripture has said that Christ comes of the seed of David,
    and out of the town of Bethlehem, where David was."
So, there was a division among the people because of Him.
And some of them would have taken Him;
but no man laid hands on Him.

131 The Sanhedrin Deliberates

  (John 7:45-8:1)

Then the officers reported to the Chief Priests and Pharisees;
who said to them,
    "Why have you not brought him?"
The officers answered,
    "No man ever spoke like this man!"
Then the Pharisees answered them,
    "Are you also deceived?
    Have any of the rulers or the Pharisees believed in him?
    These people who do not know the Law are cursed!"

Nicodemus said to them,
(he who came to Jesus by night, being one of the disciples,)
    "Does our Law judge any man,
    before it hears him, and knows what he does?"
They answered him,

"Are you from Galilee, too?
Search, look it up:
    'for out of Galilee ariseth no prophet.'"
And every man went to his own house.
Jesus went to the Mount of Olives.

132 The Adulterous Woman

(John 8:2-11)

Early in the morning He again came into the Temple,
and all the people came to Him;
and He sat down and taught them.
The Scribes and Pharisees brought Him a woman taken in adultery;
and when they had set her in the midst of the people,
They said to Him,
    "Master, this woman was taken in adultery,
    in the very act!
    Now Moses, in the Law,
    commanded that such a one should be stoned:
    but what do you say?"
They said this to tempt Him,
so that they might have grounds to accuse Him.

But Jesus stooped down,
and wrote with His finger on the ground,
as if He did not hear them.

So, when they continued questioning Him,
He got up and said to them,
    "Let he who is without sin among you
    cast the first stone at her."
Again, He stooped down,
and wrote on the ground.
And those who heard it,

being convicted by their own conscience,
left one by one,
beginning with the eldest,
until the very last.
And Jesus was left alone,
with the woman standing in the middle of the crowd.

When Jesus got up and saw none but the woman,
He said to her,
    "Woman, where are those who accused you?
    Has no man condemned you?"
She said,
    "No man, Lord."
And Jesus said,
    "Nor do I condemn you.
    Go, and sin no more."

133 Light of the World

(John 8:12-20)

Then Jesus spoke to them again, saying,
    "I am the Light of the world!
    He who follows Me shall not walk in darkness,
    but will have the Light of Life!"
So, the Pharisees said to Him,
    "You testify for yourself;
    your statement is not true!"
Jesus answered and said to them,
    "Even though I testify for Myself,
    My record is true:
    because I know where I came from,
    and where I go.
    But you cannot tell where I am from,
    and where I go.

"You judge after the flesh;
I judge no man.
And yet if I judge,
My judgment is true:
for I am not alone,
but I am with the Father who sent Me.
It is also written in your Law,
that the testimony of two men is true.
I am one,
who testifies for myself,
and the second is the Father,
who sent Me and testifies for Me."

Then said they to him,
"Where is your Father?
Jesus answered,
"You know neither Me nor My Father.
If you had known Me,
you should have also known My Father."

Jesus spoke these words in the Treasury,
as He taught in the Temple:
and no man laid hands on Him;
because His hour had not yet come.

134 The Father Sent Jesus

(John 8:21-30)

Then Jesus again said to them,
"I go My way;
and you shall seek Me
and will die in your sins!
Where I go, you cannot come."
Then the Jews said,

"Will he kill himself? After all he says,
    'Where I go, you cannot come.'"
And He said to them,
    "You are from beneath.
    I am from Above.
    You are of this world.
    I am not of this world.
    So I told you that you will die in your sins:
    because if you do not believe that I am He,
    you will die in your sins."

Then they said to Him,
    "Who are you?"
And Jesus told them,
    "Indeed,
    I AM the same as I told you
    from the Beginning!
    I have many things to say
    and to judge you for:
    but He who sent Me is true;
    and I speak to the world
    what I have heard from Him."
They did not understand that He spoke to them about the Father.

Then Jesus told them,
    "When you have lifted up the Son of Man,
    then you will know that I am He,
    and that I do nothing on my own;
    but I only speak the things My Father has taught Me.
    And He who sent Me is with Me.
    The Father has not left Me alone;
    because I always do what pleases Him."
As He spoke these words, many believed in Him.

135 Abraham's Children

(John 8:31-59)

Then Jesus said to those Jews who believed in Him,
    "If you continue in My word,
    then you are indeed My disciples;
    and you will know the truth,
    and the truth shall make you free."
They answered Him,
    "We are Abraham's seed,
    and were never in bondage to any man.
    How can you say,
        'You shall be made free?'"

Jesus answered,
    "Truly, truly, I tell you,
    whoever commits sin is the servant of sin.
    The servant does not live in the house forever:
    but the Son always remains.
    So, if the Son shall make you free,
    you shall be free indeed.
    I know that you are Abraham's seed;
    but you seek to kill Me,
    because My Word has no place in you.
    I speak of what I have seen with My Father:
    and you do what you have seen with your father."
They answered Him,
    "Abraham is our father."
Jesus told them,
    "If you were Abraham's children,
    you would do the works of Abraham.
    But now you seek to kill Me,
    a man who has told you the truth,
    which I have heard from God.

Abraham did not do this thing you do.
You do the deeds of your father."

Then they said to Him,
"We are not born of fornication;
we have one Father. God."
Jesus told them,
"If God were your Father,
you would love Me:
because I came forth from God.
Nor did I come on My own,
but instead, He sent Me.
Why do you not understand My speech?
It is because you cannot hear My Word.
You are from your father the Devil,
and you will do the lusts of your father.
He was a murderer from the Beginning,
and did not remain in the truth,
because there is no truth in him.
When he speaks a lie,
he speaks on his own:
because he is a liar and the Father of Lies.
So, because I tell you the truth,
you do not believe Me."

"Which of you proves Me guilty of sin?
And if I speak the truth,
why do you not believe Me?
He who is of God hears God's words.
Therefore, you do not hear them
because you are not from God."

Then the Jews answered Him,
"Do we not speak truly

that you are a Samaritan and have a demon?"
Jesus answered,
>   "I do not have a devil.
>   I simply honor My Father,
>   and you dishonor Me.
>   I do not seek My own glory.
>   There is one who seeks and judges.
>   Truly, truly, I tell you,
>   if a man keeps My teaching,
>   he shall never see death."

Then the Jews told Him,
>   "Now we know that you have a demon!
>   Abraham is dead, and so are the prophets!
>   But you say,
>   'If a man keeps my saying,
>   he shall never taste of death.'
>   Are you greater than our father Abraham,
>   who is dead?
>   And are you greater than the prophets,
>   who are dead?
>   Who do you make yourself out to be?"
Jesus answered,
>   "If I honor Myself,
>   My honor is nothing:
>   it is My Father who honors Me;
>   of whom you say that He is your God.
>   Yet you have not known Him.
>   But I do know Him:
>   and if I should say,
>   'I know Him not,'
>   I shall be a liar like you:
>   but I do know Him and keep His sayings.
>   Your father Abraham rejoiced to see My day.

He saw it and was glad."

Then the Jews said to Him,
    "You are not yet fifty years old,
    and you say you have seen Abraham?"
Jesus said to them,
    "Truly, truly, I tell you,
    Before Abraham was, I AM!"
Then they took up stones to cast at Him:
but Jesus hid Himself and left the Temple,
going through the midst of them,
and so, passed them by.

136 Jesus Cures a Man Born Blind
    (John 9:1-7)

As Jesus passed by,
He saw a man who was blind from his birth.
His disciples asked Him,
    "Master, who sinned?
    This man or his parents,
    so that he was born blind?"

Jesus answered,
    "Neither this man nor his parents have sinned,
    except so that the works of God should be revealed in him.
    I must do the deeds of Him who sent Me
    while it is still day.
    The night comes when no man can work.
    For as long as I am in the world,
    I am the Light of the world."

When He had spoken thus,
He spat on the ground,

and made clay of the spittle,
and He anointed the eyes of the blind man with the clay,
and said to him,

"Go, wash in the Pool of Siloam."
So, he went his way, washed, and came back seeing.

137 Neighbors Question the Cured Man

(John 9:8-12)

So the neighbors,
and those who had seen him blind before, said,

"Is this not he who sat and begged?"
Some said,

"This is he."
Others said,

"He is like him."
But he said,

"I am he!"
So, they said to him,

"How were your eyes opened?"
He answered,

"A man who is called Jesus made clay,
and anointed my eyes,
and said to me,

'Go to the pool of Siloam and wash.'
And I went and washed,
and I received sight."
Then they said to him,

"Where is he?"
He said,

"I do not know."

138 Pharisees Question the Cured Man

(John 9:13-34)

It was the Sabbath day
when Jesus made the clay and opened his eyes.
And they brought to the Pharisees
he who before this time was blind.
Then the Pharisees also asked him
how he had received his sight.
He said to them,
   "He put clay on my eyes,
   and I washed,
   and I see."
So, some of the Pharisees said,
   "This man is not of God,
   because he does not keep the Sabbath day."
Others said,
   "How could a man who is a sinner do such miracles?"
And there was a division among them.

They spoke again to the blind man,
   "What do you say about him,
   how he has opened your eyes?"
He said,
   "He is a prophet."

But the Jews did not believe
that he had been blind and received his sight,
until they called his parents.
And they asked them,
   "Is this your son,
   who you say was born blind?
   How is it that he now sees?"

His parents answered,

"We know that this is our son,
and that he was born blind:
but by what means he now sees,
we do not know.
As for who has opened his eyes,
we do not know.
He is of age so ask him!
He can speak for himself."
These are the words his parents spoke,
because they feared the Jews:
for the Jews had already agreed,
that if any man confessed that Jesus was Christ,
he would be put out of the synagogue.
That is why his parents said,
    "He is of age so ask him."

Then they again called the man who was blind
and said to him,
    "Give God the praise for your sight.
    We know that this man is a sinner."
He answered,
    "Whether he is a sinner or not,
    I do not know.
    I do know one thing,
    that I was blind,
    but now I see."

Then they again said to him,
    "What did he do to you?
    How did he open your eyes?"
He answered,
    "I have told you already,
    and you did not hear.
    So why do you want to hear it again?

Do you also want to be his disciples?"

Then they reviled him and said,
    "You are his disciple;
    but we are disciples of Moses!
    We know that God spoke to Moses.
    But as for this fellow,
    we don't know where he is from!"
The man answered them,
    "Why here is an astonishing thing,
    that you do not know where he is from,
    and yet he has opened my eyes!
    Now we know that God does not hear sinners:
    but He will hear any man
    who worships God,
    and does His will.
    It has not been heard of
    since the world began
    that any man opened the eyes
    of one who was born blind!
    This man could do nothing
    if he was not of God!"

They answered him,
    "You were altogether born in sins,
    and you think to teach us!"
And they cast him out.

139 Jesus Finds the Cured Man

    (John 9:35-10:6)

Jesus heard that they had cast him out;
and when He found him, said to him,
    "Do you believe in the Son of God?"

He answered,
    "Who is He, Lord?
    So that I might believe in Him."

And Jesus said to him,
    "You have seen Him,
    and it is He who speaks to you."
He said,
    "Lord, I believe!"
and he worshiped Him.
Jesus said,
    "I have come into this world,
    so that those who do not see,
    might see;
    and so that those who see,
    might be made blind."

Some of the Pharisees who were with Him
heard these words, and said to Him,
    "Are we also blind?"
Jesus said to them,
    "If you were blind, you would have no sin:
    but you now say,
      'We see.'
    So, your sin remains."

    "Truly, truly, I tell you,
    He who does not enter the sheepfold by the gate,
    but instead climbs up some other way,
    is a thief and a robber.
    But He who enters by the gate
    is the Shepherd of the Sheep.
    To Him the porter opens;
    and the Sheep hear His voice:

and He calls His own Sheep by name
and leads them out.
And when He takes His own Sheep out,
He goes ahead of them and the Sheep follow Him,
because they know His voice.
They will not follow a stranger,
but will flee from him,
because they do not know the voice of strangers."

Jesus spoke this parable to them,
but they did not understand what He told them.

140 Jesus the Good Shepherd

(John 10:7-21)

Then Jesus told them again,
    "Truly, truly, I tell you,
    I am the Gate for the Sheep.
    All who ever came before Me
    are thieves and robbers:
    but the Sheep did not hear them.
    I am the Gate:
    if anyone enters through Me,
    he shall be saved,
    and shall go in and out,
    and find pasture."

"The thief only comes
    to steal and to kill and to destroy.
    I have come
    so that they might have Life,
    and so that they might have it more abundantly.
    I am the Good Shepherd.
    The Good Shepherd gives His life for the Sheep.

But he who is a hireling and not the shepherd,
whose sheep are not his own,
sees the wolf coming,
and leaves the sheep and flees:
and the wolf catches them and scatters the sheep.
The hireling flees,
because he is a hireling,
and does not care for the sheep."

"I am the Good Shepherd,
and know My Sheep,
and am known by Mine.
As the Father knows Me,
even so do I know the Father:
and I lay down My life for the Sheep.
I have other Sheep, which are not of this fold.
I must also bring them, and they shall hear My voice;
and there shall be one Flock,
and one Shepherd."

"That is why My Father loves Me,
because I lay down My life,
so that I might take it again.
No man takes it from Me,
but I lay it down on My own.
I have power to lay it down,
and I have power to take it again.
I have received this Commandment from My Father."

So, again, the Jews were divided about these sayings.
Many of them said,
"He has a demon and is mad!
Why do you listen to him?"
Others said,

"These are not the words of one who has a demon!
Can a devil open the eyes of the blind?"

141 The Seventy Are Sent

(Luke 10:1-12,16)

After these things the Lord also appointed another seventy,
and sent them two by two ahead of Him,
into every city and place where He was coming.
He told them,
>"The harvest truly is great,
>but the laborers are few.
>So pray to the Lord of the harvest
>that He would send laborers out into His harvest."

"Go on your way.
I send you out as lambs among wolves.
Carry no purse, no pack, no shoes;
and greet no man along the way."

"And in whatever house you enter, first say,
>'Peace be to this house.'
If the Son of Peace is there,
your peace shall rest upon it;
if not, it shall return to you."

"And remain in the same house,
eating and drinking what they do:
for the laborer is worthy of his hire.
Do not go from house to house,
and in whatever city you enter,
if they receive you,
eat what is set before you.
Heal the sick that are within,

and tell them,
    'The Kingdom of God has come near to you.'"

"But whatever city you enter,
if they do not receive you,
go out into the streets and say,
    'Even the dust of your city,
      that sticks to our feet,
      we wipe off against you!
      But know this:
      that the Kingdom of God has come near.'
I tell you,
it shall be easier in that day for Sodom,
than for that city!
He who hears you,
  hears Me;
and he who despises you,
despises Me;
and he who despises Me,
despises Him who sent Me."

142 The Seventy Return

(Luke 10:17-24)

The seventy returned with joy, saying,
    "Lord, even the demons are subject to us through Your name!"
And He said to them,
    "I saw Satan fall like lightning from Heaven.
    I give you power to tread on serpents and scorpions,
    and over all the power of the enemy,
    and nothing at all shall hurt you!
    Even so, do not rejoice in this,
    that the spirits are subject to you,
    but instead rejoice

that your names are written in Heaven."

In that hour Jesus rejoiced in the Holy Spirit and said,
"I thank you,
Oh Father, Lord of Heaven and Earth,
that you have hidden these things from the wise and learned,
and have revealed them to infants!
Justly so, Father; for this was your will.
All is delivered to Me by My Father:
and no man knows who the Son is,
except the Father;
and who the Father is,
except the Son,
and those the Son chooses to know."

He turned to His disciples and said privately,
"Blessed are the eyes that see what you see!
For I tell you,
that many prophets and kings have desired
to see what you see,
and have not seen them;
and to hear what you hear,
and have not heard them."

143 The Parable of the Good Samaritan[18]

(Luke 10:25-37)

A certain lawyer stood up and tested Him, saying,
"Master, what shall I do to inherit eternal life?"
He said to him,
"What is written in the Law?
How do you read it?"

And he answered,

"Thou shalt love the Lord thy God
with all thy heart,
and with all thy soul,
and with all thy strength,
and with all thy mind;
and thy neighbor as thyself."
And He said to him,
    "You have answered rightly.
    Do this and you shall live."

But wanting to justify himself, he said to Jesus,
    "And who is my neighbor?"
And Jesus replied,
    "A certain man went down from Jerusalem to Jericho,
    and fell among thieves,
    who stripped him and wounded him,
    and left him half dead.
    Now, by chance,
    a certain priest came down that way:
    and when he saw him,
    he passed by on the other side.
    And, likewise, a Levite,
    when he came to the place,
    looked upon him,
    and passed by on the other side."

    "But a certain Samaritan,
    as he journeyed,
    came to where he was:
    and when he saw him,
    he had compassion for him,
    and went to him,
    and bound up his wounds,
    pouring on oil and wine,

and set him on his own beast,
and brought him to an inn,
and took care of him.
And the next day when he left,
he took out *two days wages* and gave them to the host,
and said to him,
    'Take care of him;
    and whatever more you spend,
    I will repay you when I return.'
Now, which of these three do you think
was a neighbor to him who fell among the thieves?"
And he said,
    "He who showed mercy to him."
Then Jesus said to him,
    "You go and do likewise."

144 Martha Busies Herself While Mary Listens

(Luke 10:38-42)

Now it came to pass,
as they went along their way,
that Jesus entered into a certain village:
and a certain woman named Martha welcomed him into her house.
And she had a sister named Mary,
who sat at the Lord's feet and listened as He taught.
But Martha was encumbered with so many to serve,
and came to Him and said,
    "Lord, do you not care
    that my sister has left me to serve alone?
    So, tell her to help me!"
And the Lord answered and said to her,
    "Martha! Martha!
    You are anxious and disturbed about many things:
    and only one thing is necessary.

Mary has chosen that good part,
which shall not be taken away from her."

145 The Lord's Prayer[19]

(Luke 11:1-13; Matthew 6:9-15)

And it came to pass,
that as Jesus was praying in a certain place,
when He stopped,
one of His disciples said to Him,
  "Lord, teach us to pray,
   as John taught his disciples."
And He said to them,
  "Then pray after this manner:
  When you pray, say,
      'Our Father
      Who is in Heaven,
      Holy be Your name.
      Your Kingdom come,
      Your will be done,
      On Earth
      As it is in Heaven,
      Give us this day our daily bread.
      And forgive us our offenses;
      as we forgive our offenders.
      And do not lead us into temptation,
      but deliver us from evil:
      For Yours is the Kingdom,
      and the power,
      and the glory,
      forever.
      Amen.'
  For if you forgive men their offenses,
  your Heavenly Father will also forgive you:

But if you do not forgive men their offenses,
neither will your Father forgive your offenses."

And He said to them,
    "Which of you, having a friend,
    will go to him at midnight,
    and say to him,
        'Friend, lend me three loaves;
        for a friend of mine on a journey has come to me,
        and I have nothing to set before him?"
And he shall answer from within and say,
        'Do not trouble me:
        the door is shut now,
        and my children are with me in bed;
        I cannot rise and give you this.'
I tell you,
Though he will not rise and give it to him,
because he is his friend,
yet because of his insistence
he will rise and give him as much as he needs.
And I tell you,
ask, and it will be given to you;
seek, and you shall find;
knock, and it will be opened to you."

    "For everyone who asks, receives;
and he who seeks, finds;
and to him who knocks it shall be opened.
If a son shall ask bread of any of you who is a father,
will he give him a stone?
or if he asks for a fish,
will he, instead of a fish, give him a serpent?
Or if he shall ask for an egg,
will he offer him a scorpion?

If you then,
being evil,
know how to give good gifts to your children:
how much more will your Heavenly Father give the Holy Spirit
to those who ask Him?"

146 A Woman Blesses Mary

(Matthew 6:22-23; Luke 11:27-28;33-36)

And it came to pass,
as He spoke these things,
a certain woman of the company lifted up her voice,
and said to Him,
    "Blessed is the womb that bore you,
    and the breasts which nursed you!"
But He said,
    "Rather are those blessed
    who hear the Word of God,
    and keep it!
    No man,
    when he has lit a candle,
    puts it in a secret place,
    or under a basket,
    but on a candlestick,
    so that those who come in may see the light.

    "The light of the body is the eye.
    So, if your eye is good,
    your whole body shall be full of light.
    But if your eye is evil,
    your whole body will be full of darkness.
    So, if the light that is in you is darkness,
    how great is that darkness!"

"So, take heed that the light that is in you
is not darkness.
So that if your whole body is full of light,
having no dark part,
it will be completely bright,
as when the candlelight gleams."

147 Contentious Scribes and Pharisees

(Luke 11:37-41,45,53-54)

While Jesus spoke,
a certain Pharisee asked Him to dine with him:
and He went in and sat down to eat.
And when the Pharisee saw it,
he was astonished that He had not first washed before dinner.
And the Lord said to him,
    "Now you Pharisees clean the outside of the cup and the dish;
    but your inward part is full of ravening and wickedness.
    You fools!
    Did not He who made that which is outside
    also make that which is within?
    But rather give alms of such things as you have;
    and, see that all things are clean to you."

Then one of the Scribes answered,
    'Master, saying this, you reproach us also!'
And as He said these things to them,
the Scribes and the Pharisees began to vehemently quarrel with Him,
questioning Him to answer many things:
lying in wait for Him,
and seeking to catch something out of His mouth,
so that they might accuse Him.

148 Jesus Teaches the Fear of God[20]

(Matthew 10:26-33; Luke 12:1-12)

In the meantime,
when there had gathered together
such an innumerable multitude of people
that they trampled one another,
He began to say to His disciples, first of all,
    "Beware of the leaven of the Pharisees,
    which is hypocrisy!
    For there is nothing covered that shall not be revealed;
    nor hid that will not be known.
    What I tell you in darkness,
    speak in the light:
    and what you hear in the ear,
    preach upon the housetops!"

    "And I tell you My friends,
    do fear not those who kill the body,
    yet are unable to kill the soul!
    But I will warn you whom you should fear:
    fear Him,
    whom after He has killed
    has power to destroy both soul and body in Hell!"
    Truly, I tell you:
    fear Him!"

    "Are not two sparrows sold for *a quarter*?
    Not one of them shall fall on the ground without your
    Father knowing.
    Are not five sparrows sold for *two quarters*?
    Not one of them is forgotten before God.
    Even the very hairs of your head are all numbered!
    So do not fear!
    You are of more value than many sparrows!"

"I also tell you,
whoever shall affirm Me before men,
the Son of Man will likewise affirm him,
before the angels of God,
and before My Father who is in Heaven.
But he who denies Me before men will be denied,
before the angels of God,
and before My Father who is in Heaven.
And whoever shall speak a word against the Son of Man,
shall be forgiven;
but he who blasphemes against the Holy Ghost
will not be forgiven."

"And when they bring you to the synagogues,
and to magistrates and authorities,
take no thought how or what you will answer,
or what you shall say:
for in that same moment,
the Holy Spirit shall tell you what you should say."

149 Jesus Warns against Greed

(Luke 12:13-21,35-40)

Now one of the company said to Him,
    "Master, tell my brother,
    to divide the inheritance with me!"
He said to him,
    "Man, who made Me a judge or an executor over you?"
And He told them,
    "Take heed, and beware of greed:
    for a man's life does not consist
    in the abundance of the things which he possesses."

He told them a parable,

"The ground of a certain rich man yielded plentifully:
And he thought to himself,
   "What shall I do,
   since I have no room to store my crops?"
And he said,
   "I will do this:
   I will pull down my barns,
   and build bigger ones;
   and I will store all my crops and my goods there!
   And I will say to my soul,
      'Soul,
      you have many goods laid up for many years.
      Take it easy!
      Eat, drink, and be merry!'
But God said to him,
      'You fool!
      This night your soul shall be required of you!
      Then who will have those things
      which you prepared?'
Likewise, is he who lays up treasure for himself,
and is not rich toward God."

"Let your loins be girded,
and your lights burning;
And you yourselves be like men who wait for their lord
to return from the wedding;
so that when he comes and knocks,
they may open to him immediately.
Blessed are those servants,
whom the lord shall find watching when he comes."

"Truly, I tell you,
that he shall prepare himself,
and make them sit down to dinner,

and will come out and serve them.
And if he arrives in the second watch,
or comes in the third watch,
and find them so,
blessed are those servants."

"And this know,
that if the head of the house had known
what hour the thief would come,
he would have watched,
and not have allowed his house to be broken into!
So, you be ready also:
for the Son of Man comes at an hour you do not expect."

150 Parables about Readiness[21]

(Luke 12:41-59)

Then Peter said to Him,
　"Lord, do you speak this parable to us or to all?"
And the Lord said,
　"Who then is that faithful and wise steward,
　whom his lord shall make ruler over his household,
　to give them their portion to eat in due season?
　Blessed is that servant,
　whom, when his lord comes, shall him find so doing."

"Truly, I tell you,
　that he will make him ruler over all that he has!
　But if that servant says in his heart,
　　'My lord delays his arrival';
　and shall begin to beat the menservants and maidens;
　and to eat and drink and be drunken;
　the lord of that servant will come on a day
　when he does not look for him,

and at an hour when he is not aware,
and will cut him in pieces,
and will place him with the unbelievers!"

"And that servant, who knew his lord's will,
and did not prepare himself,
nor did according to his will,
shall be flogged severely.
But he who did not know,
and did things worthy of stripes,
shall be whipped lightly.
For to whom much is given,
of him much shall be required:
and to whom men commit much,
of him they ask more."

"I have come to pour fire on the earth;
and I would have it kindled already!
But I have a baptism to be baptized with;
and I am greatly constrained until it is finished!
Do you suppose that I have come to give peace on earth?
I tell you, no!
but division instead!
For, from now on, there shall be five divided in one house,
three against two,
and two against three.
The father against the son,
and the son against the father;
the mother against the daughter,
and the daughter against the mother;
the mother-in-law against her daughter-in-law,
and the daughter-in-law against her mother-in-law."

And He also told people,

"When you see a cloud rise out of the west,
right away you say,
    'A shower is coming.'
And, so it is.
And when you see the south wind blow, you say,
    "It will be hot.'
And it comes to pass.
You hypocrites!
You can understand the face of the sky and of the earth;
but how is it that you do not recognize this season?"

"Yes! And why do you, yourselves, not judge what is right?
When you go with your adversary to the magistrate,
while you are on the way,
work diligently so that you may be free of him;
or else he will drag you to the judge,
and the judge deliver you to the officer,
and the officer cast you into prison.
I tell you,
you shall not leave there,
until you have paid the very last *dime*."

151 Jesus Speaks of Sin & Death

    (Luke 13:1-5)

There were present at that time
some who told Him of the Galileans,
whose blood Pilate had mingled with their sacrifices.
And Jesus replied to them,
    "Do you suppose that these Galileans
    were worse sinners than all other Galileans,
    because they suffered such things?
    I tell you, No!
    But, unless you repent,

you shall all perish likewise!
Or those eighteen,
slain when the tower in Siloam fell,
do you think that they were sinners
above all men who dwelt in Jerusalem?
I tell you, No!
But, unless you repent,
you shall all perish likewise!"

152 A Parable of a Fig Tree

(Luke 13:6-9)

He also told this parable:
"A certain man had a fig tree planted in his vineyard;
and he came seeking fruit on it and found none.
Then he said to the gardener,
'Look, for these three years
I have come seeking fruit on this fig tree,
and found none.
Cut it down!
Why burden the ground with it?'
And he answered him,
'Lord, let it alone this year also,
till I shall dig around it and put down manure.
Then if it bears fruit, good;
and if not, then after that you can cut it down.'"

153 Jesus Heals a Woman on the Sabbath

(Luke 13:10-17)

Now He was teaching
in one of the synagogues on the Sabbath
and there was a woman

who had a spirit of weakness for eighteen years,
and was stooped over,
and could in no way lift herself up.
When Jesus saw her,
He called her to Him, and said to Her,
    "Woman, you are released from your infirmity."
And He laid His hands on her
and she was immediately made straight,
and she praised God.

Because Jesus had healed on the Sabbath day
the master of the synagogue responded indignantly,
and told the people,
    "There are six days in which men ought to work!
    So, come then and be healed,
    and not on the Sabbath day!"
The Lord then answered him,
    "You hypocrite!
    Will not each one of you on the Sabbath
    untie his ox or his ass from the stall,
    and lead him away to water?
    Ought not this woman,
    being a Daughter of Abraham!
    whom Satan has bound these eighteen years,
    be released from this bondage on the Sabbath day?"
And when He had said these things,
all His enemies were ashamed:
and all the people rejoiced
because of all the glorious things that were done by Him.

154 The Feast of Dedication

    (John 10:22-39)

It was in Jerusalem in winter

at the Feast of the Dedication
as Jesus walked in the Temple in Solomon's Porch,
when the Jews came up around Him and said,
    "How long will you leave us in doubt?
    If you are the Christ,
    tell us plainly."
Jesus answered them,
    "I told you,
    and you did not believe.
    The works that I do in My Father's Name testify for Me.
    But as I said,
    you do not believe
    because you are not from among My Sheep.
    My Sheep hear My voice,
    and I know them,
    and they follow Me.
    I give Eternal Life to them;
    and they shall never perish,
    nor will any snatch them out of My hand.
    My Father, who gave them to Me,
    is greater than all;
    and none is able to snatch them out of My Father's hand.
    I and My Father are one."

Then the Jews again took up stones to stone him.
Jesus answered them,
    "I have shown you many good works from My Father;
    for which of these works do you stone Me?"
The Jews answered Him, saying,
    "We do not stone you for any good work;
    but for blasphemy!
    And because you, being a man,
    make yourself out to be God!"
Jesus answered,

"Is it not written in your Law,
    'I said, "You are gods?"'
If he to whom the Word of God came,
called them gods,
and the Scripture cannot be broken;
do you say of Him,
whom the Father has sanctified and sent into the world,
    'You blaspheme;'
because I said,
    'I am the Son of God?'
If I do not do the works of My Father,
then do not believe Me.
But if I do,
even though you do not believe Me,
believe the works:
so that you may know and believe,
that the Father is in Me,
and I in Him."
So, they tried again to take Him:
but He escaped out of their grasp.

155 Jesus Goes to Aenon

    (John 10:40-42; Luke 13:22-30)

He went away again beyond Jordan
to the place where John at first baptized;
and there He remained.
And many went to Him, and said,
    "John did no miracles:
    but all that John said of this man was true!"
And many believed in Him there.
And He went through the cities and villages,
teaching and journeying toward Jerusalem.
Then one said to Him,

"Lord, are there few that are saved?"

And He said to them,
    "Strive to enter at the narrow gate:
    for many, I tell you,
    will seek to enter
    and shall not be able.
    Because once the master of the house has gotten up,
    and shut the door,
    and you stand outside,
    and begin to knock at the door, saying,
        'Lord, Lord, open for us!'
    then he shall answer you,
        "I do not know where you come from:'
    Then you will begin to say,
        'We ate and drank in your presence,
        and you taught in our streets!'
    But he shall say,
        'I tell you,
        I do not know where you are from.
        Leave me,
        all you workers of evil!'"

"There shall be weeping and gnashing of teeth,
when you shall see Abraham, and Isaac, and Jacob,
and all the prophets,
in the Kingdom of God,
while you yourselves are driven out.
And they shall come from the east, and from the west,
and from the north, and from the south,
and shall be seated in the Kingdom of God.
And, behold,
some who are last shall be first,
and some are first who shall be last."

156 Pharisees Warn Jesus about Herod

(Luke 13:31-33)

That same day certain of the Pharisees came,
saying to Him,
    "Get out and leave here
    because Herod will kill you!"

And He told them,
    "You go and tell that fox,
        'Behold!
        I cast out demons,
        and I perform healings today and tomorrow,
        and the third day I shall be finished.
        Nevertheless, today I must walk,
        and tomorrow,
        and the day following:
        for it cannot be that a Prophet perishes outside of Jerusalem.'"

"Oh Jerusalem! Jerusalem!
who kills the Prophets,
and stones those who are sent to you!
How often I would have gathered your children together,
as a hen gathers her brood under her wings,
but you would not have it!
Behold! Your house is desolate!
Truly, I tell you,
you shall not see Me,
until you shall say,
    'Blessed is He who comes in the name of the Lord!'"

157 Supper in the Pharisee's Home

(Luke 14:1-6)

It came to pass,
as He went into the house of one of the chief Pharisees
to eat bread on the Sabbath day,
that they watched Him.
And there was a certain man in front of Him
who had edema.
Jesus asked the Scribes and Pharisees,
    "Is it lawful to heal on the Sabbath day?"
And they held their peace.
Then He healed him and sent him on his way.

And He said to them,
    "Which of you
      having a foal or an ox
      that has fallen into a pit on the Sabbath day,
      will not immediately pull him out?"
And they could not answer Him.

158 Supper Parables: Seating at a Wedding

(Luke 14:7-11)

Now He put a parable to those who were invited,
when He saw how they sought the best places;
telling them,
    "When you are invited by anyone to a wedding,
    do not sit down in the highest place;
    because a more honorable man than you may be invited by him.
    Then, he who invited you both shall come and say to you,
      'Give this man your place.'
    and you shall start with shame to take the lowest place.
    But when you are invited,

go and sit down in the lowliest place;
so that when he who invited you comes,
he may tell you,
    'Friend! Move higher up!'
Then you shall have honor
in the presence of those who feast with you.
For whoever exalts himself shall be humbled;
and he who humbles himself shall be exalted."

159 Supper Parables: Give to Those Who Cannot Repay

(Luke 14:12-14)

Then He also said to His host,
    "When you make a dinner or a supper,
    do not call your friends,
    nor your brothers,
    neither your kinsmen,
    nor your rich neighbors;
    or they may also invite you back,
    and you will be repaid.
    Instead, when you make a feast,
    call the poor, the maimed, the lame, the blind:
    and you shall be blessed;
    for they cannot repay you:
    but you will be repaid at the Resurrection of the Just!"

160 Supper Parables: The King's Wedding Supper

(Matthew 22:1-14; Luke 14:15-24)

And when one of those who sat at supper with him
heard these things,
he said to him,
    "Blessed is he who shall eat bread

in the Kingdom of God!"
And Jesus answered and spoke to them again in parables,
and said,
 "The Kingdom of Heaven is like a certain king,
 who hosted a marriage for his son,
 a great feast,
 and invited many
 and sent his servant at supper time,
 to say to those who were invited to the wedding,
  'Come! For all things are now ready!'
 But they would not come."

 "They each of them all began to make excuses.
 The first told him,
  'I have bought a piece of ground,
  and I must go and see it:
  I ask you to have me excused.'
 And another said,
  'I have bought five yoke of oxen,
  and I go to examine them:
  I ask you to have me excused.'
 And another said,
  'I have married a wife,
  and so, I cannot come.'"

"Again, he sent out other servants, saying,
 'Tell those who are invited,
  "Behold! I have prepared my feast!
  My oxen and my fattened calves are killed,
  and all things are ready!
  Come to the marriage!"
But they made light of it, and went their ways,
one to his farm, another to his merchandise:
and the rest took his servants,

and treated them spitefully and killed them."

"When the king heard of it,
he was furious:
and he sent forth his armies,
and destroyed those murderers,
and burned their city."

"Then the servant came and reported these things to his lord.
Then he told his servants,
    'The wedding feast is ready,
    but they who were invited were not worthy.
    Go out quickly into the streets and lanes of the city,
    and bring in the poor and the maimed,
    and the lame and the blind,
    and as many as you find,
    invite to the marriage.'
And the servant said,
    'Lord, it is done as you have commanded,
    and there is still room.'
And the lord told the servant,
    'Go out into the highways and hedges,
    and compel them to come in,
    so that my house may be filled.
    For I say unto you,
    That none of those men who were invited shall taste my feast!'
So those servants went out into the highways,
and gathered as many as they could find,
both bad and good:
and the wedding was filled with guests."

"But when the king came in to see the guests,
he saw a man there
who wore no wedding clothes,

and he said to him,
    'Friend, how did you come in here
    without wedding clothes?'
And he was speechless.
Then the king told the servants,
    'Bind him hand and foot,
    and take him away,
    and cast him into the outer darkness,
    where there shall be weeping and gnashing of teeth,
    for many are called, but few are chosen!'"

161 The Cost of Discipleship

    (Luke 14:25-35)

Now great multitudes went with Him:
and He turned, and said to them,
    "If any man comes to Me,
    and does not hate his father and mother,
    and wife and children,
    and brothers and sisters,
    yes, and His own life also,
    he cannot be My disciple.
    And whoever does not bear his cross,
    and follow Me,
    cannot be My disciple."

    "For who of you,
    intending to build a tower,
    does not sit down first,
    and count the cost,
    to know he has enough to finish it?
    Otherwise, after he has laid the foundation,
    and is unable to finish it,
    all who see it will begin to mock him, saying,

'This man began to build,
and was unable to finish.'"

"Or what king,
going to make war against another king,
does not sit down first,
and take counsel whether he is able with ten thousand
to meet him who comes against him with twenty thousand?
Otherwise,
while the other is yet a great way off,
he sends an ambassador,
and seeks conditions of peace.
So likewise,
whoever of you who does not forsake all that he has
cannot be My disciple."

162 Parables for Sinners: The Lost Sheep & the Lost Coin
(Matthew 18:12-14; Luke 15:1-8)

Now all the tax collectors and sinners drew near to hear Him.
And the Pharisees and Scribes murmured,
   "This man receives sinners,
   and eats with them!"

He told this parable to them:
   "What do you think?
   What man among you,
   having a hundred sheep,
   if he loses one of them,
   does not leave the ninety-nine in the wilderness,
   and go into the mountains after the lost one,
   until he finds it?
   And when he has found it,
   he lays it on his shoulders, rejoicing.

When he comes home,
he calls together his friends and neighbors,
saying to them,
    'Rejoice with me!
    For I have found my sheep that was lost!'

Truly, I tell you,
he rejoices more for that sheep,
than for the ninety-nine
that did not go astray.
Even so,
it is not the will of your Father who is in Heaven,
that one of these little ones should perish.
I tell you,
that there shall likewise be more joy in Heaven
over one sinner who repents,
than over ninety-nine righteous ones,
who need not repent."

"Or what woman having ten pieces of silver,
if she loses one piece,
does not light a candle,
and sweep the house,
and seek diligently until she finds it?
When she has found it,
she calls her friends and her neighbors together, saying,
    'Rejoice with me!
    For I have found the piece which I had lost!'
Likewise, I tell you,
there is joy in the presence of the angels of God
over one sinner who repents."

163 Parables for Sinners: The Prodigal Son & His Brother

(Luke 15:11-32)

And He said,

"A certain man had two sons:

And the younger of them said to his father,

'Father, give me the portion of goods that falls to me.'

And he divided his livelihood between them.

Not many days later the younger son gathered it all,

and took his journey into a far country,

and there wasted his substance with dissolute living.

And when he had spent it all,

there arose a mighty famine in that land;

and he began to be in need.

So, he went and hired himself to a citizen of that country;

and he sent him into his fields to feed swine.

And he even longed to fill his belly

with the carob pods that the swine ate:

but no man gave him anything.

And when he came to himself, he said,

'How many hired servants of my father's

have bread enough and to spare,

but I perish with hunger in this place!

I will arise and go to my father,

and will say to him,

"Father, I have sinned against Heaven,

and before you,

and am no longer worthy to be called your son.

Take me as one of your hired servants!"

"And he got up and came to his father.

But when he was still a long way away,

his father saw him,

and had compassion,

and ran and hugged his neck and kissed him.
And the son said to him,
    'Father, I have sinned against Heaven,
    and in your sight,
    and am no more worthy to be called your son...'

But the father said to his servants,
    'Quickly!
    Bring the finest robe and put it on him;
    and put a ring on his hand,
    and shoes on his feet!
    And bring the fattened calf,
    and kill it and let us eat and be merry!
    For this my son was dead,
    and is alive again!
    He was lost,
    and is found!'
And they began to rejoice."

"Now his elder son was in the field:
and as he came and drew near the house,
he heard music and dancing.
And he called one of the servants,
and asked what these things meant.
And he told him,
    'Your brother has arrived!
    And your father has killed the fattened calf,
    because he has received him safe and sound!'
And he was angry and would not go in;
so, his father came out and reasoned with him.

But he answered his father,
    'Look! I have served you for all these many years!
    I have not neglected any of your commands:

and yet you never gave me even a young goat,
so that I might celebrate with my friends!
But as soon as this son of yours has come,
who has devoured your livelihood with harlots,
for him you have killed the fattened calf!'
And he said to him,
    'Son, you are ever with me,
    and all that I have is yours.
    It was fitting that we should rejoice and be glad:
    for this your brother was dead,
    and is alive again!
    He was lost,
    and is found!'"

164 Parables for Sinners: The Unrighteous Steward

(Luke 16:1-13)

He also said to his disciples,
    'There was a certain rich man
whose steward was accused of squandering his goods.
And he called him and said to him,
    'How is it that I hear this of you?
    Give an account of your stewardship;
    for you can be steward no longer.
Then the steward said to himself,
    'What shall I do?
    For my lord takes the stewardship away from me!
    I lack strength to dig!
    I am ashamed to beg!
    I am resolved on what to do,
    so that when I am put out of the stewardship,
    others may receive me into their houses.'
So, he called every one of his lord's debtors,
and said to the first,

'How much do you owe my lord?'
And he said,
    'A hundred measures of oil.'
And he told him,
    'Quickly!
    Take your bill,
    and sit down and write fifty.'
Then he said to another,
    'And how much do you owe?'
And he said,
    'A hundred measures of wheat.'
And he told him,
    'Take your bill and write eighty.'
And the lord commended the unjust steward,
because he had done wisely:
for the children of this world,
in their generation,
are wiser than the children of light."

"And I tell you,
make friends when using unrighteous money;
so that when it fails,
you may be received into everlasting habitations.
He who is faithful with little
is also faithful with much:
and he who is deceitful with little
is also deceitful with much.
So, if you have not been faithful with unrighteous money,
who will trust you with the true riches?
And if you have not been faithful
in that which belongs to another,
who shall give you that which is your own?"

"No servant can serve two masters:

for either he will hate the one,
and love the other;
or else he will hold to the one,
and despise the other.
You cannot serve God and greed!"

165 Answering the Pharisees

(Luke 16:14-17)

The covetous Pharisees heard all these things:
and they scoffed at Him.
And He told them,
"You are those who justify yourselves before men;
but God knows your hearts!
For that which is highly esteemed among men
is an abomination in the sight of God!
The Law and the Prophets were until John.
Since that time,
the Kingdom of God is preached,
and every man pushes into it.
But it is easier for Heaven and Earth to perish,
than for one dot of the Law to fail!"

166 Parables for Sinners: The Rich Man & Lazarus

(Luke 16:19-31)

"There was a certain rich man,
who was clothed in purple and fine linen,
and feasted sumptuously every day.

And there was a certain beggar named Lazarus,
who was cast down at his gate, full of sores,
who longed to eat the crumbs that fell from the rich man's table.

Moreover, the dogs came and licked his sores.
And it came to pass, that the beggar died,
and was carried by the angels to Abraham's bosom.

The rich man also died and was buried;
and in torment in Hades,
he lifted up his eyes,
and saw Abraham afar off with Lazarus by his bosom.
He cried out and said,
    'Father Abraham!
    Have mercy on me,
    and send Lazarus,
    so that he may dip the tip of his finger in water,
    and cool my tongue;
    for I am tormented in this flame!'
But Abraham said,
    'Son, remember that you in your lifetime
    received your good things,
    and, likewise, Lazarus
    bad things:
    but now he is comforted,
    and you are tormented.
    And beside all this,
    between us and you is set a great chasm,
    so that those who would pass from here to you cannot;
    and neither can any pass to us,
    who would come from there.'

Then he said,
    'Then I beg you, Father,
    that you would send him to my father's house,
    for I have five brothers;
    so that he may testify to them,
    or else they might also come into this place of torment!'

Abraham said to him,
  'They have Moses and the Prophets;
  they can heed them.'
And he said,
  'No, Father Abraham!
  But if someone came to them from the dead
  they will repent!'
And he told him,
  'If they will not heed Moses and the Prophets,
  they will not believe even if one rose from the dead.'"

167 Parables for Sinners: The Mustard Seed

(Luke 17:1,3-10)

Then He said to the disciples,
  "It is impossible that temptations will not come:
  but woe to him through whom they come!
  Take care for yourselves!
  If your brother sins against you,
  rebuke him;
  and if he repents,
  forgive him.
  And if he sins against you seven times in a day,
  and seven times in a day turns again to you, saying,
      'I repent!'
  forgive him.

And the Apostles said to the Lord,
  'Increase our faith!'
And the Lord said,
  'If your faith was [small],
  like a grain of mustard seed,
  you might tell this sycamore-fig tree,
      'Be uprooted and be planted in the sea!'

and it would obey you.
But which of you,
having a servant plowing or shepherding,
will tell him as soon as he has come from the field,
    'Go now and sit down to dinner?'
Instead, will you not tell him,
    'Prepare my supper,
        and dress accordingly and serve me,
        as I eat and drink,
        and you shall eat and drink afterwards?'
Do you thank that servant
because he did what he was commanded?
I think not."

"So, it is likewise with you,
when you shall have done all those things
which are commanded, you say,
    'We are unworthy servants:
    who have merely done our duty.'"

168 The Sickness of Lazarus

(John 11:1-16)

Now a certain man was sick,
named Lazarus, of Bethany,
the town of Mary and her sister Martha.
(This was the same Mary who anointed the Lord with ointment,
and wiped His feet with her hair,
whose brother Lazarus was sick.)
So, his sisters sent word to Him, saying,
    "Lord, look!
    He whom you love is sick."
When Jesus heard this, He said,
    "This sickness is not fatal,

but is instead for the glory of God,
    so that the Son of God might be glorified by it."
Now Jesus loved Martha and her sister and Lazarus,
yet, when He had heard that Lazarus was sick,
He remained two days longer where He was.
Then after that He said to His disciples,
    "Let us go into Judea again."
His disciples said to Him,
    "Master! The Jews just tried to stone You!
    And You go there again?"
Jesus answered,
    "Are there not twelve hours of daylight?
    If any man walks in the day,
    he does not stumble because he sees the light of this world.
    But if a man walks at night,
    he stumbles because there is no light in him."
He said these things and then He said to them,
    "Our friend Lazarus sleeps;
    but I go so that I may awake him out of Sleep."
Then His disciples said,
    "Lord, if he sleeps,
    he shall do well!"
However, Jesus spoke of his death:
but they thought that He had spoken of taking of rest in sleep.

Then Jesus to them plainly,
    "Lazarus is dead.
    And I am glad for your sakes that I was not there,
    so that you may believe.
    Nevertheless, let us go to him."
Then Thomas, who was called The Twin, said to his fellow disciples,
    "Let us go, too,
    so that we may die with Him."

169 Jesus Comes to Bethany[22]

(John 11:17-29)

When Jesus arrived,
He found that Lazarus had already been buried for four days.
Now Bethany was near Jerusalem,
about *two miles* away:
and many of the Jews came to Martha and Mary,
to comfort them for their brother.
As soon as Martha heard that Jesus was coming,
she went and met Him:
but Mary still sat in the house.
Then Martha said to Jesus,

> "Lord, if You had been here,
> my brother would not have died!
> But I know, that even now,
> whatever You will ask of God,
> God will give it to You."

Jesus said to her,

> "Your brother shall rise again."

Martha said to Him,

> "I know that he shall rise again,
> in the Resurrection at the Last Day."

Jesus said to her,

> "I AM the Resurrection, and the Life!
> He who believes in Me,
> though he were dead,
> yet shall he live!
> Whoever lives and believes in Me
> shall never die!
> Do you believe this?"

She said to Him,

> "Yes, Lord:

I believe that You are the Christ,
the Son of God,
who must come into the world."
And when she had said so,
she went and secretly called her sister Mary, saying,
"The Master has come and calls for you!"
As soon as Mary heard that,
she rose quickly and went to Him.

170 Mary Comes to Jesus

(John 11:30-37)

Jesus had not yet arrived in town,
but was still where Martha had met Him.
When the Jews who were with Mary in the house to comfort her,
saw her rise up hastily and leave,
they followed her, saying,
"She goes to the grave to weep there."
Then when Mary arrived where Jesus was and saw Him,
she fell down at His feet, saying to Him,
"Lord, if You had been here,
my brother would not have died!"
So, when Jesus saw her weeping,
and the Jews who came with her also weeping,
He groaned in the spirit, and was troubled,
and said,
"Where have you laid him?"
They said to Him,
"Lord, come and see."
Jesus wept.
Then said the Jews,
"See how he loved him!"
And some of them said,
"Could not this man, who opened the eyes of the blind,

have caused that even this man should not have died?"

171 Jesus Raises Lazarus from the Dead
(John 11:38-44)

So, Jesus again groaned in Himself and came to the grave.
It was a cave with a stone laid over it.
Jesus said,
  "Take the stone away."
Martha, the sister of him who was dead, said,
  "Lord, by this time he stinks:
  for he has been dead for four days."
Jesus said to her,
  "Did I not say to you,
  that if you would believe,
  then you would see the glory of God?"
Then they removed the stone from the tomb.

Jesus lifted up his eyes, and said,
  "Father, I thank You that You have heard Me.
  I know that You always hear Me:
  but I say this on behalf of the people who stand by,
  so that those whom You have sent Me may believe."
And when He had said this,
he cried out with a loud voice,
  "Lazarus, come forth!"
And he who was dead came forth,
bound hand and foot with graveclothes:
and his face was bound with a cloth.
Jesus said to them,
  "Release him and let him go!"

172 The Chief Priests and Pharisees Take Council

(John 11:45-54)

Then many of the Jews who came to Mary,
and had seen the things that Jesus did,
believed in Him.
But some of them went to the Pharisees,
and told them what Jesus had done.

Then the Chief Priests and the Pharisees
gathered a council, and said,
    'What can we do?
    This man does many miracles:
    so if we leave him alone,
    all men will believe in him:
    and the Romans shall come
    and take away our position and our nation!"
And one of them, Caiaphas,
the High Priest that year, said to them,
    "You know nothing at all!
    nor do you consider that it is expedient for us
    that one man should die for the people
    so that the whole nation does not perish!"

He did not speak this on his own:
but because he was High Priest that year,
he prophesied that Jesus should die for the nation.
Not only for that nation,
But, also, that He should gather together in one
the Children of God who were scattered abroad.

Then they planned together from that day forward
to put Him to death.
So, Jesus no longer walked openly among the Jews;
but went into an area near the wilderness,

into a city called Ephraim,
and remained there with His disciples.

173 Jesus Cures Ten Lepers
(Luke 17:11-19)

It came to pass,
before He went to Jerusalem,
that He passed through the middle of Samaria and Galilee.
As He entered a certain village,
ten men who were lepers stood far off
and met Him there.
They lifted up their voices and said,
    "Jesus! Master, have mercy on us!"
And when He saw them, He said to them,
    "Go! Show yourselves to the priests."
And it came to pass,
that, as they went, they were cleansed.

One of them, a Samaritan,
when he saw that he was healed,
turned back,
and with a loud voice glorified God,
and fell down on his face at His feet,
giving Him thanks.
Jesus answering said,
    "Were there not ten cleansed?
    Where are the other nine?
    Those who returned to give glory to God,
    are not to be found,
    except for this stranger."
And He said to him,
    "Get up and go on your way.
    Your faith has made you whole!"

174 When Will the Kingdom Come?[23]

(Matthew 24:28; Luke 17:20-37)

When the Pharisees demanded that He say
when the Kingdom of God would come,
He answered them,
    "The Kingdom of God does not come visibly.
    They will not say,
    Look here! or look there!
    You see, the Kingdom of God is within you."

And He said to the disciples,
    "The days will come,
    when you will desire to see
    one of the days of the Son of Man,
    and you will not see it.
    And they shall say to you,
        'See here! or see there!'
    Do not go after them,
    nor follow them.
    For as the lightning,
    that flashes from one place in the sky,
    brightening another place in the Heavens;
    so shall the Son of Man be in His day.
    But first He must suffer many things,
    and be rejected by this generation."

    "As it was in the days of Noah,
    so, shall it be in the days of the Son of Man.
    They ate,
    they drank,
    they married wives,
    they were given in marriage,
    until the day that Noah entered into the ark,
    and the flood came,

and destroyed them all."

"Likewise, as it was in the days of Lot;
they ate, they drank;
they bought, they sold;
they planted, they built;
but the same day that Lot went out of Sodom
it rained fire and brimstone from the sky,
and destroyed them all."

"Even so shall it be
in the day when the Son of Man is revealed.
In that day,
he who shall be upon the housetop,
with his stuff in the house,
let him not come down to take it away:
and he that is in the field,
let him likewise not return back.
Remember Lot's wife!"

"Whoever shall seek to save his life
shall lose it;
and whosoever shall lose his life
shall preserve it.
I tell you,
in that night there shall be two men in one bed;
the one shall be taken,
and the other will be left.
Two women shall be grinding together;
the one shall be taken,
and the other left.
Two men shall be in the field;
the one shall be taken,
and the other left."

And they responded and said to Him,
  "Where, Lord?"
And He said to them,
  "Where the body is, the eagles gather."

175 Parables for the Pharisees: The Unjust Judge

  (Luke 18:1-8)

He spoke a parable to them
about how men should always pray
without growing weary, saying,
  "In a city there was a judge,
  who neither feared God,
  nor respected man.
  There was a widow in that city;
  and she came to him, saying,
    'Protect me from my enemy!'

  And he would not for a while:
  but afterward he said within himself,
    'Though I do not fear God, nor respect man;
    yet because this widow troubles me,
    I will protect her,
    or else she will weary me by her continual appearance.'"

And the Lord said,
  "Hear what the unjust judge said?
  Shall not God protect His own chosen,
  who cry day and night to Him,
  As if He delays answering them?
  I tell you that He will protect them speedily.
  Even so, when the Son of Man appears,
  will He find faith on the earth?"

176 Parables for the Pharisees:
The Pharisee & the Tax Collector

(Luke 18:9-14)

He told this parable
to certain who trusted in themselves:
that they were righteous,
and despised others:
    "Two men went up into the Temple to pray;
    one a Pharisee,
    and the other a tax collector.
    The Pharisee stood and prayed this way with himself,
        'God, I thank you,
            that I am not as other men are,
            extortioners, unjust, adulterers,
            or even as this tax collector.
            I fast twice in the week,
            I give tithes of all that I possess.'"

"And the tax collector,
standing far away,
would not so much as lift up his eyes to Heaven,
but struck his chest, saying,
        'God! Be merciful to me, a sinner!'
I tell you this man went down to his house justified
rather than the other:
for everyone who exalts himself
shall be humbled;
but he who humbles himself
shall be exalted."

177 Teachings on Divorce[24]

(Matthew 19:1-12; Mark 10:1-12; Luke 16:18)

It came to pass that when Jesus had finished these teachings,
He got up from there,
left Galilee,
and came to the region of Judea
beyond Jordan on the farther side.
The people gathered to Him again;
and, as was His way,
He taught them again.
And great multitudes followed Him;
and He healed them there.

The Pharisees came to Him,
testing Him, and asked,
 "Is it lawful for a man to send his wife away?"
He answered and said to them,
 "What did Moses command you?"

And they said,
 "Moses permitted the writing of a bill of divorcement,
 and to send her away."
Jesus answered and said to them,
 "Moses, because of the hardness of your heart,
 wrote you this precept
 but from the Beginning it was not so.
 Have you not read,
 that from the Beginning of the Creation
 God made them male and female.
 For this reason, a man shall leave his father and mother,
 and cleave to his wife;
 and they two shall be one flesh.
 So then, they are no more two, but one flesh.
 Therefore, what God has joined together,

let not man put asunder."

"I say to you,
unless it is for fornication,
whoever shall put away his wife,
and shall marry another,
commits adultery:
and whoever marries her who is sent away
commits adultery.
And if a woman shall send away her husband,
and be married to another,
she commits adultery."

In the house His disciples again asked Him the same question.
His disciples said to Him,
"If this the case of the man with his wife,
it is not good to marry."
But He said to them,
"Not all men can receive this saying,
except those to whom it is given.
For there are some eunuchs,
who were so born from their mother's womb:
and there are some eunuchs,
who were made eunuchs by men:
and there are eunuchs,
who [abstain as if they were] eunuchs
for the sake of the Kingdom of Heaven.
He who is able to receive it,
let him receive it."

178 Jesus Blesses the Little Children

(Matthew 19:13-15; Mark 10:13-16; Luke 18:15-17)

Then there were young little children brought to Him,

so that He might put His hands on them and pray.
They also brought infants to Him,
so that He would touch them:
and the disciples rebuked those who brought them.
But when Jesus saw it,
He was extremely displeased,
called them to Him,
and said to them,

> "Permit the little children to come to Me,
> and do not forbid them:
> for of such is the Kingdom of Heaven!
> Truly, I tell you:
> whoever does not receive the Kingdom of God
> like a little child
> in no way shall enter in!"

And He took them up in His arms,
put His hands upon them,
and blessed them.

179 The Rich Young Nobleman

(Matthew 19:16-26; Mark 10:17-27; Luke 18:18-27)

When He had gone out on the way,
a certain nobleman came running,
and knelt before Him and asked,

> "Good Master!
> What good thing shall I do
> so that I may inherit eternal life?

He said to him,

> "Why do you call me good?
> There are none good but one,
> and that is God:
> but if you will enter into Life,
> keep the commandments."

He said to Him,
 "Which?"
Jesus said,
 "You know the commandments,
 you shall not murder,
 you shall not commit adultery,
 you shall not steal,
 you shall not bear false witness,
 honor your father and your mother,
 and love your neighbor as yourself."

The young man said to Him,
 "All these things I have kept
 from my youth up!
 What do I yet lack?"
Then Jesus, looking upon him, loved Him,
and said to him,
 "One thing you lack:
 if you would be perfect,
 go on your way,
 sell whatever you have,
 and give it to the poor,
 and you shall have treasure in Heaven:
 and come,
 take up the Cross,
 and follow Me."

But when the young man heard that,
he was sad at what was said,
and went away grieved:
for he had great possessions.
He was very sorrowful
because he was very rich.

When Jesus saw that,

He was very sorrowful.

He looked around and said to His disciples,

"Truly, children, I tell you,

how hard it is for those who trust in riches

to enter into the Kingdom of God!

It is easier for a camel to go through the eye of a needle,

than for a rich man to enter into the Kingdom of God."

When His disciples heard it,

they were astonished beyond measure,

saying among themselves,

"Who then can be saved?"

And Jesus looking upon them said,

"With men it is impossible.

But not with God:

because with God all things are possible!"

180 The Disciples' Reward

(Matthew 19:27-30; Mark 10:28-31; Luke 18:28-30)

Then Peter said to Him,

"Look, we have forsaken all,

and followed You!"

So, what shall we have?"

And Jesus said to them,

"Truly I tell you,

that when the Son of Man

shall sit on the Throne of His Glory,

in the Regeneration,

you who have followed Me,

shall also sit upon twelve thrones,

judging the Twelve Tribes of Israel."

And Jesus said,
    "Truly, I tell you,
    there is no man who has left house,
    or brothers, or sisters,
    or father, or mother,
    or wife, or children, or lands,
    for My sake,
    for the Kingdom of God's sake,
    and the Gospel's,
    who shall not receive a hundredfold, manifold more,
    now,
    in this time,
    houses, and brethren, and sisters,
    and mothers, and children, and lands,
    with persecutions;
    and in the world to come,
    Eternal Life everlasting.
    But many that are first shall be last;
    and the last first."

181 A Parable of the Laborers in the Vineyard

(Matthew 20:1-16)

"For the Kingdom of Heaven is like a man
who owns an estate,
and who went out early in the morning
to hire laborers for his vineyard.
When he had agreed with the laborers
for a full day's wages that day,
he sent them into his vineyard.
And he went out about mid-morning,
and saw others standing idle in the marketplace,
and said to them;
    'You also go into the vineyard,

and whatever is fair I will give you.'
And they went on their way."

"Again, he went out about noon and mid-afternoon,
and did likewise."

"And in the late afternoon he went out,
and found others standing idle, and said to them,
    'Why do you stand here idle all day?'
They said to him,
    'Because no man has hired us.'
He said to them,
    'You also go into the vineyard;
    and whatever is fair,
    that you shall receive.'"

"So when evening had come,
the lord of the vineyard said to his steward,
    'Call the laborers,
    and give them their wages,
    beginning from the last to the first.'
And when they came who were hired in the late afternoon,
every man received a full day's wages.
But when the first came,
they supposed that they should have received more;
and, likewise, every man of them received a full day's wages."

"And when they had received it,
they murmured against the master of the house,
    'These last have worked only one hour,
    and you have made them equal to us,
    who have borne the burden and heat of the day.'"

"But he answered one of them and said,
    'Friend, I do you no wrong.

Did you not agree with me for a full day's wages?
Take what is yours and go your way:
I will give to this last the same as to you.
Is it not lawful for me to do what I want
with what is mine?
Do you see evil because I am good?'
So, the last shall be first,
and the first last:
for many are called,
but few are chosen."

182 Jesus Foretells His Death

(Matthew 20:17-19; Mark 10:32-34; Luke 18:31-34)

They were on the way going up to Jerusalem;
and Jesus went before them and they were amazed.
As they followed, they were afraid.
Again, He took the twelve aside along the way,
and began to tell them what would happen to Him, saying,
"Look, we go up to Jerusalem;
and all the things that are written by the prophets
concerning the Son of Man
shall be accomplished.
He will be delivered to the chief priests and scribes;
and they will condemn Him to death,
and deliver Him to the Gentiles.
And they shall mock Him,
and treat Him spitefully,
and scourge Him,
and spit on Him,
and kill Him:
and the third day He shall rise again."
And they understood none of these things:
and this teaching was hidden from them,

and they did not understand what was said.

183 The Sons of Zebedee

(Matthew 20:20-24; Mark 10:35-41)

Then the mother of the sons of Zebedee,
came to Him with her sons, James and John,
kneeling to Him and asking a certain thing from Him.
And He said to her,
    "What is your desire?"
She said to Him,
    "Master, grant that these my two sons may sit,
    the one on your right hand,
    and the other on the left,
    in your Kingdom!"

And He said to them,
    "What do you desire that I should do for you?"
They said to Him,
    "Grant that we may sit,
    one on your right hand,
    and the other on your left hand,
    in Your glory!"

But Jesus answered and said,
    "You do not know what you ask!
    Are you able to drink of the cup
    that I will drink,
    and to be baptized with the baptism
    that I am baptized with?"
They said to Him,
    "We are able!"
And He said to them,
    "You shall indeed drink from My cup,

and be baptized with the baptism
that I am baptized with:
but to sit on My right hand,
and on My left,
is not Mine to give,
but it shall be given to those
for whom My Father prepares it."
And when the ten heard it,
they were moved with indignation against the two brothers
and began to be greatly displeased with James and John.

184 To Serve or To Be Served[25]

(Matthew 20:25-28; Mark 10:42-45; Luke 22:24-30)

And there was also strife among them,
about which of them should be considered the greatest.
But Jesus called them to Him, and said to them,
    "You know that the royalty
    who are accounted to rule over the Gentiles
    exercise dominion and lordship over them;
    and their great ones exercise authority upon them
    and are called benefactors.
    But it shall not be so among you:
    whosoever will be greatest among you,
    let him be as the younger.
    Whosoever will be chief among you,
    let him be your servant.
    For who is greater,
    he who sits at supper,
    or he who serves?
    Is it not he who sits at supper?
    But I am among you as he who serves.
    For even the Son of Man came not to be served,
    but to serve,

and to give His life a ransom for many."

"You are the ones who have continued with Me in My trials.
And I appoint to you a Kingdom,
as my Father has appointed to Me;
so that you may eat and drink at My table in My Kingdom,
and sit on thrones judging the Twelve Tribes of Israel."

185 The Blind Men Healed in Jericho[26]

(Matthew 20:29-34; Mark 10:46-52; Luke 18:35-43)

It came to pass that as they departed,
He came near to Jericho with His disciples,
and a great multitude followed.
By the side of the highway,
two blind men sat begging.
Hearing the multitude pass by,
blind Bartimaeus, the son of Timaeus,
asked what it meant
and they told him that Jesus of Nazareth was passing by.

When he heard that Jesus passed by,
they cried out, saying,
    "Have mercy on us!
    Oh Lord, Jesus!
    You, the Son of David!"
And the multitude and those who went ahead rebuked them,
saying they should hold their peace.

But they cried out all the more, saying,
    "You, the Son of David!
    Have mercy!
    Have mercy on us,
    Oh Lord!

You, the Son of David!"
Jesus stood still,
and commanded he be called to Him,

They called the blind man, saying to him,
    "Be of good cheer!
    Rise! He calls you!"
And he threw aside his cloak,
rose, and came to Jesus.

When he had come near,
Jesus said to him,
    "What do you want Me to do for you?"
The blind man said to Him,
    "Lord, I want to receive sight.
    and that our eyes may be opened!"
So, Jesus had compassion on them,
and touched their eyes and said,
    "Go your way!
    Your faith has made you whole."
    "Receive your sight!
    Your faith has saved you."
Immediately, their eyes received sight,
and they followed Jesus along the way,
glorifying God:
and all the people, when they saw it,
gave praise to God.

186 Salvation Comes to Zaccheus

    (Luke 19:1-10)

Jesus entered and passed through Jericho
where there was a rich man named Zacchaeus,
who was the chief among the tax collectors.

He sought to see Jesus and who He was;
but could not because of the crowd,
since he was of short stature.
So, he ran ahead,
and climbed up into a sycamore tree to see Him:
because He would pass that way.
When Jesus came to the place,
He looked up and saw him, and said to him,
    "Zacchaeus, hurry and come down!
    For today I must stay at your house."
And he quickly came down,
and joyfully received Him.
And when they saw it,
they all murmured
because He went to be the guest of a sinful man.
And Zacchaeus stood, and said to the Lord:
    "See, Lord!
    I commit half of my goods to the poor;
    and if I have taken anything from any man falsely,
    I will give him back four times as much!"

Jesus said to him,
    "This day salvation has come to this house,
    for he is also a son of Abraham!
    Truly, the Son of Man comes to seek and to save
    that which was lost."

187 The First Parable of the Servants[27]

(Luke 19:11-27)

And as they heard these things,
He spoke a parable,
because He was near Jerusalem,
and because they thought that the Kingdom of God

should immediately appear.
So, He said,

"A certain nobleman went into a far country
to receive a kingdom for himself,
and then to return."

"So he called his ten servants,
and gave them *four thousand dollars in silver*,
and said to them,
'Carry on until I return.'
But his citizens hated him,
and sent a message after he left, declaring,
'We will not have this man rule over us.'"

"Now it came to pass that he returned,
having received the kingdom.
He then commanded that the servants
to whom he had given the money,
be called to him,
so that he might know how much every man had gained by trading.
The first came, saying,
'Lord, your *four hundred dollars*
has gained *four thousand dollars*.'
And he said to him,
'Well, good servant:
because you have been faithful in a very little,
now have authority over ten cities.'
And the second came, saying,
'Lord, your *four hundred dollars*
has gained *two thousand dollars*.'
And he likewise said to him,
'Now you, also, be over five cities.'

And another came, saying,

'Lord, behold, here is your *four hundred dollars*,
which I have kept laid up in a small cloth:
since I was afraid of you,
because you are a stringent man:
who takes up what you did not set down,
and reaps what you did not sow.'
And he said to him,
'Out of your own mouth I will judge you,
you wicked servant.
You knew that I was a strict man,
taking up what I did not set down,
and reaping what I did not sow:
Why then did you not put my money into the bank,
so that at my return
I might have regained my investment with interest?'
And he said to those who stood by,
'Take from him the *four hundred dollars*,
and give it to him that has *four thousand*.'
But they said to him,
'Lord, he already has *four thousand!*'

'Yet I tell you,
That everyone who has gained shall be given more;
and from he who gained nothing,
even what he kept shall be taken away from him.
But those enemies of mine,
who would not have it that I should rule over them,
bring them here and slay them before me.'"

188 The Jews Look for Jesus

(*John 11:55-57*)

The Jews' Passover was nearly at hand:
and before the Passover

many went up out of the country to Jerusalem,
to purify themselves.
Then they searched for Jesus,
speaking among themselves as they stood in the Temple,
    "What do you think,
      that he will not come to the Feast?"
Because both the Chief Priests and the Pharisees had commanded,
that if any man knew where He were,
he should tell it so that they might take him.

189 Jesus in Bethany[28]

    (Matthew 26:6-13; Mark 14:3-9; John 12:1-8)

Six days before the Passover,
Jesus came to Bethany,
where Lazarus was,
whom He raised from the dead.
Now when He was in Bethany,
in the house of Simon the Leper,
there they made Him a feast, which Martha served,
and Lazarus was one of those who sat at the table with Him.
As Jesus sat, Mary came to Him
with an alabaster box of very precious spikenard.
She broke it
and poured a pound of the costly ointment on His head,
and anointed His feet,
and wiped His feet with her hair,
and filled the house with the fragrance of the ointment.

When His disciples saw it,
one of them,
Judas Iscariot, Simon's son,
who would betray Him, said,
    "Why was this ointment not sold for a year's wages,

and given to the poor?"
He said this, not because he cared for the poor;
but because he was a thief and had the moneybag,
and kept what was put in it.
They were indignant within themselves, saying,
"What purpose did this waste of the ointment serve?
This ointment might have been sold for a great deal,
and given to the poor."
And they murmured against her.

When Jesus perceived this, then He said to them,
    "Leave her alone!
    The poor you will always have with you;
    and whenever you want
    you may do them good:
    but you will not always have Me!
    Why do you trouble the woman?
    She has done a good work for Me!
    She kept this against the day of My burying
    and poured this ointment on My body.
    In doing so, she did what she could,
    and has come beforehand to anoint My body for burial."

    "Truly, I tell you,
    wherever this gospel shall be preached in the whole world,
    there will also be this:
    that what this woman has done
    shall be told as a memorial for her."

190 The Chief Priests Plot to Kill Jesus and Lazarus

    (John 12:9-11; Luke 19:28)

When He said these things,
it was before He ascended to Jerusalem,

Thus, many people of the Jews knew that He was there.
And they came not only for Jesus' sake,
but so that they might see Lazarus also,
whom He had raised from the dead.
But the chief priests schemed
about how they might also put Lazarus to death;
since because of him
many of the Jews went to believe in Jesus.

191 Jesus Ascends toward Jerusalem

(Matthew 21:1-7; Mark 11:1-7; Luke 19:29-35; John 12:12a,14-16)

On the next day, when they drew near Jerusalem,
coming into Bethphage and Bethany,
at the Mount of Olives,
then Jesus sent two of His disciples, telling them,
    "Go into the village opposite you:
    and as soon as you have entered
    you shall find a donkey tied up,
    and a colt with her,
    on which no man has ridden.
    Untie them and bring them to Me.
    And if any man asks you,
        'Why do you untie him?'
    you shall say this to him,
        'Because the Lord has need of him.'
    and immediately he will send him here."

All this was done
so that which was spoken by the prophet
might be fulfilled, saying,
    'Tell ye the daughter of Zion,
    Behold, thy King cometh unto thee,
    meek, and sitting upon an ass,

and a colt the foal of an ass.'
His disciples did not understand these things at first:
but when Jesus was glorified,
then they remembered that these things were written about Him,
and that they had done these things to Him.
The disciples went on their way,
and did as Jesus commanded,
and found things just as He had told them,
the donkey, and the colt,
tied outside the door in a place where two roads met.

They untied him and as they were untying the colt,
certain ones of those who stood there,
the owners, said unto them,
    'Why do you untie the colt?'
And they said to them just as Jesus commanded:
    'The Lord has need of him.'
So, they put their cloaks on him and let them go.
And they brought the donkey and the colt to Jesus,
and they put their cloaks on the colt,
and they set Jesus on him.

192 Jesus Comes to Jerusalem

(Matthew 21:8-11; Mark 11:8-10; Luke 19:36-40; John 12:12b-13,17-19)

A very great multitude that had come to the feast,
heard that Jesus was coming to Jerusalem,
and went out to meet him, crying,
    "Hosanna!
    Blessed is the King of Israel
    who comes in the name of the Lord!"

And the people testified who were with Him

when He called Lazarus out of his grave
and raised him from the dead
It was also for this reason the people met Him,
because they heard that He had done this miracle.

As He went,
they spread their cloaks in the path.
Others cut down fronds from the palm trees,
and placed them in the path.

When He had come near the descent from the Mount of Olives,
the whole multitude of the disciples and those who followed
began to rejoice and to praise God with loud cheers
for all the mighty works that they had seen, saying,
　　"Blessed be the King
　　who comes in the name of the Lord!
　　Peace in Heaven,
　　and glory in the highest!"
And the multitudes that went ahead and that followed cried out, saying,
　　"Hosanna to the Son of David!
　　Blessed is He who comes in the name of the Lord!
　　Hosanna in the highest!
　　Blessed be the kingdom of our father David,
　　that comes in the name of the Lord!
　　Hosanna in the highest!"

And when He arrived in Jerusalem,
all the city was moved, saying,
　　"Who is this?"
And the multitude said,
　　"This is Jesus of Nazareth,
　　the prophet of Galilee!"

Some of the Pharisees among the multitude said to Him,
　　"Master, rebuke your disciples!"

And He answered them,
> "I tell you that if these should hold their peace,
> the stones would immediately cry out!"
So, the Pharisees said among themselves,
> "Do you see how you accomplish nothing at all?
> See! The world has gone after Him!"

193 Jesus Weeps for Jerusalem

(Luke 19:41-44)

When He came near,
And beheld the city,
He wept over it, saying,
> "If you had only known,
> even you, at least on this day,
> the things which should bring you peace!
> But now they are hidden from your eyes.
> So, the days shall come upon you,
> when your enemies shall throw down a rampart around you,
> and encircle you all around,
> and hold you in on every side,
> and shall level you to the ground,
> with your children within you!
> They shall not leave in you one stone upon another;
> because you did not know the time of your visitation!"

194 Jesus Curses a Fig Tree

(Matthew 21:18-19; Mark 11:11-14)

And Jesus entered into the Temple in Jerusalem.
The evening had come,
and when He had looked around upon all things,
He went out to Bethany with the Twelve.

Now in the morning,
when they were coming from Bethany the next day,
as He returned into the city,
He was hungry and far off, along the way,
He saw a fig tree with leaves.

He went to it in case He might find anything on it,
and found nothing on it, only leaves,
for it was not yet the time for figs.
And Jesus said to it,
    "Let no fruit grow on you!
    Let no man eat fruit from you forever after!"
Now His disciples heard it
and soon the fig tree withered away.

195 The Final Temple Cleansing

(Matthew 21:12-17; Mark 11:15-19; Luke 19:45-48)

Now they came to Jerusalem:
And Jesus went into the Temple of God,
and cast out all those who sold and bought in the Temple,
and overthrew the tables of the moneychangers,
and the seats of those who sold doves,
and would not allow any man to carry any vessel through the Temple.
Then He explained, saying to them,
    "Is it not written,
        'My house shall be called of all nations
        the house of prayer?
        but ye have made
        it a den of thieves!'"

He taught daily in the Temple
and the blind and the lame came to Him in the Temple,
and He healed them,

and the Scribes and Chief Priests heard of it.
When they saw the wonderful things that He did,
and the children crying out in the Temple, and saying,

"Hosanna to the Son of David!"
they were severely displeased,
and said to Him,

"Do you hear what they say?"
And Jesus said to them,

"Yes! Have you never read,

'Out of the mouth of babes and sucklings
thou hast perfected praise?'"
The Scribes and Chief Priests and leaders of the people
sought how they could destroy Him:
for they feared Him,
because all the people were astonished at His teachings.
And they could not determine what they could do,
since all the people were very eager to hear Him.
When evening came, He left them
And went out of the city to Bethany and stayed there.

196 The Withered Fig Tree

(Matthew 21:20-22; Mark 11:20-26)

Now in the morning, as they passed by,
they saw the fig tree was dried up from the roots.
When the disciples saw it, they were astonished and said,

"See how quickly the fig tree has withered away!
And Peter, remembering, said to Him,

"Master, see!

The fig tree which you cursed has withered away!"
And Jesus answered them,

"Have faith in God.

Truly, I tell you,

If you have faith, and do not doubt,

you shall not only do what was done to the fig tree,
but whoever shall say to this mountain,
    'Be removed,
    and be cast into the sea!'
and shall not doubt in his heart,
but shall believe that those things which he says
shall come to pass;
he shall have whatever he says.
And all things, whatever you shall ask in prayer,
believing, you shall receive.
So, I tell you,
whatever things you desire,
when you pray,
believe that you receive them,
and you shall have them.
And when you stand praying,
forgive, if you have something against any:
so that your Father, also, who is in Heaven
may forgive you your offenses.
But if you do not forgive,
neither will your Father who is in Heaven
forgive your offenses."

197 The Authority of Jesus

(Matthew 21:23-27; Mark 11:27-33; Luke 20:1-8)

They came again to Jerusalem:
and it came to pass, that on one of those days,
as He was walking in the Temple,
and teaching and preaching the Gospel,
the Chief Priests, and the Scribes, and the Elders of the people
came to Him and said,
    "By what authority do you do these things?
    and who gave you this authority?"

And Jesus answered them,
 "I also will ask you one question,
 which if you answer me,
 I will likewise tell you
 by what authority I do these things.
  'The baptism of John:
  was it from Heaven,
  or of men?'
  Answer Me."

And they reasoned with each other, saying,
 "If we say, 'From Heaven';
 he will say, 'Why then did you not believe him?'
 But if we say, 'Of men';
 we fear that all the people will stone us!
 for they are persuaded that John was indeed a prophet!"
And they answered Jesus, and said,
 "We cannot tell from where."
And Jesus answered them,
 "Then neither will I tell you
 by what authority I do these things."

198 Parable of the Two Sons

(Matthew 21:28-32)

"But what do you think of this?
A certain man had two sons;
and he came to the first and said,
 'Son, go work today in my vineyard.'
He answered and said,
 'I will not':
but afterwards, he repented and went.

And he came to the second and said likewise.

And he answered and said,
   'I go, sir':
and did not go.   ˙
Which of those two did the will of his father?"
They said to him,
   "The first."
Jesus told them,
   "Truly, I tell you,
   that the tax collectors and the whores
   enter the Kingdom of God before you.
   For John came to you in the way of righteousness,
   and you did not believe him:
   but the tax collectors and the whores believed him:
   and you,
   when you had seen it,
   did not repent afterwards,
   so that you might believe him."

199 Parable of the Wicked Husbandmen

(Matthew 21:33-46; Mark 12:1-12; Luke 20:9-19)

Now He began to teach them through parables:
   "Listen to another parable:
   There was a certain householder,
   who planted a vineyard,
   and fenced it all round,
   and dug a winepress in it,
   and built a tower,
   and leased it out to husbandmen,
   and went into a far country for a long time.

At the season when the time of the fruit drew near,
he sent his servant to the husbandmen,
to receive the fruit of the vineyard:

And they caught him,
and beat him,
and sent him away with nothing.
And again, he sent another servant to them;
and they cast stones at him,
and wounded him in the head,
and beat him also,
shamefully handled him,
and sent him away with nothing.

And again, he sent a third:
and they wounded him also,
and cast him out.
And again, he sent another;
and him they killed,
and stoned another,
and many more servants than the first;
beating some,
and killing some.

Then last of all the lord of the vineyard said,
'What shall I do?
I will send my well-beloved and son:
Perhaps they will respect him, my heir.'
But when the husbandmen saw the son,
they said among themselves,
'This is the heir!
Come, let us kill him,
and the inheritance shall be ours!'
And they took him,
and killed him,
and cast him out of the vineyard.
So, when the lord of the vineyard arrives,
what will he do to those husbandmen?"

They said to Him,
>   "He will destroy those wicked men miserably,
>   and will lease his vineyard out to other husbandmen,
>   who shall bring him the fruits in their seasons."

Jesus looked upon them and said,
>   "Did you never read in the Scriptures,
>   *'The stone which the builders rejected,*
>   *the same is become the head of the corner:*
>   *this is the Lord's doing,*
>   *and it is marvelous in our eyes!'?*
>   So, I tell you,
>   The Kingdom of God shall be taken from you,
>   and given to a people who bring forth its fruits.
>   Whoever shall fall on this stone will be broken:
>   but whoever it shall fall upon,
>   will be ground to powder."

When the Chief Priests and Pharisees had heard his parables,
they understood that He spoke of them and they said,
>   "God forbid!"

And that same hour they sought to lay hold of Him,
because they knew that He had spoken the parable against them:
but they feared the people:
who thought Him a prophet,
and so, they left Him,
and went on their way.

200 The Things That Are Caesar's[29]

>   *(Matthew 22:15-22; Mark 12:13-17; Luke 20:20-26)*

Then the Pharisees went and schemed
on how they could entangle Him in His words.
They watched Him and sent out spies,
who should pretend they were innocent men,

so that they might catch Him in His words,

to deliver Him into the power and authority of the Governor.

And they sent out their disciples with the Herodians to Him, saying,

> "Master, we know that you are true

> and teach the way of God in truth,

> nor do you care for any man:

> for you do not regard the person of men.

> So, tell us what you think.

> Is it lawful to give tribute to Caesar,

> or not?

> Shall we give,

> or shall we not give?"

But Jesus perceived their wicked craftiness, and said,

> "Why do you tempt Me, you hypocrites?

> Bring Me the tribute money.

> Bring Me a *coin*, so that I may see it."

And they produced it.

And He said to them,

> "Whose image and inscription is this?"

They said to Him,

> "Caesar's."

And Jesus answered them, saying,

> "So, pay Caesar the things that are Caesar's,

> and God the things that are God's."

They were astonished at His answer,

and could not catch Him in His words in front of the people:

and held their peace, left Him, and went on their way.

201 Sadducees Question the Resurrection

(Matthew 22:23-33; Mark 12:18-27; Luke 20:27-39)

The same day certain Sadducees,

who deny that there is any resurrection;

came and questioned Him, saying,
    "Master, Moses wrote to us,
        'If a man dies, having no children,
        his brother shall marry his wife,
        and raise up seed unto his brother.'
    Now there were seven brethren:
    and the first took a wife,
    and dying,
    left no posterity.
    The second married her, and died,
    nor did he leave any posterity:
    Likewise, the third,
    and all the seven,
    and left no posterity.
    Last of all the woman also died.
    So, in the resurrection,
    when they shall rise,
    whose wife shall she be among them?
    for the seven had her as wife."

Jesus answered them, saying,
    "You err,
    not knowing the Scriptures,
    nor the power of God.
    The children of this world marry,
    and are given in marriage.
    But those who shall be accounted worthy to reach that world,
    and the resurrection from the dead,
    do not marry,
    and are not given in marriage.
    Nor can they die again:
    for they are like the angels in Heaven;
    and are the Children of God,
    being the Children of the Resurrection.

But regarding the Resurrection of the Dead
have you not read in the Book of Moses,
how in the bush God said to him,
> *'I am the God of Abraham,*
> *and the God of Isaac,*
> *and the God of Jacob?'*

God is not the God of the dead,
but of the living:
for all are alive to Him.
So, you err greatly."

Then certain Scribes replied saying,
> "Master, you have spoken well!"

When the multitude heard this,
they were astonished at His teaching.

202 The Scribes and Pharisees Test Jesus

(Matthew 22:34-40; Mark 12:28-34; Luke 20:40)

When the Pharisees had heard
that He had silenced the Sadducees,
they were gathered together.

Then one of the Scribes among them,
having heard them reasoning together,
and perceiving that He had answered them well,
asked Him a question, testing Him, saying,
> "Master, which is the first and great commandment in the Law?"

Jesus said to him,
> *"'Hear, O Israel;*
> *The Lord our God is one Lord:*
> *Thou shalt love the Lord thy God*
> *with all thy heart,*
> *and with all thy soul,*

and with all thy mind,
and with all thy strength.'
This is the first and greatest commandment.
And the second is like it,
'*Thou shalt love thy neighbor as thyself.'*
There is no other commandment greater than these.
On these two commandments
depend all the Law and the Prophets."

And the Scribe said to Him,
"Well, Master, you have told the truth:
for there is one God;
and there is none other but He:
And to love him with all the heart,
and with all the understanding,
and with all the soul,
and with all the strength,
and to love his neighbor as himself,
is more than all whole burnt offerings and sacrifices."
And when Jesus saw that he answered wisely,
He said to him,
"You are not far from the Kingdom of God."
And after that they dared not ask Him any question at all.

203 Christ Is David's Son?

(Matthew 22:41-46; Mark 12:35-37; Luke 20:41-44)

While the Pharisees were gathered together,
as He taught in the Temple, Jesus asked them,
"What do you think of the Christ?
Whose son is He?"
They said to Him,
"The Son of David."
And He said to them,

"How can the Scribes say that Christ is David's son?
For David himself, by the Holy Spirit,
said in the Book of Psalms,
>'The LORD said unto my Lord,
>>"Sit thou on my right hand,
>>till I make thine enemies thy footstool.'"
So, if David calls Him, Lord,
how is He his son?"
The common people gladly heard Him.
And no man was able to answer Him even a word.
Nor did any man from that day forward
dare to ask Him any more questions.

204 Woe to the Scribes & Pharisees[30]

*(Matthew 23:1-39; Mark 12:38-40;
Luke 11:42-44,46-52,13:34-35,20:45-47)*

Then Jesus spoke to the multitude, and to His disciples, saying
"The Scribes and the Pharisees sit in the Seat of Moses.
So, whatever they order you to observe,
observe it and do it;
but do not do as they do:
for they say,
but they do not do.
They tie heavy grievous burdens onto men's shoulders;
but they themselves will not lift one of their fingers to move them.
Instead, they do all their works to be seen by men.
They make their phylacteries broad,
and lengthen the fringes of their clothing."

"Woe to you, Pharisees!
for you love the uppermost rooms at feasts,
and the chief seats in the Synagogues,
and greetings in the markets,

and to be called of men,
    'Rabbi, Rabbi.'"
Then in the audience of all the people
He said to His disciples,
    "But do not let yourselves be called 'Rabbi':
    for One is your Master,
    Christ alone;
    and you are all brothers.

    "Call no man your father on Earth:
    for One alone is your Father,
    who is in Heaven.

    But he who is greatest among you shall be your servant.
    Whoever shall exalt himself
    shall be humbled;
    and he who humbles himself
    shall be exalted."

And He told them as He taught,
    "Beware of the Scribes,
    who love to go about in long robes,
    and love greetings in the marketplaces,
    and the chief seats in the Synagogues,
    and the uppermost rooms at feasts:
    Who devour widows' houses,
    and make long prayers for a show:
    the same shall receive greater damnation!"

    "Woe to you, also, you Scribes!
    because you have taken away the key of knowledge:
    you yourselves did not enter,
    and you hindered those who were entering!"

    "Woe to you Scribes and Pharisees!

Hypocrites!
–because you shut up the Kingdom of Heaven against men:
you neither go in yourselves,
nor do you permit those who are entering to go in!"

"Woe to you Scribes and Pharisees!
Hypocrites!
–because you traverse sea and land
to make one proselyte,
and when he is made,
you make him twice the child of Hell
than yourselves!"

"Woe to you, you blind guides, who say,
    'Whoever swears by the Temple,
    it is nothing;
    but whoever swears by the gold of the Temple,
    he is bound by his oath.'
You blind fools!
What is greater, the gold
or the Temple that sanctifies the gold?"

"And [you also say],
    'Whoever shall swear by the Altar,
    it is nothing;
    but whoever swears by the gift that is upon it,
    he is bound by his oath.'
You blind fools!
What is greater, the gift
or the Altar that sanctifies the gift?
Therefore, whoever swears by the Altar,
swears by it and by all things upon it!
And whoever swears by the Temple,
swears by it and by Him who dwells within!

And whoever swears by Heaven,
swears by the Throne of God,
and by Him who sits upon it!"

"Woe to you Scribes and Pharisees!
Hypocrites!
–because you pay tithes of mint and anise and cumin,
and rue and all manner of herbs,
and have omitted the weightier matters of the Law,
judgment, mercy, faith,
and the love of God.
You ought to have done these,
and not left the other undone.
You blind guides!
Who strain at a gnat and swallow a camel!"

"Woe to you Scribes and Pharisees!
Hypocrites!
–because you clean the outside of the cup and of the platter,
but within they are full of extortion and excess.
You blind Pharisee!
first clean what is within the cup and platter,
so that the outside may be clean also."

"Woe to you Scribes and Pharisees!
Hypocrites!
– because you are like whitewashed tombs,
which indeed appear outwardly beautiful
but within are full of dead men's bones,
and all uncleanness!
Just so do you also appear outwardly righteous to men,
but you are full of hypocrisy and sin within!"

"Woe to you Scribes and Pharisees!
Hypocrites!

–because you are like unseen graves,
and the men who walk over them
are not aware of them!"

"Woe to you Scribes and Pharisees!
Hypocrites!
–because you build the tombs of the prophets,
and adorn the tombs of the righteous,
and your fathers killed them!
And you say,
>   'If we had been in the days of our fathers,
>   we would not have partaken with them
>   in the blood of the prophets.'

Truly, you bear witness
that you admit the deeds of your fathers:
because they indeed killed them,
and you build their tombs.
So, you are witnesses against yourselves
that you are the children of those who killed the prophets.
Fill up, then, the measure of your fathers!"

"You serpents!
You generation of vipers!
How can you escape the damnation of Hell?
So, the wisdom of God also said,
>   '... *behold,*
>   *I send unto you prophets, and wise men,*
>   *and apostles, and scribes:*
>   *and some of them ye shall kill and crucify;*
>   *and some of them shall ye scourge in your synagogues,*
>   *and persecute them from city to city:'*
so that upon you may come
all the righteous blood of all the prophets

that was shed upon the earth
from the foundation of the world,
from the blood of righteous Abel,
to the blood of Zachariah, son of Barachiah,
whom you slew between the Temple and the Altar.
Truly, I tell you,
all these things shall be required of this generation!"

"Oh, Jerusalem! Jerusalem!
You who kills the prophets,
and stones those sent to you!
How often would I have gathered your children together,
even as a hen gathers her chicks under her wings,
and you would not have it!"

"Behold!
Your house is left to you desolated.
For I tell you that you shall not see Me after this,
until you come to say,
    'Blessed is He who comes in the name of the Lord!'"

205 The Poor Widow[31]

(Mark 12:41-44; Luke 21:1-4)

Jesus sat over across from the Treasury,
and He looked up,
and saw how the people dropped money into the Treasury:
and many who were rich dropped in a great deal.
And there came a certain poor widow,
and she threw in two *coins*,
worth *about a quarter*.
He called His disciples to Him and said,
    "Truly, I tell you:
    this poor widow has given more

than all those who have given into the Treasury,
because all these contributed to the offerings of God
out of their abundance,
but in her poverty
she has given all she had to live on."

206 The Disciples Admire the Temple

(Matthew 24:1-2; Mark 13:1-2; Luke 21:5-6)

As Jesus went out of the Temple,
His disciples came to Him
to show Him the buildings of the Temple.
One of His disciples said to Him,
    "Master,
    see what manner of stones and what buildings are here,
    adorned with precious stones and gifts!"
And Jesus said to them,
    "As for all these great buildings and things you see:
    truly, I tell you,
    the days will come,
    when there shall not be left here one stone upon another,
    that shall not be thrown down."

207 The End Shall Come

(Matthew 24:3-14; Mark 13:3-13; Luke 21:7-19)

As He sat upon the Mount of Olives
over across from the Temple,
the disciples Peter and James and John and Andrew
came to Him and asked Him privately,
    "Master, when shall these things be?
    What shall be the sign of your coming and the end of the world
    when all these things shall come to pass?"

And Jesus answered them,
 "Take care that no man deceives you.
 For many shall come in My name, saying,
  'I am Christ';
 and shall deceive many.
 The time draws near,
 so do not go after them."

 "You shall hear of wars
 and rumors of wars and commotions:
 see that you are not troubled or terrified:
 for all these things must come to pass,
 but the end is not yet."

Then He said to them,
 "Nation shall rise against nation,
 and kingdom against kingdom:
 and there shall be famines, and pestilences,
 and troubles and earthquakes in various places,
 and fearful sights and great signs from Heaven.
 All these are the Beginning of Sorrows."

 "But take hold of yourselves.
 Before all of these,
 they shall lay their hands on you,
 and persecute you.
 So, take heed to yourselves:
 for they shall deliver you to councils,
 and into prisons,
 and you shall be beaten in the synagogues:
 and you shall be brought before rulers and kings
 for My name's sake,
 and testify against them.
 Then they will deliver you up to be afflicted,

and will kill you:
and you shall be hated of all nations for My name's sake."

"So, when they lead you and deliver you up,
settle it in your hearts
to take no thought beforehand what you shall say.
Don't premeditate either:
but whatever shall be given to you in that hour;
say that,
for it is not you who speaks,
but the Holy Spirit.
I shall give you a mouth and wisdom,
which all your adversaries will not be able to debate or resist."

"Now the brother shall betray the brother to death,
and the father betray the son;
and children shall rise up against their parents,
and cause them to be put to death.
And then shall many be offended,
and shall betray one another,
and shall hate one another.
And many false prophets shall rise,
and shall deceive many.
And because wickedness shall increase,
the love of many shall grow cold."

"You shall be hated by all men for My name's sake:
but not a hair of your head shall perish.
In your patience you gain your souls.
He who shall endure to the end,
is he who shall be saved.
And this Gospel of the Kingdom
must first be preached in all the world
as a witness to all nations;

and then the end shall come."

208 Jesus Foretells the Fall of Jerusalem[32]

(Matthew 24:15-27; Mark 13:14-23; Luke 21:20-24)

"So, when you shall see the Abomination of Desolation,
spoken of by Daniel the prophet,
stand where it ought not, in the Holy Place,
(whoever reads, let him understand:)
and when you shall see Jerusalem surrounded with armies,
then know that its desolation is near!

"Then let those who are in Judea flee to the mountains;
and let those who are in the middle of it go out;
and do not let those who are in the countryside enter in.
Let him who is on the housetop
not come down to take anything out of his house:
Nor let him who is in the field
return back to take his clothes.
And woe to those who are with child,
and to those who feed infants in those days
for there shall be great distress in the land,
and wrath upon this people!"

"But pray that your evacuation not be in the winter,
nor on the Sabbath day.
For these are the days of vengeance,
and all that is written shall be fulfilled.
They shall fall by the edge of the sword,
and shall be led away captive into all nations:
and Jerusalem shall be trampled down by the Gentiles,
until the season of the Gentiles is complete.
For then there shall be great tribulation,
such as has never been

since the Beginning of the Creation which God created
up until that time,
no, nor ever shall be again."

"Unless the Lord had shortened those days,
there should be no flesh saved.
But for the elect's sake,
whom He has chosen,
those days shall be shortened.
For these will be the days of vengeance,
that all things which are written
may be fulfilled."

"And then if any man shall say to you,
    'Look, here is Christ!' or,
    'Look, He is there!'
do not believe him!
For there shall arise false Christs and false prophets,
showing great signs and wonders;
so much so, that, if it were possible,
they shall seduce and deceive the very elect.
But you take notice!
See, I have foretold all things.

So, if they say,
    'Look, He is in the desert!'
do not go forth:
    'Look, He is in the secret chambers!'
do not believe it.
For as the lightning comes out of the east,
and shines even to the west;
so, too, shall be the coming of the Son of Man."

209 The Second Coming

(Matthew 24:29-31; Mark 13:24-27; Luke 21:25-28)

"Immediately after the tribulation of those days
the sun shall be darkened,
and the moon shall not give her light,
and the stars shall fall from Heaven,
and upon the Earth."

"There will be distress and perplexity of nations,
at the sea and the roaring waves.
Men's hearts will fail them for fear,
and for looking toward those things which are coming on the Earth:
and even the powers of the Heavens shall be shaken."

"And then the sign of the Son of Man shall appear in Heaven:
and then all the Tribes of the Earth shall mourn.
They shall see the Son of Man coming in the clouds of Heaven
with power and great glory.
And He shall send His angels with a great sound of a trumpet,
and they shall gather His elect together from the four winds,
from the uttermost part of the Earth
to the uttermost part of Heaven.
And when these things begin to come to pass,
then look up! Lift up your heads!
because your redemption draws near!"

210 Parable of the Fig Tree

(Matthew 24:32-33; Mark 13:28-29; Luke 21:29-31)

And He told them a parable;
"Now learn a parable of the fig tree.
See the fig tree, and all the trees,
as they now shoot forth.

His branch is still tender and puts out leaves.
You yourselves see and know
that summer is now near at hand.
So, likewise, when you see all these things come to pass,
you will know that the Kingdom of God is near at hand,
even at the doors."

211 Watch and Pray

(Matthew 24:34-39,43-51; Mark 13:30-37; Luke 21:32-36)

"Truly, I tell you,
this generation shall not pass away,
until all these things are fulfilled.
Heaven and Earth shall pass away,
but My words shall not pass away.
But of that day and hour, no man knows,
no, not even the angels of Heaven,
nor even the Son,
but only My Father.
You take notice!
Watch and pray:
for you do not know when the time is!"

"But as the days of Noah were,
so, too, shall be the coming of the Son of Man.
For as in the days that were before the Flood
they were eating and drinking,
marrying and giving in marriage,
until the day that Noah entered the Ark,
and they knew nothing until the Flood came,
and took them all away.
So, too, shall be the coming of the Son of Man."

"But know this,

that if the man of the house had known
what time of night the thief would come,
he would have watched,
and would not have let his house be broken into.
So, you be ready also!
Because the Son of Man comes
in an hour you do not expect.
Who, then, is a faithful and wise servant,
whom his lord has made ruler over his household,
to give them food in due time?
That servant is blessed
whom shall be found doing that when his lord appears.
Truly, I tell you,
that he shall make him in charge of all his goods."

"But if that evil servant shall say in his heart,
    'My lord delays his coming';
and shall begin to beat his fellow-servants,
and to eat and drink with the drunken;
the lord of that servant shall come
in a day when he does not expect him,
and in an hour when he is unaware,
and shall cut him to pieces,
and establish his fate with the unbelieving hypocrites:
and there shall be weeping and gnashing of teeth."

"And take notice of yourselves,
unless at any time your hearts be burdened
with debauchery and drunkenness,
and the anxieties of this life,
and so that day comes upon you unawares.
For as a snare it shall come down on all them
that dwell on the face of the whole Earth."

"For the Son of Man is as a man taking a far journey,
who left his house,
and gave authority to his servants,
and to every man his job,
and commanded the doorman to watch."
So, you must watch:
for you do not know when the master of the house comes,
at evening, or at midnight,
or at the cock-crowing, or in the morning:
unless coming suddenly
he finds you sleeping."

"So, you must watch
and always pray that you may be counted worthy
to escape all these things that shall come to pass,
and to stand before the Son of Man.
And what I say to you,
I say to all,
    'Watch!'"

212 Parable of the Ten Virgins

   (Matthew 25:1-13)

"Then the Kingdom of Heaven will be like ten virgins,
who took their lamps,
and went out to meet the bridegroom.
Five of them were wise,
and five were foolish.
Those who were foolish took their lamps,
but took no oil with them.
However, the wise took bottles of oil with their lamps.
While the bridegroom was delayed,
they all grew sleepy and slept."

"Suddenly, there was a cry at midnight,
    'Look! The bridegroom has come!
    Go out to meet him!"
Then all those virgins arose and trimmed their lamps.
And the foolish said to the wise,
    'Give us some of your oil;
    because our lamps have gone out!'"
"But the wise answered, saying,
    'No there may not be enough for us and you!
    Instead, go to the merchants
    and buy some for yourselves.'
While they went to buy,
the bridegroom came;
and those who were ready
went in with him to the marriage:
and the door was shut."

"Afterward the other virgins also came, saying,
    'Lord! Lord!
    Open to us!'
But he answered, saying,
    'Truly, I tell you,
    I do not know you.'"

"So, watch!
for you know neither the day nor the hour
in which the Son of Man comes!"

213 The Second Parable of the Servants[33]

    (Matthew 25:14-30)

"The Kingdom of Heaven is like a man
traveling into a far country,
who called his own servants,

and entrusted his goods to them.
To one he gave *five hundred thousand dollars,*
to another *two hundred thousand,*
and to another *one hundred thousand;*
to every man each according to his ability;
and immediately took his journey.
Then he who had received the *five hundred thousand*
went and traded with them,
and made *five hundred thousand more.*
And, likewise, he who had received *two hundred thousand,*
he also gained another *two hundred thousand.*
But he who had received *one hundred thousand*
went and dug in the earth,
and hid his lord's money.
After a long time
the lord of those servants came,
and settled with them."

"And so, he who had received *five hundred thousand dollars*
came and brought another *five hundred thousand,* saying,
    'Lord, you gave me *five hundred thousand.*
    Look, beside that I have gained *five hundred thousand.*'
His lord said to him,
    "Well done, good and faithful servant!
    You have been faithful over a few things;
    I will make you ruler over many things.
    Share in the joy of your lord!'

"He also who had received *two hundred thousand* came and said,
    'Lord, you gave me *two hundred thousand.*
    Look, beside that I have gained *two hundred thousand.*'
His lord said to him,
    'Well done, good and faithful servant;
    You have been faithful over a few things;

I will make you ruler over many things.
Share in the joy of your lord!'"

"Then he who had received the *one hundred thousand* came and said,
'Lord, I knew that you are a hard man,
reaping where you have not sown,
and gathering where you have not scattered:
And I was afraid,
and went and hid your *investment* in the earth.
Look, there you have what is yours.'
His lord answered and said to him,
'You wicked and lazy servant!
You knew that I reap where I did not sow,
and gather where I have not scattered.
So, you ought to have invested my money with the brokers,
and then at my coming
I would have received my capital with interest.
So, take the *one hundred thousand* from him,
and give it to him who has *a million dollars.*'"

"For everyone who has gained shall be given more,
and he shall have abundantly:
but from him who has gained nothing
even what he has shall be taken away.
And the unprofitable servant you will cast into outer darkness:
where there shall be weeping and gnashing of teeth."

214 The Sheep and the Goats

(Matthew 25:31-46)

"When the Son of Man shall come in His glory,
and all the holy angels with Him,
then He will sit upon the throne of His glory:
And all nations shall be gathered before Him:

and He shall separate them from one another,
as a shepherd divides his sheep from the goats.
He shall set the sheep on his right hand,
but the goats on the left."

"Then the King shall say to them on His right hand,
    'Come, you blessed of My Father,
    inherit the Kingdom prepared for you
    from the foundation of the world!
    For I was hungry,
    and you gave Me food.
    I was thirsty,
    and you gave Me drink.
    I was a stranger,
    and you took Me in.
    Naked,
    and you clothed Me.
    I was sick,
    and you visited Me
    I was in prison,
    and you came to Me.'"

"Then the righteous shall answer Him,
    'Lord,
    when did we see You hungry,
    and fed You?
    or thirsty,
    and gave You drink?
    When did we see You as a stranger,
    and took You in?
    or naked,
    and clothed You?
    Or when did we see You sick,
    or in prison,

and come to You?'"

"And the King shall answer and say to them,
    'Truly I tell you,
    Inasmuch as you have done it
    to one of the least of these My brethren,
    you have done it to Me.'"

"Then He shall also say to them on the left hand,
    'Depart from Me, you accursed,
    into the everlasting fire,
    prepared for the devil and his angels:
    For I was hungry,
    and you gave Me no food:
    I was thirsty,
    and you gave Me no drink:
    I was a stranger,
    and you did not take Me in:
    naked,
    and you did not clothe Me:
    sick,
    and in prison,
    and you did not visit me.'"

"Then they shall also answer Him,
    'Lord, when did we see you
    hungry, or thirsty, or as a stranger,
    or naked, or sick, or in prison,
    and did not minister to you?'"

"Then He shall answer them,
    'Truly I tell you,
    just as you did nothing
    for one of the least of these,
    you did nothing for Me.'

And these shall go away
into everlasting punishment:
but the righteous
into Life Eternal."

215 The Hour Has Come

(Luke 21:37-38; John 12:20-50)

In the daytime He was teaching in the Temple
and at night He went out
and stayed in the mount that is called the Mount of Olives.
Early in the morning all the people came to hear Him in the Temple,
and there were certain Greeks among them
who came up to worship at the Feast.
So, these came to Philip,
who was of Bethsaida of Galilee,
and petitioned him, saying,
        'Sir, we want to see Jesus!'

Philip came and told Andrew
and again, Andrew and Philip told Jesus.
Jesus answered them,
        "The hour has come
        in which the Son of Man should be glorified.
        Truly, truly, I tell you,
        unless a kernel of wheat falls into the ground and dies,
        it stays alone:
        but if it dies,
        it brings forth much fruit.
        He who loves his life shall lose it;
        and he who hates his life in this world
        shall keep it through to Life Eternal.
        If any man would serve Me,
        let him follow Me;

and where I am,
there my servant shall be also.
If any man serves Me,
My Father honors him.
Now My soul is troubled;
and what shall I say,
    'Father, save Me from this hour'?
but it was for this cause I have come to this hour.
Father, glorify your name!"
Then came there a voice from Heaven, saying,
    "I have both glorified it,
    and will glorify it again."

So, the people who stood near and heard it
said that it thundered:
others said,
    "An angel spoke to Him!"
Jesus answered and said,
    'This voice did not come for My sake,
    but for yours.
    The judgment of this world is now!
    The prince of this world shall now be cast out!
    And I,
    if I am lifted up from the Earth,
    will draw all to Me."
He said this, signifying what death He would die.
The people answered Him,
    "We have heard out of the Law
    that Christ lives forever.
    How can you say,
        'The Son of Man must be lifted up'?
    Who is this Son of Man? "

Then Jesus said to them,

"For just a little while,
the Light is with you.
Walk while you have the Light,
or darkness may come upon you:
for whoever walks in darkness
does not know where he goes.
While you have the Light,
believe in the Light,
that you may be the Children of Light."
These things Jesus said and departed,
and hid Himself from them.

Even though He had done so many miracles before them,
they still did not believe in Him:
so that the saying of Isaiah the prophet would be fulfilled,
in which he said,
    "Lord, who hath believed our report?
    and to whom hath the arm of the Lord been revealed?"
So, they could not believe,
because again Isaiah had said,
    "He hath blinded their eyes,
    and hardened their heart;
    that they should not see with their eyes,
    nor understand with their heart,
    and be converted, and I should heal them."
Isaiah said these things of Him,
when he saw His glory.

Nevertheless, among the chief rulers many also believed in Him;
but they did not confess their belief Him,
because the Pharisees would put them out of the Synagogue:
and they loved the praise of men more than the praise of God.

Jesus cried out and said,

"He who believes in Me,
believes not in Me,
but in Him who sent Me.
And he who sees Me
sees Him who sent Me.
I am come as a Light into the world,
so that whoever believes in Me should not stay in darkness."
"If any man hears My words, and does not believe,
I do not judge him:
because I did not come to judge the world,
but to save the world."

"He who rejects Me, and does not receive My words,
has one who judges him:
the Word that I have spoken,
the same shall judge him in the Last Day.
For I have not spoken by My own will;
but by that of the Father who sent Me."

"He commanded Me,
in what I should say,
and what I should speak.
And I know that His commandment is Life Everlasting.
Therefore, whatever I speak
is just as the Father said to Me.
So, do I speak."

216 Jesus Foretells the Day of Crucifixion

(Matthew 26:1-5 Mark 14:1-2; Luke 22:1-2)

Two days before the Feast of the Passover,
and of unleavened bread:
it came to pass,
when Jesus had finished all these sayings,

He said to His disciples,

"You know that after two days will the Feast of the Passover,
and the Son of Man will be betrayed to be crucified."

Then the Chief Priests, and the Scribes, and the Elders of the people,
assembled together into the palace of the High Priest,
whose name was Caiaphas,
scheming that through craft and subtlety,
they might take Jesus and kill Him.
But because they feared the people, they said,

"Not on the Feast Day,
or there may be an uproar!"

217 Judas Conspires to Betray Jesus[34]

(*Matthew 26:14-16; Mark 14:10-11; Luke 22:3-6*)

Then Satan entered into one of the Twelve, called Judas Iscariot,
And he went on his way, to the Chief Priests and captains,
conspiring to betray Him to them.
And he said to them,

"What will you give me,
to deliver him to you?"

When they heard it, they rejoiced,
and they covenanted with him
for thirty *pieces of silver*.
He promised to betray Him to them,
and from that time sought opportunity
in the absence of the multitude.

218 Peter and John Prepare for Passover

(Matthew 26:17-19; Mark 14:12-16; Luke 22:7-13)

Now it was the first day of the Feast of Unleavened Bread,
when the Passover must be killed.
The disciples came to Jesus, saying to Him,
　　"Where do you want us to prepare for You to eat the Passover?"
And He said,
　　"Go into the city and prepare the Passover for us to eat,
　　There you shall meet a man carrying a pitcher of water.
　　Follow him
　　and wherever he goes in,
　　say to the man of the house,
　　　　'The Master says,
　　　　　　"My time is at hand;
　　　　　　I will keep the Passover at your house
　　　　　　with My disciples.
　　　　　　Where is the guest chamber,
　　　　　　where I shall eat the Passover?"'
　　And he will show you a large upper room
　　furnished and prepared.
　　Make things ready for us there."

And He sent two of His disciples, Peter and John,
and they went out into the city,
and did as Jesus had charged them;
and found it as He had told them:
and they made things ready for the Passover.

219 Jesus Washes Peter's Feet

(Matthew 26:20; Mark 14:17; Luke 22:14; John 13:1-20)

Now when the evening had come,
before the Feast of the Passover,

when Jesus knew that His hour had come
that He would depart out of this world to the Father,
having loved His own who were in the world,
He loved them to the end.

He sat down with the Twelve Apostles,
and supper being ended,
the Devil,
having now put into the heart of Judas Iscariot, Simon's son,
to betray Him;
and Jesus,
knowing that the Father had given all things into His hands,
and that He came from God and went to God;
rose from supper,
and laid His clothing aside,
and took a towel and wrapped Himself.
After that He poured water into a basin,
and began to wash the disciples' feet,
and to wipe them with the towel which He wore.

Then He came to Simon Peter:
and Peter said to Him,
    "Lord, do you wash my feet?"
Jesus answered and said to him,
    "What I do, you do not now understand;
    but afterwards you shall know."

Peter said to Him,
    "You shall never wash my feet!"
Jesus answered him,
    "If I do not wash you,
    you have no part with Me."

Simon Peter said to Him,
    "Lord, then wash not only my feet,

but my hands and my head, too!"
Jesus said to him,
    "He who is washed needs only to wash his feet,
    but is clean otherwise:
    and you are clean,
    but not all of you."
For He knew who would betray Him, so, He said,
    "You are not all clean."

So, after He had washed their feet,
and had put on His clothing,
and had sat down again,
He said to them,
    "Do you know what I have done to you?
    You call me Master and Lord:
    and you say rightly;
    for so I am.
    If I, your Lord and Master,
    have washed your feet,
    then you also ought to wash each other's feet.
    For I have given you an example,
    that you should do as I have done to you."

    "Truly, truly, I tell you,
    the servant is not greater than his Lord;
    neither is he who is sent greater than He who sent him.
    If you know these things,
    you are happy if you do them.
    He who receives whomever I send
    receives Me;
    and he who receives Me
    receives Him who sent Me."

    "I do not speak of all of you:

I know whom I have chosen:
but so that the Scripture may be fulfilled,
    'He that eateth bread with Me
    hath lifted up his heel against Me.'
Now I tell you before it happens,
so that, when it has come to pass,
you may believe that I am He.

220 The Lord's Supper

(Matthew 26:26-29; Mark 14:22-25; Luke 22:14-20;
1 Corinthians 11:24-25)

And when the hour had come,
He sat down,
and the Twelve Apostles sat with Him.
And He said to them,
    "I have greatly desired to eat this Passover with you,
    before I suffer.
    I tell you, I will not eat it again,
    until it is fulfilled in the Kingdom of God."

And as they were eating,
Jesus took bread,
and when He had given thanks,
blessed it,
broke it,
and gave it to the disciples, and said,
    "Take, eat;
    this is My Body,
    which is given and broken for you.
    Do this in remembrance of Me.

In the same way, when He had eaten, He took the cup,
gave thanks and gave it to them, and He said,

"Take this,
and divide it among yourselves:
Drink all of it;
for this cup is the New Testament in My Blood,
which is shed for many
for the remission of sins.
Do this as often as you drink it,
in remembrance of Me.
But, truly, I tell you,
I will not drink again of this fruit of the vine,
until that day when I drink it new with you
in My Father's Kingdom."
and they all drank of it.

221 Jesus Foretells the Betrayal

(Matthew 26:21-25; Mark 14:18-21; Luke 22:21-23; John 13:21-26)

When Jesus had said this,
He was troubled in spirit,
And as they sat and ate, Jesus declared,
   "Truly, truly, I tell you,
   one of you
   who eats with Me
   shall betray Me."
And they were exceeding sorrowful,
and began every one of them to say to Him,
one by one,
   "Is it I?"
and another said,
   "Lord, is it I?"

And He answered and said,
   But, behold,
   the hand of him who betrays Me

is with Me on the table.
It is one of the Twelve,
One who dips his hand with Me in the dish,
is the same who shall betray Me.
The Son of Man indeed goes,
as it is written of Him:
but woe to that man by whom the Son of Man is betrayed!
It would be good for that man if he had never been born!"

Then the disciples looked at one another,
wondering of whom He spoke.
And they began to inquire among themselves,
which of them it was who would do this thing.

Now there was leaning against Jesus
one of His disciples, whom Jesus loved.
So, Simon Peter beckoned to him
to ask of whom He spoke.
He then, leaning against Jesus, said to Him,
    "Lord, who is it?"
Jesus answered,
    "It is he to whom I shall give a sop,
    when I have dipped it."
And when He had dipped the sop,
He gave it to Judas Iscariot, the son of Simon.
Then Judas, who betrayed him, answered and said,
    "Master, is it I?"
He said to him,
    "As you have said."

222 Judas Leaves as Night Falls

(John 13:27-30)

Afterwards, Satan entered into him.

Then said Jesus to Judas,
    "What you do, do quickly."
Now no man at the table knew why He said this to him.
Because Judas had the moneybag some of them thought
that Jesus had merely told him
to buy what was needed for the Feast
or to give something to the poor.
Then Judas, having received the sop,
immediately went out just as night had fallen.

223 A New Commandment

    (John 13:31-35)

So, when Judas had gone, Jesus said,
    "Now the Son of Man is glorified,
    and God is glorified in Him.
    If God is glorified in Him,
    then God shall also glorify Him in Himself,
    and shall glorify Him immediately."

    "Little children,
    just a little longer am I with you.
    You shall seek Me:
    and just as I told the Jews,
        'Where I go, you cannot come;'
    so now I also say to you.
    I give you a new Commandment:
    that you love one another!
    Just as I have loved you,
    you also love one another.
    By this shall all men know that you are My disciples,
    if you have love one for another."

224 Jesus Foretells Peter's Denials

(Matthew 26:31-35; Mark 14:27-31; Luke 22:31-34; John 13:36-38)

Simon Peter said to Him,
    "Lord, where are you going?"
Jesus answered him,
    "Where I go, you cannot follow Me now;
    but you shall follow Me afterwards."
Peter said to Him,
    "Lord, why can I not follow you now?
    I will lay down my life for your sake!"
And Jesus said to him,
    "Will you lay down your life for My sake?
    Simon, Simon. Look!
    Satan desires to have you
    and to sift you like wheat!
    But I have prayed for you,
    that your faith will not fail:
    and when you are converted,
    to strengthen your brothers."

And he said to Him,
    "Though all shall fall away,
    yet I will not!"
They all said likewise.

And the Lord said,
    "Truly, truly, I tell you,
    this day, even this night,
    before the cock crows twice,
    you shall deny Me thrice."
But he spoke all the more vehemently,
    "Lord, I am ready to go with You,
    both into prison, and to death.
    Even if I should die with you

I will not deny you in any way!"

Then Jesus said to them all,
 "All of you shall fall away this night because of Me:
 for it is written,
  'I will smite the shepherd,
  and the sheep of the flock
  shall be scattered abroad.'
 But after I have risen again,
 I will go before you into Galilee."

225 Jesus Warns His Disciples to Prepare

   (Luke 22:35-38)

He said to them,
 "When I sent you without purse, and money, and shoes,
 did you lack anything?"
And they said,
 "Nothing."
Then He said to them,
 "But now, he who has a purse,
 let him take it, and likewise his money.
 And he who has no sword,
 let him sell his cloak and buy one!
 For I tell you,
 that what is written must still be accomplished in Me,
  'And He was reckoned among the transgressors:'
 because the things concerning Me have a conclusion."
And they said,
 "Lord, look, here are two swords."
And He said to them,
 "It is enough."

226 Many Mansions

(John 14:1-4)

"Do not let your hearts be troubled!
You believe in God,
believe also in Me!
There are many mansions in My Father's house.
If this was not true,
I would have told you.
I go to prepare a place for you!
If I go to prepare a place for you,
I will come again
and welcome you as one of My own;
so that where I am,
you may be also.
Where I go, you know,
and the way I go, you know."

227 The Way, the Truth, and the Life

(John 14:5-7)

Thomas said to Him,
  "Lord, we do not know where you go,
  so how can we know the way?"
Jesus said,
  "I AM
  the Way,
  the Truth,
  and the Life.
  No man comes to the Father, except by Me.
  If you had known Me,
  then you should have known My Father also.
  From now on you know Him,
  and have seen Him."

228 Another Comforter

(John 14:8-21)

Philip said to Him,
    "Lord, show us the Father, and that will convince us."
Jesus said,
    "Have I been with you so long a time,
    and yet you have not known Me, Philip?
    He who has seen Me has seen the Father!"

    "How can you say,
        'Show us the Father?'
    Do you not believe that I am in the Father,
    and the Father is in Me?
    The words that I speak to you
    I do not speak on My own.
    The Father who dwells in Me does the works!
    Believe Me that I am in the Father,
    and the Father is in Me:
    or else believe Me for the sake of the works themselves."

    "Truly, truly, I tell you,
    He who believes in Me,
    shall also do the works that I do.
    He shall do greater works than these,
    because I go to My Father
    and whatever you shall ask in My Name,
    that I will do,
    so that the Father may be glorified in the Son.
    If you shall ask anything in My Name,
    I will do it!"

    "If you love Me,
    keep My Commandments.
    I will pray to the Father,

and He shall give you another Comforter,
that He may remain with you forever;
the Spirit of Truth Himself;
whom the world cannot receive,
because it neither sees Him,
nor knows Him:
but you know Him;
for He dwells with you,
and shall be in you."

"I will not leave you without comfort:
I will come to you.
Just a little longer,
and the world will see Me no more;
but you do see Me.
Because I live,
you also shall live.
At that time,
you shall know that I am in My Father,
and you in Me,
and I in you."

"Those who hold My Commandments,
and keep them,
are those who love Me.
And those who love Me
shall be loved by My Father,
and I will love them,
and they shall see My face."

229 Keep My Words

(John 14:22-31)

Judas (not Judas Iscariot), said to Him,

"Lord, how is it that You will reveal Yourself to us,
and not to the world?"
Jesus answered him,
"If a man loves Me,
he will keep My words:
and My Father will love him,
and we will come to Him,
and make our home with Him.
He who does not love Me
does not keep My sayings."

"The Word which you hear is not Mine.
It is the Father's Word, who sent Me.
I have said these things to you,
while I am still here with you.
But the Comforter,
who is the Holy Spirit,
whom the Father will send in My Name,
He shall teach you everything,
bringing everything to your memory,
everything I have said to you."

"I leave you with peace.
My peace I give you.
I do not give to you as the world gives.
Do not let your hearts be troubled or afraid!
You heard how I told you,
    'I go away,
    and come again to you.'
If you loved Me,
you would rejoice,
because I said,
    'I go to the Father!'
for My Father is greater than I am!"

"Now I have told you before it comes to pass,
so that when it has come to pass,
you might believe.
After this I will not talk with you much:
because the Prince of this World is coming,
but has no part of Me.
Yet, so that the world may know that I love the Father,
and that I do just as the Father commands Me: get up!
Because we go to meet it!"

230 The True Vine

(John 15:1-16:33)

"I am the True Vine,
and My Father is the Gardener.
Every branch in Me that is not fruitful,
He takes away.
And every branch that is fruitful,
He prunes so that it may be more fruitful.
Now you are clean through the Word
that I have spoken to you."

"Abide in Me, and I in you.
Just as the branch is not fruitful on its own,
unless it abides in the Vine,
nor can you bear fruit,
unless you abide in Me.
I am the Vine.
You are the branches.
He who abides in Me,
and I in Him,
will be very fruitful."

"But, without Me, you can do nothing.

If a man does not abide in Me,
He is cast away as a branch and withers.
Men gather them and throw them into the fire
and they are burned.
If you abide in Me,
and my Word abides in you,
you can ask what you desire,
and it shall come to pass for you."

"Here is how My Father is glorified:
in that you are very fruitful.
This is how you will be My disciples.
Just as the Father has loved Me,
so, have I loved you."

"Abide in My love!
If you keep My Commandments,
you shall abide in My love;
just as I have kept My Father's Commandments,
and abide in His love.
I have told you these things,
so that My joy might abide in you,
and so that your joy might be full."

"This is My Commandment:
Love one another,
just as I have loved you!
No man has greater love than this:
that a man lays down his life for his friends.
You are My friends.
If you do whatever I command you,
afterwards, I will not call you slaves:
because the slave does not know his lord's business.
But I have called you friends,

because everything that I have heard from My Father
I have made known to you.
You have not chosen Me,
but I have chosen you and ordained you,
so that you should go and be fruitful,
so that your fruit should abide,
and so that whatever you shall ask from the Father,
in My Name,
He may give it to you."

"These things I command you,
so that you love one another!
If the world hates you,
you know that it hated Me before it hated you.
If you were of the world,
the world would love his own.
You are not of the world,
because I have chosen you out of the world.
That is why the world hates you."

"Remember the word I told you,
      'The servant is not greater than His lord.'
If they have persecuted Me,
then they will also persecute you.
If they have recorded My words,
then they will also record yours.
They will do all this to you for My Name's sake,
because they do not know Him who sent Me.
If I had not come and spoken to them,
they would not have sinned.
But now they have no cloak for their sin."

"He who hates Me
also hates My Father.

If I had not done works among them
that no other man did,
they would not have sinned.
But now, they have both seen and hated
both Me and My Father.
This only came to pass so that the Word might be fulfilled
which is written in their Law,
    'They hated Me without a cause.'
But when the Comforter has come,
whom I will send to you from the Father,
the Spirit of Truth, Himself,
who proceeds from the Father.
He shall testify about Me.
You, also, shall testify,
because you have been with Me from the start."

"I have told you these things
so that you would not fall away.
They shall put you out of the Synagogues.
Yes! the time comes when whoever kills you
will think that he does God's work!
They will do these things to you,
because they have neither known the Father nor Me.
But I have told you these things
so that when the time comes,
you may remember that I told you so."

"I did not tell you these things from the first,
because I was with you.
But now I am on My way to Him who sent Me;
and none of you asks Me,
    'Where do you go?'
But because I have told you these things,
sorrow has filled your heart.

Nevertheless, I tell you the truth.
It is best for you that I do go away:
because if I do not go away,
the Comforter will not come to you;
but if I depart,
I will send Him to you."

"When He has come,
He will convict the world of sin,
and of righteousness,
and of judgment.
Of sin,
because they do not believe in Me.
Of righteousness,
because I go to My Father
and you will no longer see Me.
Of judgment,
because the Prince of this World is judged!"

"I still have many things to tell you,
but you cannot handle them now.
However, when He, the Spirit of Truth, has come,
He will guide you into all truth:
because He shall not speak on His own,
but whatever He shall hear,
He shall speak,
and He will show you things to come.
He shall glorify Me:
because He shall receive from Me,
and shall reveal to you."

"All things that the Father has are Mine.
That is why I said
        'He shall receive from Me,

and shall reveal to you.'
Just a little longer and you shall not see Me.
and then just a little later and you shall see Me,
because I go to the Father."

Then some of His disciples said among themselves,
    "What is He telling us,
        'Just a little longer and you shall not see Me.
        and then just a little later and you shall see Me,'
        and, 'Because I go to the Father?'"
So, they said,
    "What is He saying,
        'A little longer?'
    We cannot understand what He is saying."

Now, Jesus knew that they wanted to question Him and said,
    "Do you ask each other why I said,
        'Just a little longer and you shall not see Me.
        and then just a little later and you shall see Me'?

"Truly, truly, I tell you,
that you shall weep and wail,
but the world shall rejoice.
You shall be sorrowful,
but your sorrow shall be turned into joy.
A woman in labor has anguish,
because her hour has come.
But as soon as she has delivered the child,
she no longer remembers the anguish,
because of her joy that a child is born into the world.

"So, you will have anguish now:
but I will see you again,
and your heart shall rejoice,
and no man will take your joy from you.

In that day you shall not question Me."

"Truly, truly, I tell you,
whatever you shall ask the Father in My Name,
He will give it to you!
So far you have asked nothing in My Name.
Ask, and you shall receive,
so that your joy may be full!
I have told you these things in parables:
but the time comes
when I shall no longer speak to you in parables.
Instead, I shall clearly reveal to you the will of the Father.
In that day, you shall ask in My Name.
I do not tell you that I will pray to the Father for you,
because the Father Himself loves you,
because you have loved Me,
and have believed that I came forth from God.
I came forth from the Father,
and came into the world.
Again, I tell you,
I leave the world and go to the Father."
His disciples said to Him,
"See, now You speak plainly, not in parables!
Now are we sure that You know all things
and that no man needs to question You!
By this we believe that You came forth from God!"
Jesus answered,
"You believe now?
Behold! The hour comes!
Indeed, it is now here,
in which you shall be scattered,
every man on his own,
and shall leave Me alone.
Yet I am not alone,

because the Father is with Me.
I have told you these things,
so that you might have peace in Me.
You shall have tribulation in the world:
but be cheerful!
I have overcome the world!"

231 Jesus Prays for His Disciples

(John 17:1-26)

Jesus said these things
and then lifted up His eyes to Heaven, saying,
 "Father, the hour has come!
 Glorify your Son,
 so that your Son may also glorify You:
 because you have given Him power over all flesh,
 so that He should give Eternal Life to all
 whom You have given Him."

 "This is Life Eternal,
 that they might know You,
 the only true God,
 and Jesus Christ, whom You have sent.
 I have glorified You on Earth:
 I have finished the work You gave Me to do.
 And now, Oh Father!
 Glorify Me with Your own Self,
 with the glory which I had with You before the world was.
 I have revealed Your Name to the men
 whom You gave Me out of the world.
 They were Yours,
 and You gave them to Me;
 and they have kept Your Word.
 Now they have known

that all things and whatever You have given Me
are from You.
For I have given them the Words which You gave Me;
and they have received them,
and have known surely that I came forth from You,
and they have believed that You indeed sent Me."

"I pray for them.
I do not pray for the world,
but instead, for those You have given Me:
because they are Yours.
All of Mine are Yours,
and Yours are Mine;
and I am glorified in them.
Now, I am no longer in the world,
but these are still in the world
and I go to You."

"Holy Father,
keep through Your own Name
those whom You have given Me,
so that they may be one,
as are We.
While I was with them in the world,
I kept them in Your Name.
I have kept those You gave Me,
and lost none of them
except the Son of Damnation;
so that the Scriptures might be fulfilled."

"Now I come to You;
and I say these things while still in the world,
so that they might have My joy fulfilled in themselves.
I have given them Your Word;

and the world has hated them,
because they are not of the world,
just as I am not of the world.
I do not pray that You should take them out of the world,
but instead that You should keep them from the evil of it.
They are not of the world,
just as I am not of the world.
Sanctify them through Your Truth.
Your Word is Truth!"

"Just as You have sent Me into the world,
I have also sent them into the world.
For their sake I sanctify Myself,
so that they also might be sanctified through the Truth."

"Neither do I pray for these alone,
but, also, for those who shall believe on Me
through their testimony;
so that they all may be one,
just as You, Father, are in Me,
and I in You;
so that they also may be one in Us;
so that the world may believe that You have sent Me."

"The glory which you gave Me
I have given them;
so that they may be one,
even as We are one;
I in them,
and You in Me,
so that they may be made perfect in one;
and so that the world may know that You have sent Me,
and have loved them,
as You have loved Me."

"Father,
I desire that they also,
whom You have given to Me,
will be with Me where I am;
so that they may behold My glory,
which you have given Me:
for You loved Me before the foundation of the world."

"Oh, Righteous Father,
the world has not known You:
but I have known You,
and these have known that You have sent Me.
I have declared Your Name to them,
and will continue to declare it:
so that the love with which You have loved Me
may be in them,
and so that I may be in them!"

232 The Garden of Gethsemane

(Matthew 26:30,36-46; Mark 14:26,32-42; Luke 22:39-46; John 18:1)

When Jesus had spoken these words,
and they had sung a hymn,
He went out with His disciples over the Brook Kidron,
to the Mount of Olives,
where was a garden called Gethsemane.
He entered, as was His habit,
and His disciples also followed Him.
When He was at the place,
He said to the disciples,
    "You sit here,
    while I go and pray over there.
    Pray that you do not enter into temptation."

He took with Him Peter and the two sons of Zebedee,
James and John,
and began to be greatly apprehensive, sorrowful, and very troubled.
Then He said to them,
    "My soul is exceedingly sorrowful, even to death.
    Wait here, and watch with Me."
And He went forward a little farther,
and was withdrawn from them about a stone's cast,
and knelt down,
and fell on His face on the ground and prayed,
    "Abba! Oh, My Father!
    All things are possible for You!
    If it is possible,
    if you are willing,
    let this hour pass from Me!
    Take this cup away from Me!
    Nevertheless, not My will,
    but Yours be done."
And an angel from Heaven appeared there to Him,
strengthening Him.

Being in an agony He prayed more earnestly:
and His sweat fell in great drops of blood
down to the ground.

And He rose up from prayer and came to the disciples,
and found them asleep in their sorrow,
and said to Peter,
    "Simon, do you sleep?
    What? Could you not watch with Me one hour?
    Why do you sleep?
    Get up!
    Watch and pray,
    so that you do not enter temptation:

the spirit indeed is willing and is truly ready,
but the flesh is weak."

He went away a second time,
and prayed, saying,
    "Oh, My Father!
    Even if this cup may not pass away from Me,
    unless I drink it,
    Your will be done."

And when He returned and found them asleep again:
for their eyes were heavy,
they did not know how to answer Him.
He left them,
and went away again,
and prayed the third time,
saying the same words.
Then He came to His disciples, and said to them,
    "Sleep and take your rest hereafter."
    [You have slept] enough.

    "Behold, the hour is at hand,
    when the Son of Man is betrayed into the hands of sinners.
    Rise up, let us go.
    Look! he who betrays Me is at hand."

233 Judas Leads the Mob

    (Matthew 26:47-50a; Mark 14:43-45; Luke 22:47-48; John 18:2-3)

One of the twelve, Judas, who betrayed Him, knew the place:
for Jesus often resorted there with His disciples.
And immediately, while He was still speaking,
Judas, having received a band of men and officers
from the Chief Priests and Scribes

and Pharisees and Elders of the people,
came leading a great mob
with lanterns and torches and swords and staves.

He who betrayed Him had given them a token, saying,
    "Whoever I kiss,
    he is that very man.
    Hold him tightly!
    Take him and lead him away safely."

As soon as Judas had come,
he went right away to Him,
and drew near Jesus and said,
    "Hail, Master! Master!"
and kissed Him.

And Jesus said to him,
    "Friend Judas.
    Where have you come from?
    Do you betray the Son of Man with a kiss?"

234 Jesus Awes the Mob

(John 18:4-9)

So, Jesus, knowing all that should happen to Him,
went forward and said to them,
    "Whom do you seek?"
They answered,
    "Jesus of Nazareth."
Jesus told them,
as well as Judas,
who betrayed Him, and stood with them,
    "I AM HE!"
Then, just as He told them,

"I AM HE!"
they fell backward to the ground.

Then He asked them again,
  "Whom do you seek?"
And they said,
  "Jesus of Nazareth."
Jesus answered,
  "I have told you that I am He.
  So, if you are looking for Me,
  let these go their way":
so that His words might be fulfilled,
  "Of those whom You gave Me I have lost none."

235 Peter Maims Malchus

  (Matthew 26:50b-54; Mark 14:46-47; Luke 22:49-51; John 18:10-11)

Then they came,
and laid hands on Jesus and took Him.
When they who were around Him saw what would follow,
they said to Him,
  "Lord, shall we strike with the sword?"

One of those who were with Jesus,
Simon Peter, having a sword,
stretched out his hand, drew his sword,
and struck Malchus, a servant of the High Priest's,
and cut off his right ear.

Then Jesus said to Peter,
  "Sheathe your sword!
  All those who choose the sword shall perish by the sword!
  Do you think that I cannot now pray to my Father,
  and He shall instantly give Me more than twelve legions of angels?

But how else shall the Scriptures be fulfilled
that it must be so?
The cup which my Father has given Me,
shall I not drink it?"

And Jesus said,
"Permit this much."
And He touched his ear and healed him.

236 Jesus Is Arrested

(Matthew 26:55-56; Mark 14:48-52; Luke 22:52-54b; John 18:12)

At that time, Jesus answered and said to the mob,
and to the Chief Priests and officers of the Temple and the Elders,
who had come to Him,
"Have you come out as against a thief
with swords and staves to take Me?
I sat daily with you teaching in the Temple.
You reached out with no hands against Me:
and you did not lay hold on Me
and you did not take Me.
But the Scriptures must be fulfilled.
This is your hour in the power of Darkness."
All this was done,
so that the Scriptures of the Prophets might be fulfilled.
Then all the disciples forsook Him and fled.
The cohort of soldiers, their Captain, and the Jewish officials,
took Jesus and bound Him.

Following Him, there was a certain young man,
who had a linen cloth wrapped about his naked body;
and the young men grabbed him:
but he left the linen cloth and fled naked from them.

Then they took Him and led Him away,
and brought Him into the High Priest's house,
and Peter followed from afar.

237 Jesus Is Taken to The High Priest

(Matthew 26:57; Mark 14:53; Luke 22:54a; John 18:13-14,24)

Those who had laid hold of Jesus
led Him away to Caiaphas the High Priest.
With him were assembled
all the Chief Priests and the Elders and the Scribes.
They led him away to Annas, first,
for he was the father-in-law of Caiaphas,
who was the High Priest that same year.
Annas sent Him bound to Caiaphas.
Now Caiaphas was he who counseled the Jews,
that it was expedient that one man should die for the people.

238 Peter Follows

(Matthew 26:58; Mark 14:54; Luke 22:54; John 18:15-16)

From afar, Simon Peter followed Jesus to the High Priest's palace,
and stood at the door outside.
Another disciple followed Jesus:
and went in with Jesus into the palace of the High Priest,
because that disciple was known to the High Priest.
That disciple went out
and spoke to the girl who kept the door,
and brought Peter in to see the conclusion.
Peter went in and sat with the servants
and warmed himself at the fire.

239 Peter's First Denial

(Matthew 26:69-70; Mark 14:66-68; Luke 22:55-57; John 18:17-18)

As Peter was in the palace below,
and stood with the servants and officers,
who had made a fire of coals in the middle of the hall,
for it was cold and they warmed themselves.
Peter sat down among them and warmed himself.

When the girl who kept the door,
one of the maids of the High Priest,
saw Peter warming himself by the fire,
she looked at him earnestly and said,
 "Are you not also one of this man's disciples?
 You were also with Jesus of Galilee!"

But he denied it in front of all of them, saying,
 "Woman, I am not!
 I don't know him,
 and I don't know what you're talking about!"
He went out to the porch and the cock crowed.

240 The High Priest Interrogates Jesus

(John 18:19-23)

The High Priest then asked Jesus
about His disciples and His doctrine.
Jesus answered,
 "I spoke openly to the world.
 I always taught in the Synagogue and in the Temple,
 where the Jews always go;
 and I have said nothing in secret.
 Why do you ask Me?
 Ask those who heard Me

what I have told them.
See! They know what I said."

When He had said this,
one of the officers who stood by
struck Jesus with the palm of his hand, saying,
"Do you answer the High Priest like that?"
Jesus answered,
"If I have spoken evil,
declare what was wrong:
but if good,
then why do you strike Me?"

241 Peter's Second Denial

(Matthew 26:71-73; Mark 14:69-70; Luke 22:59; John 18:25)

When Simon Peter went out to the porch,
another maid saw him,
and said to those who were there,
"This man was also with Jesus of Nazareth!
He is one of them!"

Just afterwards, he stood and warmed himself.
So, another standing nearby looked at him and said,
"You are a Galilean and even talk like one!
Surely you are also one of his disciples!"

Again, he denied it with an oath,
"Man, I am not!
I do not know the man!"
And about an hour or so later
another confidently agreed, saying,
"It is true. This man also was with him:
for he is a Galilean."

242 The False Witnesses

(Matthew 26:59-61; Mark 14:55-59)

The Chief Priests, and Elders, and all the Council
sought for testimony against Jesus
to put Him to death;
and found none.
Indeed, though many false witnesses testified against Him,
their testimonies did not agree together.
At last, there arose two certain men who were false witnesses,
and gave false testimony against Him, saying,
    "We heard him say,
        'I will destroy this Temple of God
        that is made with hands,
        and within three days
        I will build another
        made without hands.'
But neither did their testimony agree together.

243 The High Priest Condemns Jesus

(Matthew 26:62-66; Mark 14:60-64; Luke 22:66-71)

As soon as it was day,
the elders of the people and the Chief Priests and the Scribes
came together,
and led Him into their council, asking,
    "Are you the Christ?"
And He said to them,
    "If I tell you,
    you will not believe:
    and if I also ask you,
    you will not answer Me,
    nor will you let Me go."
And the High Priest stood up in the midst, and asked Jesus,

"Have you no answer
  to what these have witnessed against you?"
But Jesus held his peace and gave no answer.

Again, the High Priest asked Him, saying,
  "I adjure you by the living God:
  Tell us if you are the Christ, the Son of God!
  Are you the Christ, the Son of the Blessed?"
And Jesus said,
  "You say that I am.

Then they all asked,
  "Are you then the Son of God?"
And Jesus said,
  "I AM. Moreover, I say to you,
  hereafter you shall see the Son of Man
  sitting on the Right Hand of Power,
  and coming in the clouds of Heaven."

Then the High Priest tore his clothes, and said,
  "He has spoken blasphemy!
  What need have we for any further witnesses?
  See! Now you have heard the blasphemy!
  What do you think?
  For we ourselves have heard it from his own mouth!"
And they all condemned Him to be guilty of death.

244 Jesus Is Beaten in the Sanhedrin[35]

(Matthew 26:67-68; Mark 14:65; Luke 22:63-65)

The servants who held Jesus
mocked Him and struck Him.
Then they spat in his face and beat Him.
And when they had blindfolded Him,

other struck Him on the face with the palms of their hands,
and questioned Him, saying,

> "Prophesy to us, you Christ!
> Who hit you?"

And they spoke many other blasphemous things against Him.

245 Peter's Third Denial

(Matthew 26:74-75; Mark 14:71-72; Luke 22:60-62; John 18:26-27)

One of the servants of the High Priest,
being related to the man whose ear Peter cut off, said to him,

> "Didn't I see you in the garden with him?"

Then he began to curse and to swear, saying,

> "Man, I don't know what you're talking about!
> I don't know who you're talking about!"

Immediately, while he was still speaking,
the cock crowed the second time.
And the Lord turned and looked upon Peter.
Then Peter remembered the word Jesus said to him,

> *"Before the cock crows twice,*
> *you shall deny me thrice."*

And when he realized it,
he went out and wept bitterly.

246 The Hall of Judgment

(Matthew 27:1-2; Mark 15:1; John 18:28)

Now morning had come,
and immediately all the Chief Priests
consulted with the Elders of the people
and the Scribes and the whole Council,
and took counsel against Jesus to put Him to death.
It was very early, and they bound Jesus

and led Him away from Caiaphas
and delivered Him to the Hall of Judgment,
to Pontius Pilate the Governor.
So that they could eat the Passover
they did not go into the Hall, themselves,
where they would be defiled.

247 Thirty Pieces of Silver[36]

(Matthew 27:3-10)

When Judas, who had betrayed Him,
saw that He was condemned,
he then repented and returned the thirty *pieces of silver*
to the Chief Priests and Elders, saying,
    "I have sinned because I have betrayed innocent blood!"
And they said,
    "What is that to us?
    See to that yourself!"
And he threw down the *pieces of silver* in the Temple,
and departed, going and hanging himself.

The Chief Priests took the *silver pieces* and said,
    "It is not lawful to put them in the Treasury,
    because it is the price of blood."
They took counsel,
and bought the potter's field with them,
to bury strangers in.

So that field was called,
"The Field of Blood" to this day.
Then that which was spoken by Jeremiah the prophet was fulfilled,
    "And they took the thirty pieces of silver,
    the price of him that was valued,
    whom they of the children of Israel did value;

And gave them for the potter's field,
as the Lord appointed me."

248 Pilate Interrogates Jesus

(Matthew 27:11-14; Mark 15:2-5; Luke 23:1-7; John 18:29-38a,39)

The whole multitude of them rose up and led Him to Pilate.
Pilate went out to them and said,
    "What accusation do you bring against this man?"
They answered and said to him,
    "If he was not a malefactor,
    we would not have delivered him to you."
Then Pilate said to them,
    "You take him,
    and judge him according to your law."
But the Jews said to him,
    "It is not lawful for us to put any man to death."
So, were the words of Jesus fulfilled,
foretelling what death He would die.
And they began to accuse Him, saying,
    "We found this fellow subverting the nation,
    and forbidding the giving of tribute to Caesar,
    saying that he, himself, is Christ, a King!"

Then Pilate entered the Hall of Judgment again.
Jesus stood before the Governor
and Pilate asked Him,
    "Are you the King of the Jews?"
Jesus answered Him,
    "It is as you say.
    But do you ask this for yourself,
    or did others tell this to you about Me?"
Pilate answered,
    "Am I a Jew?

Your own nation and the Chief Priests
have delivered you to me.
What have you done?"

Jesus answered,
 "My Kingdom is not of this world.
 If My Kingdom were of this world,
 then My servants would fight,
 so that I would not be delivered to the Jews.
 But, for now, My Kingdom is not from here."

And when He was accused,
by the Chief Priests and Elders,
of many things
He gave no answer.
Then said Pilate to Him,
 "Do you not hear how many things
 they testify against you?"
But Jesus never answered with so much as a word,
so that the Governor was greatly astonished.

So, Pilate said to Him,
 "Are you a king then?"
Jesus answered,
 "You ask if I am a king.
 To this end I was born,
 and for this cause I came into the World,
 so that I should testify to the Truth.
 Everyone who is of the Truth hears My voice."
Pilate said to Him,
 "What is truth?"

And when he had said this,
he went out again to the Jews,
to the Chief Priests and to the people,

and said to them,
  "I find no fault at all in this man."
And they were even more fierce, saying,
  "He stirs up the people,
    teaching throughout all the Jewish lands,
    beginning from Galilee to this place!"

When Pilate heard of Galilee,
he asked if the man was a Galilean.
As soon as he knew that He belonged to Herod's jurisdiction,
he sent Him to Herod,
who, at that time, was also in Jerusalem.

249 Herod Interrogates Jesus

(Luke 23:8-12)

When Herod saw Jesus,
he was exceedingly glad:
since he had wanted to see Him for a long time,
because he had heard many things about Him,
and he hoped to see Him do some miracle.

Then he questioned Him with many words;
but He gave him no answer.
And the Chief Priests and Scribes stood and vehemently accused Him.

And Herod, with his men of war, held Him in contempt,
and mocked Him,
and dressed Him in a gorgeous robe,
and sent Him back to Pilate.
That very day, Pilate and Herod became friends together.
Before this, they were opposed to one another.

250 Pilate Seeks to Pardon Jesus

(Matthew 27:15-23; Mark 15:6-13; Luke 23:13-23; John 18:38b-40)

Now at that feast
the Governor's custom was to release one prisoner to the people,
whoever they desired.
There was one, a notorious prisoner,
a robber called Barabbas,
who lay imprisoned with the rebels,
who had joined him in murder and insurrection.
And the mob cried out
and required he do as he had always done for them.

So, when they were assembled,
Pilate said to them,
      "You have a custom,
      that I should release one to you at the Passover.
      So, is it your will that I release to you the King of the Jews?
      Whom would you have me release to you?
      Barabbas, or Jesus, who is called Christ?"
For he knew that they had delivered Him due to envy.
Then they all cried again, saying,
      "Not this man, but Barabbas."

When he had sat down on the judgment seat,
his wife sent to him, saying,
      "Don't you do anything to that righteous man!
      –I was tormented with dreams today about Him!"

But the Chief Priests and Elders persuaded the crowd
that they should ask for Barabbas,
and destroy Jesus.

And Pilate again said to them,
      "What then is your will

that I shall do to him
whom you call Christ,
the King of the Jews?"
And they cried out again,
"Let him be crucified!
Crucify him!"
Then Pilate said to them,
"Why, what evil has he done?"
And they cried out more intensely,
"Crucify him!"

When he had called together
the Chief Priests and the rulers and the people,
Pilate said to them,
"You brought this man to me,
as one who misleads the people:
and after examining him before you,
I find no fault in this man
regarding your accusations against him.
No, nor did Herod:
for I sent you to him and, see,
nothing worthy of death was found by him.
I will therefore flog him and release him."
(For it was a necessity that he must release one to them at the Feast.)

And they cried out all at once, saying,
"Away with this man,
and release Barabbas to us!"
(Who was imprisoned for a certain murder,
and for sedition in the city.)

So Pilate, who was willing to release Jesus,
spoke to them again.
But they cried, saying,

"Crucify him! Crucify him!"
And he said to them a third time,
    "Why, what evil has he done?
    I have found no cause of death in him!
    So, I will flog him, and let him go!'
And they instantly raised loud voices,
demanding that He be crucified.
And their voices and those of the Chief Priests prevailed.

251 A Crown of Thorns

(Matthew 27:27-30; Mark 15:16-19; John 19:1-3)

Then Pilate had Jesus flogged.
The soldiers of the governor took Jesus
and led him away into the common hall, called the Praetorium;
and gathered the whole band of soldiers.
They stripped Him
and then clothed Him with a robe of scarlet and purple.
When they had braided a crown of thorns,
they put it on His head
and a reed in His right hand,
and they bent the knee before Him in worship
and mocked Him.
They began to salute Him, saying,
    "Hail, King of the Jews!"
They spit on Him
and took the reed and struck Him on the head
and they hit Him with their hands.

252 Behold the Man!

(John 19:4-7)

So, Pilate went out again and told them,

"Look! I bring him out to you,
so that you may know that I find no fault in him."
Then Jesus came out,
wearing the crown of thorns and the purple robe.
And Pilate said to them,
"Behold the man!"

So, when the Chief Priests and officers saw Him,
they cried out, saying,
"Crucify him! Crucify him!"
Pilate told them,
"You take him and crucify him:
because I find no fault in him."
The Jews answered,
"We have a law and by our Law he ought to die,
because he makes himself out to be the Son of God."

253 Pilate Again Interrogates Jesus

(John 19:8-12)

So, when Pilate heard that,
he was even more afraid;
and went into the Hall of Judgment again
and said to Jesus,
"Where are you from?"
But Jesus gave him no answer.
Then Pilate said to Him,
"You will not speak to me?
Do you not know that I have power to crucify you,
and have power to release you?"
Jesus answered,
"You could have no power at all against Me,
unless it was given to you from above:
thus, he who delivered Me to you has the greater sin."

And from then on, Pilate sought to release Him:
but the Jews cried out, saying,
    "If you let this man go,
    you are not Caesar's friend!"
    Whoever makes himself out to be a king
    speaks against Caesar!"

254 Pilate Sentences Jesus[37]

    (Matthew 27:24-26; Mark 15:14-15; Luke 23:24-25; John 19:13-16)

So, when Pilate heard those words,
he brought Jesus out,
and sat down in the judgment seat
in the place that is called the Pavement,
but in the Hebrew, "Gabbatha."

It was the preparation of the Passover,
near mid-morning:
and he said to the Jews,
    "Behold your King!"
But they cried out,
    "Away with him!
    Away with him!
    Crucify him!"
Pilate said to them,
    "Shall I crucify your King?"
The Chief Priests answered,
    "We have no king but Caesar!"

When Pilate saw that he could not prevail,
and that, instead, a riot was being started,
he took water,
and washed his hands in front of the multitude, saying,
    "I am innocent of the blood of this just person!

See to it yourselves!"
Then answered all the people, who said,
"His blood be on us,
and on our children!"

And so, Pilate, willing to placate the people,
gave the sentence they demanded
and released to them, whom they wanted,
Barabbas,
who was imprisoned for sedition and murder,
and delivered Jesus,
whom he had flogged,
to be crucified as was their will.
And they took Jesus and led Him away.

255 Simon of Cyrene Bears the Cross

(Matthew 27:31-32; Mark 15:20-21; Luke 23:26; John 19:17a)

After they had mocked Him,
they took the purple robe off Him
and put His own clothing on Him
and led Him away to crucify Him.
Bearing His cross, He went forth.
As they came out,
they found and laid hold of a man of Cyrene,
by the name of Simon,
the father of Alexander and Rufus,
and they compelled him to bear the cross following Jesus.

256 The Daughters of Jerusalem

(Luke 23:27-32)

And following Him,

there was a great company of people,
and of women,
who were also wailing and lamenting for Him.

Jesus turned to them and said,
    "Daughters of Jerusalem,
    do not weep for Me,
    but weep for yourselves,
    and for your children.
    For, behold,
    the days are coming, in which they shall say,
        'Blessed are the barren,
        and the wombs that never bare,
        and the breasts which never suckled!'
    Then they shall begin to say to the mountains, 'Fall on us!'
    and to the hills, 'Cover us!'
    For if they do these things in a green tree,
    what shall be done in the dry?"

257 The Place of the Skull[38]

(Matthew 27:33-34; Mark 15:22-23; Luke 23:33a; John 19:17b)

And they came to Calvary,
a place which is called in the Hebrew, "Golgotha,"
that is to say, "The Place of The Skull.",
They gave him *wine vinegar* to drink mingled with *bitter myrrh*:
and when He had tasted,
He would not receive it and drink it.

258 The Crucifixion of Jesus

(Matthew 27:37-38; Mark 15:25-28; Luke 23:32,33b,38; John 19:18-22)

It was mid-morning,
and they led Him there with two others, thieves.
They crucified Him there with the malefactors,
the one on His right hand,
and the other on His left,
with Jesus in between.
And the Scripture was fulfilled, which said,
　　"And He was numbered with the transgressors."
Pilate wrote a title,
and the superscription of his accusation was written
and set up over His head on the cross
in letters of Greek, and Latin, and Hebrew,
　　"THIS IS JESUS OF NAZARETH
　　THE KING OF THE JEWS."
Then many of the Jews read this title,
since the place where Jesus was crucified was near the city.

Then the Chief Priests of the Jews said to Pilate,
　　"Do not write, 'The King of the Jews;'
　　but that he said, 'I am King of the Jews.'"
Pilate answered,
　　"What I have written I have written."

259 The Soldiers Divide His Clothes

(Matthew 27:35-36; Mark 15:24; Luke 23:34; John 19:23-24)

Then Jesus said,
　　"Father, forgive them;
　　for they do not know what they do."

Then the soldiers who crucified Jesus
took His clothes and made four portions,
a portion for each soldier;
in addition to His robe.
Now the coat was seamless,
woven from the top throughout.
So, they said among themselves,
    "Let's not tear it,
    but cast lots for whose it shall be."
And they divided His clothes by casting lots for them,
to decide what every man should take.

Thus, that which was spoken by the prophet, was fulfilled,
    "They parted my garments among them,
    and upon my vesture did they cast lots."
So, the soldiers did these things
and, sitting down,
they watched Him there.

260 Behold Your Mother

    (John 19:25-27)

By the cross of Jesus there stood His mother,
and His mother's sister,
Mary the wife of Cleophas,
and Mary Magdalene.
So, when Jesus saw His mother,
and the disciple whom He loved standing by,
He told His mother,
    "Dear woman, behold your son!"
Then He said to the disciple,
    "Behold your mother!"
And from that hour that disciple took her into his own home.

261 The Multitude Mocks Jesus[39]

(Matthew 27:39-43; Mark 15:29-32a; Luke 23:35-37)

As the people stood watching
those who passed by railed at Him and reviled Him,
wagging their heads and saying,
> "Ah! You who would destroy the Temple
> and rebuild it in three days,
> save yourself!
> If you are the Son of God,
> come down from the cross!"

Likewise, the Chief Priests with the Scribes and Elders,
also mocked Him, saying,
> "He saved others
> but cannot save himself!
> If he is Christ, the King of Israel,
> the chosen of God,
> let him now come down from the cross,
> so that we may see.
> Then we will believe him!
> He trusted in God?
> Let Him deliver him now,
> if He will have him since he said,
> > 'I am the Son of God!'"

And the soldiers also mocked Him,
coming to Him and offering Him *wine vinegar*, and saying,
> "If you are the King of the Jews save yourself!"

262 Jesus and the Thieves

(Matthew 27:44; Mark 15:32b; Luke 23:39-43)

The thieves who were crucified with Him,
also reviled Him,

and cast the same words in His teeth.
And one of the malefactors who was hanged
railed on Him, saying,
>"If you are Christ,
>save yourself and us!"

But the other answered and rebuked him, saying,
>"Do you not fear God,
>seeing how you are condemned the same way?
>And we indeed justly so,
>because we receive the due reward of our deeds:
>but this man has done nothing wrong."

And he said to Jesus,
>"Lord, remember me
>when you come into Your Kingdom."

And Jesus said to Him,
>"Truly I tell you,
>Today you shall be with Me in Paradise."

263 The Sun Was Darkened[40]

>*(Matthew 27:45-50; Mark 15:33-37; Luke 23:44-45a,46; John 19:28-30)*

When it was about noon,
the sun grew dark
and the darkness was over all the land
until the middle of the afternoon.
At that time, Jesus cried with a loud voice,
>"Eloi! Eloi!
>Lama sabachthani?"

which is, being interpreted,
>*"My God! My God!*

Why have you forsaken Me?"

After this, some of them that stood by,
when they heard it, said,
    "Look! He calls Elijah!"
Jesus, knowing that all things were now accomplished,
so that the Scripture would be fulfilled, said,
    "I thirst."

Now a vessel full of *wine vinegar* sat there,
and immediately, one ran and filled a sponge with the vinegar,
and put it on a hyssop reed,
and gave it Him to drink.
The rest said,
    "Let it be!
    Let us see whether Elijah will come to save him!"

When Jesus had thus received the *wine vinegar,*
He cried with a loud voice,
    "It is finished!
    Father! Into your hands I commend My Spirit!
And having said this,
He bowed His head,
and gave up the spirit.

264 Signs & Wonders with the Death of Jesus

    (Matthew 27:51-56; Mark 15:38-41; Luke 23:45b-47,49)

And, behold,
the Veil of the Temple was torn in two
from the top to the bottom;
and the earth quaked,
and the rocks were split.
The graves were opened;

and many bodies of the saints who slept
arose and came out of the graves after His resurrection,
and went into the Holy City,
and were seen by many.

Now when the Centurion,
and those who were with him,
watching and standing across from Jesus,
saw that He cried out so, and gave up the spirit,
and saw the earthquake,
and those things that happened,
they feared greatly and glorified God, saying,
    "Certainly, this was a righteous man!
    Truly, this man was the Son of God!"
And all the people who came together to that sight,
seeing the things that happened,
struck their breasts and departed.

Far away,
watching these things,
stood all His acquaintances,
and the many women that served Jesus
and followed Him from Galilee.
Among them was Mary Magdalene,
and Mary the mother of James the Lesser and of Joseph,
and Salome the mother of Zebedee's children,
and many other women who came up with Him to Jerusalem.

265 Confirming the Death of Jesus

(John 19:31-37)

Because it was the Preparation,
and so that the bodies would not remain on the cross
on a day of High Sabbath,

the Jews asked Pilate to have their legs broken,
and that they could be taken away.
Then the soldiers came,
and broke the legs of the first
and then of the other who was crucified with Him.

When they came to Jesus,
seeing that He was dead already,
they did not break His legs.
But one of the soldiers with a spear pierced His side,
and immediately blood and water came out.
He who saw it testified,
and his testimony is true:
and he knows that he speaks truth,
so that you might believe.
Because these things were done,
so that the Scripture should be fulfilled,
   "A bone of Him shall not be broken."
And again, another Scripture that said,
   "They shall look on Him whom they pierced."

266 Joseph of Arimathea

   (Matthew 27:57-58; Mark 15:42-45; Luke 23:50-52; John 19:38)

After this, because it was the Preparation,
that is, the day before the Sabbath,
when evening was near,
there came a rich man of Arimathea, named Joseph,
a good and righteous man:
an honorable Counselor
(who had not consented to the advice and deeds of the others)
who also waited for the Kingdom of God,
and who was also himself Jesus' disciple,

but secretly for fear of the Jews.
He went in boldly to Pilate,
and begged for the body of Jesus.

Pilate could not believe He was already dead:
and called the Centurion to him.
He asked him whether He was already dead.
When he knew it from the Centurion,
then Pilate gave him permission
and commanded the body to be delivered to Joseph.
So, he came and took the body of Jesus.

267 Nicodemus and Joseph Bury Jesus[41]

(Matthew 27:59-61; Mark 15:46-47; Luke 23:53-56; John 19:39-42)

And Nicodemus,
who at the first came to Jesus by night,
also came there,
and brought a mixture of myrrh and aloes
weighing *about seventy-five pounds*.
And when Joseph had taken the body of Jesus,
he wrapped it with the spices
in fine clean linen he had bought,
in the burial custom of the Jews,
and laid it in his own new tomb,
which he had carved out in the rock,
and in which no one had ever been buried.
He rolled a great stone to the door of the tomb and departed.
They laid Jesus this way
because of the Jews' Preparation Day:
since the tomb was nearby,
in the garden in the place where He was crucified.

That day was the Preparation,

and the Sabbath drew on.
And there was Mary Magdalene,
and the other Mary, the mother of Joseph,
sitting over across from the tomb.
And they saw where He was laid;
the women who came with Him from Galilee,
followed and also saw the tomb,
and how His body was laid.
They left and prepared spices and ointments;
and then rested on the Sabbath day according to the commandment.

268 Roman Soldiers Guard the Tomb

(Matthew 27:62-66)

Now the next day, following the day of the Preparation,
the Chief Priests and Pharisees came together to Pilate, saying,
    "Sir, we remember what that deceiver said
    while he was yet alive,
        'After three days I will rise again.'
    So, command the tomb be made secure until the third day,
    or his disciples may come by night
    and steal him away
    and say to the people,
        'He has risen from the dead!'
    so that the last error shall be worse than the first."
Pilate said to them,
    "You may have a watch.
    Go your way.
    Make it as secure as you can."
So, they went and made the tomb secure,
sealing the stone and setting a watch.

269 The Stone Is Rolled Away

(Matthew 28:2-4)

And, behold,
there was a great earthquake:
for the angel of the Lord descended from Heaven,
and came and rolled back the stone from the door,
and sat upon it.
His countenance was like lightning,
and his robe was as white as snow:
and the keepers trembled in fear of him,
and became as dead men.

270 The Women Return at Dawn

(Matthew 28:1,5-7; Mark 16:1-7; Luke 24:1-8; John 20:1)

At the end of the Sabbath,
as it began to dawn toward the first day of the week,
Mary Magdalene,
Mary, the mother of James,
and Salome,
had bought sweet spices,
so that they could come to the tomb and anoint Him.

They came to the tomb when it was still dark,
very early in the morning, at the rising of the sun.
And they said among themselves,
　　'Who shall roll away the stone for us
　　from the door of the tomb?'
for it was very large.
And when they looked,
they saw that the stone was rolled away from the tomb.
They entered in
and did not find the body of the Lord Jesus.

And it came to pass,
as they were much perplexed by this,
two men stood by them in shining robes:
and they were afraid,
and bowed down their faces to the earth,

They said to them,
    "Why do you seek the Living among the Dead?
    He is not here,
    but has risen!
    Remember how He spoke to you
    when He was still in Galilee, saying,
        'The Son of Man must be delivered
        into the hands of sinful men,
        and be crucified,
        and the third day rise again'?"
And as they remembered His words,
they saw a young man sitting on the right side,
clothed in a long white robe;
and they were afraid.

And the angel said to the women,
    'Do not be afraid!
    for I know that you seek Jesus of Nazareth,
    who was crucified.
    He is not here,
    for He is risen, as He said!"
    Come, see the place where the Lord lay!"

    "Go your way quickly,
    and tell His disciples and Peter
    that He has risen from the dead.
    He goes ahead of you into Galilee.
    You shall see Him there,

as He said to you.
Lo! I have told you!"

271 Peter and John See the Empty Tomb

(Matthew 28:8; Mark 16:8; Luke 24:9-12; John 20:2-11a)

Mary Magdalene and Joanna,
and Mary the mother of James,
and other women that were with them,
left quickly and fled from the tomb with fear and great joy;
for they trembled and were amazed.

Nor did they say anything to anyone,
for they were afraid,
and ran to bring word to His disciples,
to the Eleven Apostles,
and to all the rest.
But their story seemed to them like nonsense,
and they were not believed.

Then Mary Magdalene ran and came to Simon Peter,
and to the other disciple whom Jesus loved, and said to them,
      "They have taken the Lord away out of the tomb,
      and we do not know where they have laid Him."

So, Peter got up and went out,
running together with the other disciple to the tomb.
The other disciple outran Peter,
and came to the tomb first.
He stooped down and looked in,
and saw the linen clothes lying there,
but did not go in.

Then Simon Peter came, following him,

and went into the tomb,
and stooped down,
and saw the linen clothes laid by themselves.
The kerchief that was about his head,
was not lying with the linen clothes,
but was folded together in a place by itself.
Then the other disciple,
who came first to the tomb,
also went in,
and he saw and believed.

But they still did not know the Scripture,
that He must rise again from the dead.
Then the disciples departed,
wondering at what had come to pass,
and went away again to their own home.
But Mary stood weeping outside the tomb.

272 Jesus First Appears[42]
(Matthew 28:9-10; Mark 16:9-11; John 20:11b-18)

Now when Jesus had risen early the first day of the week,
He appeared first to Mary Magdalene,
out of whom He had cast seven devils.

As she wept,
she stooped down,
looking into the tomb,
and saw two angels in white sitting there,
one at the head and the other at the feet,
where the body of Jesus had lain.
And they said to her,
    'Woman, why do you weep?
She said to them,

'Because they have taken away my Lord,
   and I do not know where they have laid Him.'

And when she had said this,
she turned herself around,
and saw Jesus standing there,
and did not know that it was Jesus.
Jesus said to her,
   "Woman, why do you weep?
   Whom do you seek?"
She, supposing him to be the gardener, said to Him,
   "Sir, if you have carried Him away,
   tell me where you have laid Him,
   and I will take Him away."
Jesus said to her,
   "Mary!"
She turned herself and said to him,
   "Rabboni!"
which is to say,
   "Master!"
Jesus said to her,
   "Do not cling to Me;
   for I have not yet ascended to My Father.
   Instead, go to My brethren,
   and say to them that,
      'I ascend to My Father and your Father;
      and to My God and your God.'"

As *the women* went to tell His disciples,
behold, Jesus met them, saying,
   "All hail!"
And they came and held Him by the feet,
and worshiped Him.

Then Jesus said to them,
 "Do not be afraid!
 Go tell My brothers
 that they must go into Galilee,
 and there they shall see Me."

Mary Magdalene came and told those who had been with Him,
as they mourned and wept,
that she had seen the Lord,
and that He had spoken these things to her.
And when they had heard that He was alive,
and had been seen by her,
they did not believe.

273 The Guards Report to the Chief Priests

(Matthew 28:11-15)

Now, while they were on their way,
observe that some of the watch came into the city,
and explained to the Chief Priests all that had happened.
After they assembled with the Elders
and took counsel,
they gave a great deal of money to the soldiers, saying,
 "You say,
  'His disciples came by night,
   and stole him away while we slept.'
 And if this comes to the Governor's ears,
  we will persuade him to keep you secure."
So, they took the money,
and did as they were instructed:
and this saying is commonly reported among the Jews until this day.

274 On the Road to Emmaus[43]

(Mark 16:12-13; Luke 24:13-35)

Afterwards, He appeared in another form to two of the disciples,
as they walked that same day,
into the country, to a village called Emmaus,
which was *about seven miles* from Jerusalem.
And they talked together
of all these things which had happened.
And it came to pass,
that while they talked and debated,
Jesus Himself appeared in another form,
and drew near,
and went with them.

But their eyes were held back
so that they would not know Him.
And He said to them,
    "What kind of talk is this
    that you have with each other
    as you walk in sadness?"
One of them, whose name was Cleopas, answered Him,
    "Are you only a stranger in Jerusalem,
    and have not known
    the things which have come to pass there these days?"
And He asked,
    "What things?"
And they said,
    "All about Jesus of Nazareth!
    He was a prophet,
    mighty in deed and word
    before God and all the people.
    The Chief Priests and our rulers
    delivered him to be condemned to death,

and have crucified him!
But we trusted that he was the one
who would have redeemed Israel.
Besides all this,
today is the third day
since these things were done.

Yes! And we were astonished
by certain women, also of our company,
who were at the tomb early.
When they did not find his body,
they came saying that they had also seen a vision of angels,
who said that he was alive!
And certain of those who were with us
went to the tomb,
and found it just as the women had said.
But they did not see him."

Then He said to them!
    "Oh, fools!
    and slow of heart
    to believe all that the prophets have spoken!
    Ought not Christ to have suffered these things,
    and to enter into His glory?"
And beginning at Moses and all the prophets,
He expounded all the Scriptures to them:
the things concerning Himself.

They drew near to the village where they went:
and He made as if He would have gone further.
But they constrained Him, saying,
    "Stay with us:
    for it is nearly evening,
    and the day is almost spent."

And He went in to stay with them.
And it came to pass,
as He sat at dinner with them,
He took bread and blessed it,
and broke it,
and gave to them.
Their eyes were opened and they knew Him
and He vanished out of their sight.

They said one to another,
    "Didn't our hearts burn within us,
      while He talked with us along the way,
      and as He opened the Scriptures to us?"
And they got up that same moment
and returned to Jerusalem,
and found the Eleven gathered together
with those who were with them,
and told it to the rest of them, saying,
    "The Lord is risen indeed,
      and has appeared to Simon!"
And they told what was done along the way,
and how He was known to them in the breaking of bread.
But they did not believe them either.

275 Jesus Appears to the Disciples

(Mark 16:14; Luke 24:36-43; John 20:19-25)

Afterwards, the same day, the first day of the week, at evening,
the doors were shut where the disciples were gathered
for fear of the Jews.
As they talked, while they sat eating,
Jesus Himself appeared to the Eleven
and stood in their midst,
and said to them,

"Peace be with you!"
But they were terrified and full of fear,
and supposed that they had seen a spirit.
And He reproached them for their unbelief and hardness of heart,
because they did not believe those who had seen Him
after He had risen.

He said to them,
    "Why are you troubled?
    and why do thoughts arise in your hearts?
    Behold My hands and My feet,
    and that it is I, myself:
    handle Me and see;
    for a spirit has no flesh and bones,
    as you see that I have!"
And when He had said this,
He showed them His hands and His feet.
And while for joy and wonder they still did not believe,
He said to them,
    "Have you any food here?"
They gave Him a piece of a broiled fish and a piece of honeycomb.
And He took it and ate in front of them.
Then the Disciples rejoiced when they knew it was the Lord.
Then Jesus said to them again,
    "Peace be with you.
    As my Father has sent Me,
    even so do I send you."
And when He had said this,
He breathed on them, and said to them,
    "Receive the Holy Ghost:
    Whose sins you forgive,
    they are forgiven;
    and whose sins you restrain,
    they are restrained."

Thomas, one of the twelve, called "The Twin",
was not with them when Jesus came.
So, the other disciples told him,
    "We have seen the Lord!"
But he told them,
    "Unless I see the mark of the nails in His hands,
    and put my finger into the nail prints,
    and place my hand into His side,
    I cannot believe."

276 Jesus Appears to Thomas

(John 20:26-29)

Eight days afterwards
His disciples were inside,
and Thomas was with them.

Jesus came then,
though the doors were shut,
and stood among them and said,
    "Peace be with you."
Then He said to Thomas,
    "Reach here with your finger and search My hands;
    and reach here with your hand and thrust it into My side.
    Do not be faithless but believing instead."
Thomas answered and said to Him,
    "My Lord and my God!"
Jesus told him,
    "Thomas, you have believed because you have seen Me.
    Blessed are those who have not seen and yet have believed."

277 Jesus Appears by the Sea

(John 21:1-14)

After these things, at the Sea of Tiberias,
Jesus again showed Himself to the disciples
and He showed Himself in this way.

There were gathered there Simon Peter,
Thomas the Twin,
Nathanael of Cana in Galilee,
the sons of Zebedee,
and two others of His disciples.

Simon Peter said to them,
    "I am going fishing."
They said to him,
    "We are going with you, too."
They went out and immediately got into a ship;
and that night they caught nothing.

But when the morning had come,
Jesus stood on the shore,
but the disciples did not know that it was Jesus.
Then Jesus said to them,
    "Children, do you have any fish?
They answered Him,
    "No!"
He told them,
    "Cast the net on the right side of the ship
    and you shall find fish!"

So, they cast and now they were not able to draw the net
because of the multitude of fishes.
So, the disciple beloved of Jesus told Peter,
    "It is the Lord!"

Now when Simon Peter heard that it was the Lord,
he wrapped his fisher's coat around himself since he was naked,
and cast himself into the sea.
The other disciples came in the little ship;
dragging the net with fishes,
because they were only a hundred yards from land.
As soon as they came ashore,
they saw a fire of coals there,
and fish laid upon it with bread.
Jesus said to them,
    "Bring some of the fish you just caught."
Simon Peter went and drew the net to land
full of one hundred fifty-three large fish,
and though there were so many,
the net was not broken.
Jesus said to them,
    "Come and eat!"
Knowing that it was the Lord,
none of the disciples dared ask Him,
    "Who are you?"
Jesus then came and took bread and fish and gave it to them.
Now this was the third time
that Jesus showed Himself to His disciples,
after He had risen from the Dead.

278 Feed My Sheep

    (John 21:15-23)

So, when they had eaten, Jesus said to Simon Peter,
    "Simon, son of Jonah, do you love Me more than these?"
He said to Him,
    "Yes, Lord. You know that I love You."
He said,
    "Feed My Lambs."

He said to Peter a second time,
    "Simon, son of Jonah, do you love Me?"
He said to Him,
    "Yes, Lord. You know that I love You."
He said,
    "Feed My Sheep."

He said to Peter a third time,
    "Simon, son of Jonah, do you love Me?"
Peter was grieved because He said to him a third time,
    "Do you love Me?"
And he said to Him,
    "Lord, You know all things.
    You know that I love you."
Jesus said to him,
    "Feed My Sheep.
    Truly, truly, I tell you,
    when you were young, you dressed yourself,
    and walked where you wanted.
    but when you are old, you shall stretch out your hands,
    and another shall dress you,
    and carry you where you do not want to go."
He said this,
signifying the death by which Peter should glorify God.
After He had said this, He said to him,
    "Follow Me."

Then Peter turned around and saw following them
the disciple whom Jesus loved,
the one who leaned upon Him at supper and said,
    "Lord, who is it who betrays You?"
Seeing him, Peter said to Jesus,
    "Lord, what shall this man do?"
Jesus said to him,

"If I desire that he lingers until I come,
what is that to you?
You follow Me."
Then this saying spread among the brethren,
that this disciple should not die:
but Jesus did not tell him that he would not die;
but [instead],
"If I desire that he lingers until I come,
what is that to you?"

279 Go into All the World

(Matthew 28:16-20; Mark 16:15-18; Luke 24:44-49)

Then the eleven disciples went away into Galilee,
to a mountain where Jesus had directed them.
And when they saw Him,
they worshiped Him:
but some doubted.

Jesus came and said to them,
"All power is given to Me in Heaven and in Earth.
You, therefore, go into all the world,
and preach the Gospel to every creature,
and teach all nations,
baptizing them
in the name of the Father,
and of the Son,
and of the Holy Spirit:
Teaching them to observe all that I have commanded you.
He who believes and is baptized
shall be saved;
but he who does not believe
shall be damned."

"These signs shall follow those who believe;
In My Name they shall cast out devils;
they shall speak with new tongues;
They shall take up serpents;
and if they drink any deadly thing,
it shall not hurt them;
they shall lay hands on the sick,
and they shall recover."

And He said to them,
"These are the words which I spoke to you,
while I was still with you,
that all things must be fulfilled,
which were written
in the Law of Moses,
and in the Prophets,
and in the Psalms,
concerning Me."

Then He opened their comprehension,
so that they might understand the Scriptures,
and said to them,
"Thus, it is written
and, thus, it behooved Christ to suffer,
and to rise from the dead on the third day:
so that repentance and remission of sins
should be preached in His name among all nations,
beginning at Jerusalem.
You are witnesses of these things."

"And, behold,
I send the promise of My Father upon you.
So, linger in the city of Jerusalem,
until you are endued with power from on high.

And, behold,
I am with you always,
even to the end of the world.
Amen."

280 Jesus Ascends into Heaven[44]

(Mark 16:19-20; Luke 24:50-53; Acts 1:1b-12)

Jesus taught until the day He was taken up.
He gave commandments to the Apostles,
whom He had chosen:
to whom also He showed Himself,
by many infallible proofs,
to be alive after His passion,
and spoke of the things pertaining to the Kingdom of God:
being seen by them for forty days.

He led them out as far as to Bethany,
and He lifted up His hands and blessed them.
Being assembled together with them,
He commanded that they should not leave Jerusalem,
　　"Wait for the promise of the Father,
　　which you have heard from Me.
　　John truly baptized with water;
　　but you shall be baptized with the Holy Spirit
　　not many days from now."

So, when they gathered,
they asked Him,
　　"Lord, will you now restore the Kingdom to Israel again?"
And He said to them,
　　"It is not for you to know the times or the seasons,
　　which the Father has put in His own power.
　　But you shall receive power,

after the Holy Spirit has come upon you:
and you shall be witnesses for Me
both in Jerusalem, and in all Judea, and in Samaria,
and to the uttermost part of the earth."

It came to pass, after the Lord had spoken to them,
while He blessed them, He was parted from them.
While they looked, He was taken up;
and a cloud received Him out of their sight,
and He was carried up into Heaven,
and sat on the Right Hand of God.

And while they looked earnestly toward Heaven as He went up,
two men stood by them in white robes, who also said,
"You men of Galilee,
Why do you stand gazing up into Heaven?
This same Jesus,
who is taken up from you into Heaven,
shall likewise appear in same way
as you have seen Him go into Heaven!"

Then they returned with great joy to Jerusalem from Mount Olivet,
which is a Sabbath day's journey from Jerusalem.
And they worshiped Him and were continually in the Temple,
praising and blessing God.
And they went out and preached everywhere,
the Lord working with them,
and confirming the Word with signs that followed.
Amen.

281 This Testimony Is True[45]

(John 20:30-31, 21:24-25)

This is from the disciples who testified
and wrote these things:

and we know that this testimony is true.

In the presence of His disciples
Jesus truly did many other signs
which are not written in this book,
which, if every one of them should be written,
we suppose that not even the world itself
could contain the books that should be written.

But these are written,
so that you might believe
that Jesus is the Christ,
the Son of God;
and that believing
you might have life through His Name.
Amen.

ENDNOTES

1 Foreword

As mentioned in the Foreword, Blue Letter Bible publishes a "Harmony of The Gospels" chart that I found instructive. They forwarded information to me about the source material they used, which I traced back to a still earlier publication by the same author. Please find below, the citation and the URL to the Google scan of the book in the library of the University of Illinois at Urbana-Champaign.

Nevin, Alfred, 1816-1890: The Holy Bible: containing the Old and New Testaments / (Philadelphia: A.J. Holman, 1879), also by Alexander Cruden.

Online Book

https://babel.hathitrust.org/cgi/pt?id=uiug.30112114853911;view=1up;seq=66;-size=125;skin=default

2 1 Preamble

(Mark 1:1; Luke 1:1-4)

Theophilus is deleted from Luke's Preamble and the personal pronoun indicating the writer has been made plural. This work is a compilation from multiple accounts, and it seemed best to paraphrase the Scriptures in that way.

3 2 In the Beginning

(John 1:1-5,10-18)

Here the mention of John the Baptist in John 1:6-9 has been moved to Vignette 4 for a better chronological and narrative flow. This kind of paraphrasing was used similarly throughout the work.

4 3 The Genealogy of Jesus

(Matthew 1:1-17; Luke 3:23-38)

There are four major theories that explain the apparent divergence of the genealogies offered by Matthew and Luke.

1) One or both genealogies are either fiction or error.
This theory presupposes Scripture cannot be trusted and I reject it.

2) Luke provides the line of Mary and Matthew that of Joseph.

This is a notion for which I found little support and which has difficulties in terms of the count of generations.

3) Joseph had two fathers after a levirate marriage by two brothers, of different fathers, to Joseph's mother.

There is a very interesting and not implausible Sixth Century theory that Joseph had two legal fathers. This could take place with Joseph's mother having married two half-brothers (the first not siring a son before dying) who each had a different father, one descended from Nathan and the other from Solomon. Thus, genetically through Matthew and legally through Luke the lineages of both fathers were traced from Joseph to David. This still does not resolve the generation count.

4) Luke provides the lineage of Joseph and Matthew that of Mary.

I have decided to follow the word of Clement, who was the student of Polycarp, who was the student of John the Apostle, in whose home Mary lived out her days. His teaching was that Mary's was the lineage that Matthew described.

"And in the Gospel according to Matthew, the genealogy which begins with Abraham is continued down to Mary the mother of the Lord."

(From: STROMATA: CHAPTER XXI.— THE JEWISH INSTITUTIONS AND LAWS OF FAR HIGHER ANTIQUITY THAN THE PHILOSOPHY OF THE GREEKS.)

Others also theorize that Matthew was first written in Aramaic and then translated into Greek.

Thus, Matthew 1:16 [And Jacob begat Joseph the husband of Mary, of whom was born Jesus, who is called Christ.] originally used the Aramaic word "gowra" (which could mean father), which, in the absence of vowel markings, was read by the Greek translator as "gura" (husband). In any case, an early understanding that Matthew traced Mary's genealogy would explain why the contradiction between Matthew and Luke apparently escaped notice until the 3rd century.

(Andrew Gabriel Roth, Proofs of Peshitta Originality in the Gospel According to Matthew & the Gowra Scenario: Exploding the Myth of a Flawed Genealogy.)

This explanation, that Mary was the ward of a father/protector or kinsman redeemer who was her legal father, whose name was Joseph (not Jacob, her grandfather), would also make the "fourteen generations" Matthew cites in 1:17 complete.

To my thinking, this explanation harmonizes all issues. I have reversed the order of Matthew's Scriptures to present the lineage going back, as Luke did. ~RWG

5   4   John the Baptist Was Sent

(John 1:6-9)

See Vignette #2.

6   24   The First to Follow

(John 1:35-51)

This vignette follows John's use of Cephas and the Greek interpretation of Peter, but adds the English interpretation of "Rock".

7   25   Water Made into Wine

(John 2:1-12)

John 2:6 states that there were 6 water pots which each held 2 or 3 (μετρητής) metrētēs or between 20 and 30 gallons. The total volume of liquid was between 120 and 180 gallons. In the interest of some analysis, we can split the difference at 150 gallons of water made into wine.

The VIVINO website provides the range of wine prices. An "average bottle" is nearly $16 dollars. A very good wine is just over twice that. The most excellent bottles you can purchase run about 33 times as much as the average bottle. So, if Jesus had just created average wine for this wedding, it would have been worth $9,600 at today's prices. If a very good wine, such as you might find in a quality wine store, then His gift was worth at least $19,200. If the wine Jesus created was the very best of the very best, then His wedding gift was worth more than $316,800! In any case, this was a kingly gift!

8   26   The First Cleansing of the Temple

(John 2:13-25)

The Synoptic Gospels describe Jesus cleansing the Temple at the end of His ministry. John describes such an event at the beginning of it. For all we know, Jesus may have done this not only more than once, but more than twice. I believe that the Gospels record two such occasions, each of which also differ in detail from the other.

9 52 Sermon on the Mount

(Matthew 5:1)

Three different passages of Luke were blended into the Sermon on the Mount as found in Matthew. Portions of Matthew's account were moved for better harmony to other vignettes. Doubtless, Jesus may have preached the same subject matter more than once. Choices of this kind where made to avoid repetition.

10 57 Sermon on the Mount: Be Reconciled

(Matthew 5:21-26)

Jesus says to reconcile with your adversary on the way to court, or you may have to pay your last quadrans (κοδράντης) a Roman coin worth one quarter of an as, which was worth a little over a dollar in 2020 US currency. While the term "quarter" would be a more accurate paraphrase here, the expression "pay your last dime/penny" is more familiar. Also, in Vignette 150, the same sentiment is expressed using a lepton, a coin worth half a quadran, which is there also paraphrased with "dime". So, "dime" is used here instead.

11 63 Sermon on the Mount: Do Not Be Anxious

(Matthew 6:25-34, Luke 6:22-40)

Jesus uses the measurement "cubit" which was the length of a forearm from elbow to fingertips, standardized at about 18 inches (44 centimeters). The nearest modern term conveying the spirit of the lesson is the imperial unit the "foot" which is used in this paraphrase. To say "a foot and a half" would be more accurate, but the Carpenter was not measuring anything here and the lesson is better served by the less accurate term.

12 74 The Sinful Woman of The City

(Luke 7:36-50)

This vignette is often considered part of the similar story in Bethany, told in the other three Gospels. I am now of the opinion that these are two separate incidents in two different times and places. Two of the similarities (the common name of Simon and the common use of alabaster containers) are not hard to believe. In a YouTube.com video series "A Very Challenging "Contradiction" in the Gospels: The Mark Series pt 57 (14:1-12)", Bible teacher Mike Winger also offered that, in Bethany, Mary's use of her hair to wash and annoint Jesus' feet in the home of Simon the Pharisee could likely enough have been inspired by the previous act of worship of the woman in the home of Simon the Leper, in Galilee. It was a blessing that his unsearched and unsolicited video was recommended to me by a YouTube algorithm just before I wrapped up the proofreading of this work.

13 88 Jesus Casts Out the Demon, Legion

(Matthew 8:28-34; Mark 5:1-20; Luke 8:26-39)

These accounts individually describe either one possessed man or two men. It is reasonable to think that there were two men encountered, but that one of them received special attention. I've adjusted the personal pronouns to reflect this.

14 98 Jesus Feeds Five Thousand Men

(Matthew 14:15-21; Mark 6:35-44; Luke 9:12-17; John 6:5-14)

On this occasion, Jesus fed the multitude from the loaves and fishes that a boy carried. On another, he fed the great crowd from bread and fish that the disciples had. These were two separate events and so no attempt was made to harmonize them.

The disciples remarked that 200 denarion (a denarius being Roman silver coin worth about a day's pay for a soldier or a laborer) would not buy enough bread. Their math holds up pretty well! One wonders if that happened to be how much was in the moneybag that Judas carried...

In the First Century, a Roman modius (about two gallons) of wheat provided bread for ten for a day at a traditional "Fair Price" of 12 assarii. A denarius was worth 16 assarii, so 200 denarion would buy 5,333 one pound loaves, bread enough for barely more than half the 5,000 men (who needed about 2 pounds of bread each day). This does not consider the needs of the women and children also present.

It is an "apples to oranges" comparison to attempt to compare wages across twenty centuries, not to mention the purchasing power of those wages when considering the cost of bread. This work simply equates the denarius with a day's labor for the sake of readability. In that same spirit, a little more simple math gives us another way to paraphrase this sum. 200 days pay, divided by 28 days in a month, gives us 7.14, or a little over "seven months pay" as an approximate value of the disciple's rough estimate.

15 100 Jesus Walks on Water

(Matthew 14:24-33; Mark 6:47-52; John 6:16-21)

John tells us that the disciples had rowed 25 or 30 stadios (τά σταδια) when they encountered Jesus out on the lake. A stadion was a measure of about 606 modern feet, derived from the length of a foot race in a Greek stadium. Twenty-five stadios is 15,150 feet, or just under three miles, and thirty would be 18,180, or nearly three and a half miles. Splitting the difference is 16,665 feet, or just over three miles. For the sake of readability, and since there is more than half a mile between the two estimates, this work will simply say, "about three miles". This would put them in the middle of the lake, which is where Matthew said they were.

Mathew and Mark both tell us this event happened during the "fourth watch" of the night, which in Roman times was the time between 3:00 AM and 6:00 AM. John tells us it was dark. We are told that they saw Him walking on the water and Mark says that Jesus saw them rowing hard.

There are some interesting possibilities which come to mind. We know that this event happened soon after the death of John the Baptist, which was on the birthday of Herod Antipas. There is a belief that this was perhaps two or three weeks after Purim and one or two weeks before Passover. This would mean that the moon was between First Quarter and Waxing Gibbous, getting brighter every night and moving farther in the sky from the sun. In the hours before sunrise, a growing moon would have been in the western sky between zenith and the horizon.

Perhaps we can assume that Peter and the rest of the experienced Galilean fisherman might not have gotten on a boat to row in complete darkness if it was overcast and they had any notion that a fierce wind was about to blow against them. When they started, there might have at least been some decent moonlight from the east. Jesus saw them rowing across the lake, stopped in the middle, exhausting themselves against the wind. By the time He reached them, they may have seen His form lit by the moon in the darkness as He approached from the east. (No wonder they thought He was a spirit!) As Peter's struggle with his faith played out on the water, dawn may have begun to light the sky a little.

16   119   Jesus Miraculously Pays Taxes

(Matthew 17:24-27)

Jesus tells Peter to fish for a stater (στατήρ), a "standard" silver coin, the Greek tetradrachma, that would be enough for two to pay the annual Temple Tax of half a shekel, or two drachma, each. Here this is paraphrased "a silver coin worth a shekel".

17   124   Forgiveness

(Matthew 18:21-35)

It is difficult to value ancient currencies and commodities by modern standards. One day of work for a soldier was a silver drachma or denarius, 3.9 grams of silver, worth less than four dollars on the day this is written, but it would buy a modius (about two gallons) of wheat, or bread enough for ten days. Even that price varied by location. In this work, the price of silver will be used to create the appropriate sense of scale.

According to the 1906 Jewish Encyclopedia, the "heavy common talent", used in New Testament times, was 58.944 kg (129 lb 14 oz). The August 9, 2020 spot value of silver was $28.50. In modern times, ten thousand talents of silver would be valued at $59,223,000. One hundred silver denarii, at 3.9 grams each (13.7569 oz. total) would be worth only $392.07 that same day. For readability and scale, we will express these sums as "nearly sixty million dollars" and "not quite four hundred dollars".

18   143   The Parable of the Good Samaritan

(Luke 10:25-37)

Jesus cited the amount the Samaritan left with the innkeeper as "two denarii" which would be the pay of a soldier or a laborer for two days. It is expressed here as two "days wages".

19   145   The Lord's Prayer

(Luke 11:1-13; Matthew 6:9-15)

This section was moved from Matthew's account of the Sermon on the Mount and blended here with Luke's for better narrative flow.

20 148 Jesus Teaches the Fear of God

(Matthew 10:26-33; Luke 12:1-12)

A quadran (κοδράντης) is a Roman coin worth one quarter of an as, which was worth a little over a dollar in 2020 US currency. So, the term "quarter" is used instead.

21 150 Parables about Readiness

(Luke 12:41-59)

A lepton (λεπτόν) is a Roman coin worth one eighth of an as. The term "dime" is used instead, in this one place.

22 169 Jesus Comes to Bethany

(John 11:17-29)

A stadion was a measure of about 606 modern feet, derived from the length of a foot race in a Greek stadium. Fifteen stadios is 9,090 feet, or less than two miles

23 174 When Will the Kingdom Come?

(Matthew 24:28; Luke 17:20-37)

Luke 17:37 has sometimes been translated using the word "vultures" Greek: aetos (ἀετός) which actually means "eagles". I don't see the need to change this meaning. Matthew 24:28 uses the word "carcass". This is different from Luke, who used the word (σῶμα) sōma, "body". Matthew 24:28 is cited here to avoid redundancy later in the narrative.

24 177 Teachings on Divorce

(Matthew 19:1-12; Mark 10:1-12; Luke 16:18)

Luke's recording of Jesus teaching about divorce is included in this vignette for narrative flow.

25   184   To Serve or To Be Served

(Matthew 20:25-28; Mark 10:42-45; Luke 22:24-30)

The conversation in Luke about this subject seems out of place in the Last Supper vignette and harmonizes better with the chronologically earlier description of it in Matthew and Mark.

26   185   The Blind Men Healed in Jericho

(Matthew 20:29-34; Mark 10:46-52; Luke 18:35-43)

This vignette resolves Scriptures in a way similar to the matter of the demon possessed men among the Gaddarenes. We are told there are two blind men, but only one is said to be doing the talking, so both are included but dialogue is attributed to Bartimaus.

27   187   The First Parable of the Servants

(Luke 19:11-27)

While I have often moved descriptions of parables to avoid redundancy, these are similar parables in structure but teach slightly different lessons, so, I have chosen to retain both. In this first of these two similar parables, written by Luke, the servants are all given the same amount of money but achieve different results. The unprofitable servant loses the job he had and does not advance. This perhaps applies to the Kingdom in this life.

28   189   Jesus in Bethany

(Matthew 26:6-13; Mark 14:3-9; John 12:1-8)

For readability, and to preserve the paraphrasing method in this vignette, the phrase "sold for three hundred denarii" becomes "sold for a year's wages". This is a fairly close approximation when 52 sabbaths as well as other holy days are subtracted from the days in a year. Could "300 denarii" have been a colloquial expression for "a year's wages"? Both Mark and John noted it.

29   200   The Things That Are Caesar's

(Matthew 22:15-22; Mark 12:13-17; Luke 20:20-26)

Jesus calls for a "denarius" to be brought to Him. Rather than express a particular sum, the word is paraphrased as "coin".

30   204   Woe to the Scribes & Pharisees

(Matthew 23:1-39; Mark 12:38-40; Luke 11:42-44,46-52,20:45-47)

Luke twice recorded the maledictions of Jesus against the Scribes and the Pharisees. They are all combined here with the similar reports of Matthew and Mark.

31   205   The Poor Widow

(Mark 12:41-44; Luke 21:1-4)

Mark records that the widow threw in "two leptons" which were worth only a "quadran". The paraphrase uses "coins" instead of leptons and "a quarter" instead of quadran.

32   208   Jesus Foretells the Fall of Jerusalem

(Matthew 23:1-39; Mark 12:38-40; Luke 11:42-44,46-52,13:34-35,20:45-47)

Matthew 24: 28 has sometimes been translated using the word "vultures" Greek: aetos (ἀετός) which actually means "eagles". I don't see the need to change this meaning. Matthew uses the word (πτῶμα) ptōma or "carcass". This is different from Luke, who used the word "body".

33   213   The Second Parable of the Servants

(Matthew 25:14-30)

This similar parable, as written by Matthew, perhaps applies to the Kingdom in the next life, and to the lack of reward, not to mention punishment, that unprofitable, false servants will see. In this second of these two similar parables, the profitable servants are all given differing amounts of money and each doubles the investment he received.

In this parable, weights of silver are once again entrusted to some servants for investment. One "heavy common talent" in that day would be worth $59,223 at

2020's spot silver price. For readability and to keep the proportions the same, I have expressed the sums as if a talent were the equivalent today of one hundred thousand dollars and once used the term "investment".

34   217   Judas Conspires to Betray Jesus

(Matthew 26:14-16; Mark 14:10-11; Luke 22:3-6)

"Pieces of silver" is a close translation of "*argyrion*" (ἀργύριον). This may have meant silver *shekels* or *drachma*. This paraphrase retains the traditional phrase.

35   244   Jesus Is Beaten in the Sanhedrin

(Matthew 26:67-68; Mark 14:65; Luke 22:63-65)

Luke's slightly earlier placement of the beating and mocking of Jesus in the Sanhedrin is combined here with the reports of Matthew and Mark.

36   247   Thirty Pieces of Silver

(Matthew 27:3-10)

Matthew tells us that Judas betrayed Jesus for the price of thirty "argyrion" (ἀργύριον) or silver-pieces. This may have meant silver *shekels* or *drachma*. This paraphrase retains the traditional expression.

37   254   Pilate Sentences Jesus

(Matthew 27:24-26; Mark 15:14-15; Luke 23:24-25; John 19:13-16)

I have adopted a view expressed in the following excerpts of a paper by Dr. James Davis on the subject.

"The Time of Jesus' Death and Inerrancy: Is Harmonization Plausible?"

https://bible.org/article/time-jesus-death-and-inerrancy-harmonization-plausible

This paper was presented on November 21 at the 2013 annual meeting of the Evangelical Theological Society in Baltimore, Maryland.

"Mark 15:25 reads that Jesus was crucified at the third hour. Under a Jewish or common reckoning time system, which started the day at sunrise, Jesus was crucified at about nine in the morning. However, in the Gospel of John, John writes that Jesus was at his final trial before Pilate at [about the sixth hour] (John 19:14).

If John was using the same time reckoning system as Mark, Jesus was not yet on the cross around noontime that day."

"Sabastian Bartina and C.K. Barrett raise the possibility that John 19:14 had an original reading of the third hour and an early transcriptional error between the letters of gamma (Γ= 3) and digamma (F = 6) account for the time discrepancy in the accounts.

Sebastian Bartina, S.J., "Ignotum Episemon Gabex," Verbum Domini 36 (1958), 16-37. C. K. Barrett, The Gospel According to St. John – An Introduction with Commentary and Notes on the Greek Text (2nd ed; Philadelphia: The Westminster Press, 1978), 545.

"Peter of Alexandria [Bishop of Alexandria starting in about 300 AD] indicates that the correct reading of "third" in John can be verified with the original extant manuscript,

"'For Christ our Passover was sacrificed for us,' as has been before said, and as that chosen vessel, the apostle Paul, teaches. Now it was the preparation, about the third hour, as the accurate books have it, and the autograph copy itself of the Evangelist John, which up to this day has by divine grace been preserved in the most holy church of Ephesus, and is there adored by the faithful"

(Peter of Alexander, Fragments from the Writings of Peter 5.7).

(The Ante-Nicene Fathers 6:282.)

Davis recommends that it would perhaps be a good idea .... for Bible translations to put the textual variant of "three" in John 19:14, something to the effect that a few manuscripts have it. This seems warranted due to the possibility of a transcriptional error and testimony of the church fathers.

38 257 The Place of the Skull

(Matthew 27:33-34; Mark 15:22-23; Luke 23:33a; John 19:17b)

Matthew tells us that they gave Jesus "oxos" (ὄξος), a sour, vinegary, wine drank by the Roman soldiers, and that this was mixed with "cholē" (χολή), bile or gall or wormwood or a bitter tasting thing, possibly myrrh.

Mark tells us that they gave Jesus "oinos" (οἶνος), wine and that this was mixed with "smyrnizō", (σμυρνίζω), flavored with myrrh.

Volume 49 Number 3, May/June 1996 of "Archaeology", published by the Archaeological Institute of America, states that myrrh was used as a medicine since ancient times and an Italian laboratory has verified that it has pain relieving properties, possibly interacting with opioid receptors in the brain.

This paraphrase harmonizes the reports with the terms "sour wine" and "bitter myrrh".

39   261   The Multitude Mocks Jesus

(Matthew 27:39-43; Mark 15:29-32a; Luke 23:35-37)

Matthew tells us that they gave Jesus "oxos" (ὄξος), a sour, vinegary, wine drank by the Roman soldiers. This is paraphrased "wine vinegar". (Please see Endnote 38.)

40   263   The Sun Was Darkened

(Matthew 27:45-50; Mark 15:33-37; Luke 23:44-45a,46; John 19:28-30)

Matthew, Mark, and John tell us that they gave Jesus "oxos" (ὄξος), a sour, vinegary, wine drank by the Roman soldiers. This is paraphrased ""wine vinegar". (Please see Vignette 37.)

41   267   Nicodemus and Joseph Bury Jesus

(Matthew 27:59-61; Mark 15:46-47; Luke 23:53-56; John 19:39-42)

John tells us that Nicodemus brought about one hundred "lítra" (λίτρα), of burial spices. A litra was about 12.5 ounces, so one hundred would be 78.15 pounds. This is paraphrased as a modern measure of 75 pounds. This was, by any standard, a kingly burial and cost Nicodemus dearly.

The aloes referred to here may be the spice that comes from (Aquilaria agallocha), Aloeswood or Agarwood.

At this writing, Egyptian Myrrh, can be purchased in bulk at $457.90 per pound, or $17,171.25 for 37.5 pounds. 2010 prices for superior pure aloeswood was as high as $100,000/kg according to "Flavour and Fragrance Journal" 26(2):73–87. On Amazon, the premium oil is $1,187.94 per ounce. At that price, for 37.5 pounds, the cost would still be $712,764 for a total of both spices being $729,935.25! A kingly burial indeed, not counting the tomb of Joseph!

42   272   Jesus First Appears

(Matthew 28:9-10; Mark 16:9-11; John 20:11b-18)

This vignette is assembled to show how Mary Magdelene had more interaction with Jesus, but how all the women were indeed involved in these graveside appearances.

43   274   On the Road to Emmaus

(Mark 16:12-13; Luke 24:13-35)

Luke reports that these two disciples were walking sixty "stadios" (οἱ στάδιοι) from Jerusalem to Emmaus. A stadion was a measure of about 606 modern feet, derived from the length of a foot race in a Greek stadium. This is a distance measured today as 6.8864 miles, or as paraphrased, "about seven miles."

44   280   Jesus Ascends into Heaven

(Mark 16:19-20; Luke 24:50-53; Acts 1:1b-12)

Luke's more detailed account of Jesus departing into Heaven continues in the Acts of the Apostles and is included here.

45   281   This Testimony Is True

(John 20:30-31, 21:24-25)

The personal pronoun indicating the authorship has been made plural. This work is a compilation from multiple accounts, and it seemed best to paraphrase this Scripture in that way.